Identity Theory

All people derive particular identities from their roles in society, the groups they belong to, and their personal characteristics. Introduced almost thirty years ago, identity theory is a social psychological theory in the field of sociology that attempts to understand identities, their sources in interaction and society, their processes of operation, and their consequences for interaction and society. The theory brings together in a single framework the central roles of both meaning and resources in human interaction and purpose. This book describes identity theory, its origins, the research that supports it, and its future direction. It covers the relation between identity theory and other related theories as well as the nature and operation of identities. In addition, the book discusses the multiple identities that individuals hold from their multiple positions in society and as well as the multiple identities activated by many people interacting in groups and organizations. And, it covers the manner in which identities offer both stability and change to individuals. Co-authored by the developers of the theory, this book accessibly presents decades of research in a single volume, making the full range of this powerful new theory understandable to readers at all levels.

IDENTITY THEORY

Peter J. Burke and Jan E. Stets

OXFORD
UNIVERSITY PRESS
2009

OXFORD

UNIVERSITY PRESS

Oxford University Press, Inc., publishes works that further
Oxford University's objective of excellence
in research, scholarship, and education.

Oxford   New York
Auckland   Cape Town   Dar es Salaam   Hong Kong   Karachi
Kuala Lumpur   Madrid   Melbourne   Mexico City   Nairobi
New Delhi   Shanghai   Taipei   Toronto

With offices in
Argentina   Austria   Brazil   Chile   Czech Republic   France   Greece
Guatemala   Hungary   Italy   Japan   Poland   Portugal   Singapore
South Korea   Switzerland   Thailand   Turkey   Ukraine   Vietnam

Library of Congress Cataloging-in-Publication Data
Burke, Peter.
Identity theory / Peter J. Burke and Jan E. Stets.
   p.   cm.
Includes bibliographical references and index.
ISBN 978-0-19-538827-5; 978-0-19-538828-2 (pbk.)
1. Identity (Psychology)   I. Stets, Jan E.   II. Title.
BF697.B855 2009
155.2—dc22   2008046390

Printed in the United States of America
on acid-free paper

To our students and to the students who follow them.

Preface

This book had its beginnings almost fifteen years ago when we were on sabbatical at the University of Iowa. Over the years, we kept promising ourselves that we would get back to finishing it, but inevitably other research projects, journal articles, and book chapter obligations got in the way. Those who tend to write research articles will understand this. This past year we took the Nike slogan "Just Do It!" seriously and began a flurry of writing that culminated in this book. Ironically, the long delay has proven to be beneficial for this book. Over the years, our ideas and work in identity theory have matured theoretically and methodologically, and we have discovered some fascinating patterns given our empirical results. These insights keep us excited in forging ahead to discover more. Thus, on the one hand, the current book is much better, more developed, and more complete than it would have been if we wrote it many years earlier. On the other hand, in taking time out to write this book, we realized that there was much more that needed to be developed in identity theory. This realization makes it clear that we are working with a rich theory that has still more to say about the self and the self-society relationship.

We admit that an important reason behind writing this book at this time is to give scholars within sociology and across the social sciences a clear and organized statement on identity theory in sociological social psychology. To date, no such book exists. Over time, we became increasingly frustrated with this fact, so we decided it was time to provide one. Identity theory research has been scattered across numerous journals, book chapters, and conference papers, and we wanted to provide a place where scholars could obtain a clear and organized understanding of the theory. We think we have accomplished this goal although our readers are the ultimate judge of this.

We also think it is important to make this theory more accessible to a wide array of scholars and even to those outside of the academy who simply wish to learn more about the self. We hope we have come close to meeting this loftier goal.

We received much help and encouragement in writing this book. We are especially grateful to the students in our graduate social psychology seminar at the University of California, Riverside. The students read each of the chapters and provided us with useful feedback. The book is better because of their insights, and we thank each of them, including Emily Asencio, Michael Carter, Allison Cantwell, Christine Cerven, Jesse Fletcher, Michael Harrod, Richard Niemeyer, Shelley Osborn, and Yvonne Thai. They are much relieved that this is finally in print!

We also are indebted to George McCall who wrote the foreword. We have always admired his work, and we have learned much from him. We also would like to thank Sheldon Stryker. The work that served as the basis for this book all began with Sheldon's ideas about the nature of identities and the relationship between identity and society. His support and encouragement have meant a great deal. Together, Sheldon Stryker and George McCall were the earliest thinkers on identity theory in sociology. We hope we have added some important ideas to their already forward-looking thinking. And we hope that students of identity theory will continue to push this theory theoretically, methodologically, and empirically so that we have a better understanding of self and the intricate interplay of self and society.

Contents

Foreword

For more than thirty years now, Peter Burke has been perhaps the most insightful symbolic interactionist around, as his emphasis on the correlated meaning of identities and of behaviors (ideas consolidated for most of that time within an adaptation of William Powers's perceptual control theory) has allowed Burke not only to incorporate earlier thinking about identities (such as my own) but also to conduct a fruitful program of empirical research on these previously airy topics. Throughout this extensive period, Burke has enjoyed numerous coauthorships, but for nearly half of those years, his most consistent collaborator by far has been Jan Stets, his close colleague and wife. For these two to have jointly produced the current volume on identity theory is a most fortunate development for every potential reader.

The concept of identities (i.e., who one is) is best developed within structural symbolic interaction theories, of course, but Burke's differentiating fundamental insight lies in applying to identities Powers's perceptual control theory—that for human beings it is not the control of output or behavior that matters (as it does in most cybernetic theories) so much as the control of perceptions (or input). That is to say, humans maintain a steady and stable environment in the face of disturbances, and they do so by changing their actions (output) to make their perceptions (input) match a reference standard. In what seems a simple move, Burke makes measured identities serve as such a reference point, and from there he and his collaborators elaborate a rich and powerful theory. Understanding and accepting these ideas is difficult for most social scientists because they are so unfamiliar. Burke and Stets do a masterful job of explicating these basic ideas that are so central to their version of identity theory.

Burke has elsewhere contended that what best sets apart many contemporary theories in social psychology is that they have developed, not through the thinking of one eminent theorist, but rather through cumulative testing and building in systematic agendas of research. Key here is that "the ideas in these theories are subject to continuous testing through active programs of research" (Burke 2006c, p. xi). Indeed, over the past couple of decades the Burke/Stets research group has been arguably the most productive we have in sociological social psychology, conducting a systematic and mature program of both survey and laboratory research that supports and extends identity theory. It is one of the greatest strengths of this book that Burke and Stets demonstrate in such detail just how this program of empirical research serves to test, elaborate, and expand the core theoretical model.

In fact, this book seeks to pull together for the first time—and to build upon—the many articles and chapters that constitute their highly ambitious and compelling program of theoretical development and empirical research. Burke and Stets systematically and clearly explicate that program—a real challenge in view of its very size, involving as it does at least twenty-seven different coauthors and some twenty different publication outlets. Many readers who are familiar with only one or a few contributions of this program will find quite astonishing the scope, integrity, and power of identity theory that receives full systematic exposition here for the very first time.

The first three chapters of this book nicely assemble, explicate, and evaluate all the background concepts the authors will need. Chapter 1 locates the idea of identities relative to the key concepts of structural symbolic interaction—such as self, language, and interaction. All three of these are subtly transformed within identity theory, but especially the concept of interaction, which has to be viewed as taking place among identities rather than among persons and centering on the meanings of the behaviors rather than the behaviors themselves. Chapter 2 reviews the historical roots of identity theory, not only in symbolic interaction, but also, just as crucially, in the cybernetics perspective. Chapter 3 builds on these historical roots to examine how contemporary versions of identity theory actually developed, culminating (thus far) in Burke's perceptual control theory emphasis.

Chapter 4 is the heart of the book, in which Burke and Stets explicate their fundamental perceptual control theory of identities—with its implications and explanations for stress and self-esteem—and review the research program's many studies on that model's central process of identity-verification.

The following five chapters relate adaptations of that core model to deal with major and quite obvious complications that simple model faces; and in spelling out each of those elaborations, Burke and Stets helpfully review their empirical support within the extensive program of research.

The final chapter confronts questions of where that theoretical development might next go and how the research program might adapt to those directions. Closely related to these two emphases, an appendix usefully details past and current measures of the major identity concepts—useful because the Burke/Stets program of research has been so extensive and methodologically variable that many researchers need a good road map.

In summary, this book not only enjoys the most expert authorship but also pulls together and systematically explicates the cumulative theoretical research tradition of identity theory, perhaps the most significant in sociological social psychology today. Every scholar (current or prospective) in any branch of social psychology could profit immensely by a careful reading of this most important and timely book.

George J. McCall

Identity Theory

1

Agency and Social Structure

What does it mean to be who you are? An identity is the set of meanings that define who one is when one is an occupant of a particular role in society, a member of a particular group, or claims particular characteristics that identify him or her as a unique person. For example, individuals have meanings that they apply to themselves when they are a student, worker, spouse, or parent (these are roles they occupy), when they are a member of a fraternity, when they belong to the Democratic Party, when they are Latino (these are memberships in particular groups), or when they claim they are outgoing individuals or moral persons (these are personal characteristics that identify themselves as unique persons). People possess multiple identities because they occupy multiple roles, are members of multiple groups, and claim multiple personal characteristics, yet the meanings of these identities are shared by members of society. Identity theory seeks to explain the specific meanings that individuals have for the multiple identities they claim; how these identities relate to one another for any one person; how their identities influence their behavior, thoughts, and feelings or emotions; and how their identities tie them in to society at large.

Identities characterize individuals according to their many positions in society, and it is important to note as we move through the chapters in this book that both the individual and society are linked in the concept of identity. In a broad sense, this is a book about the relationship between the individual and society. Although much of our focus will be on the individual, it is always to be remembered that the individual exists within the context of the social structure. As Cooley (1902) pointed out, the individual and society are two sides of the same coin. Like Coleman (1990), Stryker (1980 [2002]), and others, it is our view that society (social structure) is created

3

by the actions of individuals, though it is recognized that these actions are produced in the context of the social structure they create and are influenced by this context. There is, thus, an elaborate system of mutual influences between characteristics of the individual and characteristics of society. This being true, we need to understand both the nature of the individuals who are creating society as well as the nature of the society in which the individuals are acting.

The dependence of society on the individuals that make it up can be seen in the following thought experiments. Imagine a society in which the average intelligence or IQ was 60—that is, a society with individuals who are very different from the individuals in our own society, whose average IQ is 100. Most of these individuals could barely take care of themselves, let alone form the complex web of social relations we take for granted. Such a society would be nothing like our own; change the nature of the individuals and the nature of society changes. A similar thought experiment shows the dependence of the individual on the society in which he or she lives. Imagine the kind of individual you might become if you lived in a changed (different) society, for example, Nazi Germany or in an Eskimo clan at the turn of the century. Imagine how different you would become growing up in such a society; the nature of the individual depends upon the society in which he or she lives.

It is on the first half of this picture that we will concentrate: the nature of the individuals and the basis of their actions and action choices, that is, their motivations. However, we do not intend to neglect the social structural side of the picture entirely, for the nature of the individuals and what they do depends in large part on the social structural positions in which they are located. What we have to say in these chapters is built on the emerging perspective known as structural symbolic interaction (Stryker 1980 [2002]).

Some Thoughts on Social Structure

Sociologists are interested in understanding the nature of social structure—its forms and patterns, the ways it develops and transforms itself. We have always been somewhat surprised, however, to learn that sociologists often do not have the same phenomenon in mind when talking about social structure and sometimes end up talking past one another. For some, social structure is an idea about how the behavior of individuals ought to be patterned. For others, it is the actual patterns of behavior of those individuals. Initially, we want to emphasize the latter position and thus distinguish between social structure and ideas about social structure.[1] We also want to be clear that in discussing patterns of behavior we have available many different levels of analysis in looking at those patterns, which is a key point in understanding the link between the individual and social structure. At one level, we can look at the patterns of behavior of one individual over time and come to know that individual, and by pooling several such patterns across similar individuals, we can come to know individuals of a certain type. This does not tell us about social structure. At another level, we can look at the patterns of behavior across and between individuals such as store clerks and shoppers to see how those patterns fit with the patterns of others such as other store clerks and higher management to create the larger patterns of behavior of the whole store. At a higher level still, we can look at how different stores relate to one another and to the companies that supply them. It is these larger, interindividual pattern and intergroup patterns that can be thought to constitute social structure.

In this book, we will be talking about how people act to protect and verify their conceptions of who they are. In this vein, for example, Jason, a scientist, may act in ways that make it clear to himself, as well as to others, that he is careful, analytic, logical, experimentally inclined, and so on. In doing this, Jason is engaging in a variety of patterns of action and interaction that conveys these images. These are individual patterns of behavior; they help us understand the individual scientist, Jason. They do not speak to our understanding of social structure. However, these same patterns of behavior may be part of a larger, social structure. We may note, for example, that persons who do the things Jason does, and do them well, are elected to higher positions in their scientific organizations. If we step back and take an even broader view, we may see that there is a flow of such persons as Jason into positions of prominence within their scientific societies and, indeed, perhaps into positions of eminence in policy and governmental circles. From these positions of power, they may help maintain boundaries between such scientists and others as well as help keep resources flowing to the groups and organizations to which they belong. This flow of persons into positions of importance through the mechanism of elections and appointments is part of the social structure, as are the mechanisms that support and sustain this flow of persons, goods, and services.

The actions are still being taken by individuals, but we now see them in a very different way. We see the social structures that emerge from individual actions, as those actions are patterned over time and across persons. In this way, social structure is a very abstract idea. It is not something that we experience directly. Our senses are not well tuned to these patterns as they occur over time and across persons (not to mention across space as well). Nevertheless, we can become aware of them and study them. Indeed, many of the patterns are well recognized, named, and attended to. They enter our everyday language as things like General Motors, the New York Yankees, the Brown family, and Milwaukee. Some are recognized but are harder to point to, such as "the working class" or "the country club set," which do not have a legal status and do not maintain offices or locations. We can only point to individuals who may contribute to the patterns of behavior that constitute the structure. Some structures we tend not to see at all (without special effort and thought) such as the patterns of action that block access of

African Americans to the educational system or the patterns of actions that create the "glass ceiling" in organizations preventing qualified women from rising to positions of power and authority. Nevertheless, these too are parts of social structure, and it is the job of sociologists to discover, attend to, and understand these patterns.

The task we have set for ourselves in this book is to introduce a basis for understanding social structure, in the sense we have begun to outline above, as arising from the actions of individual agents or actors and as feeding back to those agents to change them and the way they operate. However, to do so requires us, at least, to understand the agents or actors that are producing the actions, the patterns that constitute social structure. Depending upon the nature of the agents, we would have a variety of forms of social structures. If our agents had full information and were perfectly rational, we would have very different forms of social organization than if our agents were acting without full information or acting with misinformation or making decisions not on the basis of rationality, but perhaps on the bases of self-interest, fear, love, cowardice or some combination of these other motives.

To accomplish this task we have set for ourselves, we will have to deal more directly with understanding the individual actor, but, as sociological social psychologists, we want to keep in mind that our actor is always embedded in the very social structure that is being created by that (and other) actor(s). For this, we review some ideas about the nature of the actors or agents that are producing the behavior in which we are ultimately interested.

Agents

Agents are actors. In sociological parlance, agents have been referred to by a number of terms and have had a variety of properties. We refer to "individuals," to "actors," to "person and other." Generally speaking, the terms "individual," "actor," "person," and "other" refer to individual human beings, though at times "actor" has been used to refer to a corporate entity (see Coleman 1990). Sociologists, like people in general, have attempted to represent the world as they see it, and they have tried to build theories to account for human behavior and patterns of interaction among humans. In these theories, the agent is the entity that acts. Agents have a variety of properties and these properties help us understand both the different types of agents and the different kinds of actions they may take. For example, actors (agents) whose legitimate means to a goal is blocked may resort to illegitimate (criminal) means (Merton 1957); actors who interact frequently with one another come to like one another (Homans 1950). Resorting to criminal activity, interacting, and liking are actions that agents may take under predictable conditions.

What is seldom talked about, however, is the fact that when agents are human beings, the agent who resorts to criminal activity in one context may be the agent who interacts frequently and is a best friend in another context.

A theory of criminality has little to do with a theory of sentiments and inter-actions. We all recognize this, but our theories generally ignore it. Our theo-ries are, in fact, not about whole human beings. They are theories about aspects of human beings, and each aspect appears (in our theories) to have little to do with the other aspects.

Role theory (see Linton 1936; Nadel 1957) has recognized this and does not claim to be about people, but only about those aspects of people (or interaction systems) that are called roles. What is confusing in role theory is that it is not always clear that it has anything to do with "people." Roles are often described in terms of their structural features (for example, how they relate to other roles) or their behavioral features (for example, what behaviors are accomplished by the role) or their expectational features (for example, what behaviors are expected, that is, prescribed and proscribed) by the role. In talking about relationships, behaviors, and expectations, we avoid dealing with people altogether. However, we have also thrown away a notion of agent. To avoid this problem, whenever an agent is needed to actu-ally take some action, hold an expectation, or be in a relationship, the per-son is brought back into the theory as part of the background. Persons take actions as holders of a particular role, but the focus is on the role and the actions. Persons hold expectations, but it is the content of the expectations and the implications of that content for behavior that is important—not the person who holds those expectations or who engages in the behavior.

When persons become important in role theory it is usually because of the recognition that persons may hold multiple roles and therefore may be agents in multiple systems of interaction. The question then is how these multiple agencies are accomplished and what consequence they have. Here, for example, we may be looking at role conflict and the stress that a person feels when serving as an agent in incompatible interaction systems (Burke 1991). Or we may be looking at the way in which being an agent in several interaction systems serves to enhance and energize the person (e.g., Thoits 1983). In these cases, there is explicit recognition of the multiple agencies that may exist within a single person. This approach will be taken in this book. *"Person" becomes the link between the various agencies that exist within the person.* For example, Mary is a teacher and a mother. Mary may gain information in her role as a teacher that can be passed on to herself as a mother in order to help her children learn something. In this case, "teacher" is linked to "mother" by being in the same person. Teacher and mother are each agents that can act independently or jointly or can interact with each other.

Sometimes the agent is a person in a generic relationship with other per-sons, for example, in an exchange relationship. In this case, particular roles are not relevant except as they emerge from the nature of the exchange rela-tionship itself. For example, one person may be more dependent upon the other for the attainment of various exchange outcomes because there are fewer alternatives. If there is only once grocery store in town, I am likely more dependent on the store than the store is on me. In exchange relationships, the behavioral decisions that are made by each agent are understood to be a function of the nature of the exchange relationship, the position of each agent in that relationship, and the nature of human problem-solving under the specified conditions (Cook and Rice 2003). Supposedly, the way in which humans solve problems holds across various roles and positions in society as long as they have the stated characteristics, for example, of power dependency (Emerson 1962).

Sometimes the agent is a person in a generic relationship with his or her environment generally, for example, in a learning situation in which reinforcements are applied following behavioral decisions. In this case, particular roles are not relevant, nor are particular relationships with other persons at all. Studying agents in this kind of learning situation, researchers seek knowledge and understanding of agency in its least contextualized format. How do persons choose actions in a very abstract setting?

These last two examples of the study of agency (in exchange relationships and in learning situations) come from research that is conducted in laboratory settings for the most part. In such settings, the purpose is to control as many factors as possible in order to understand the nature of human agency in the idealized conditions usually expressed in theories. Of course, it is recognized that these idealized conditions do not include anything about the fact that humans can act as agents in many systems simultaneously. As a result, the distinction between person and agent is blurred or lost. Yet this ability of humans to act as agents in many systems simultaneously (as we will see) may be key to our understanding of social structure. Person and agent are thus not synonymous, and it is imperative to distinguish carefully between them in our theories.

Although both person and agent are abstract concepts, empirical instances of persons are easily visible to our senses. Empirical instances of agents as separate from persons are not. We must be trained to see them, just as we had to be trained to see the relationship between the earth and the sun. Our senses "see" the sun traveling across the sky; they do not "see" the earth rotating on its axis. Yet the earth rotating on its axis has a better fit with the rest of astronomy and physics than the sun traveling across the sky and has come to be accepted if not experienced.

This distinction between person and agent is central to identity theory. In identity theory, an identity is an agent. Each person has many identities, for example, friend, parent, worker, church member, and club member; and each of these identities is an agent. Part of what makes interaction and the social system work is the fact that different identities *within* persons engage in transactions (as the example mentioned above of Mary who is a teacher and a mother) as well as different identities *between* persons (for example, between Mary the teacher and Veronica the mother of one of Mary's sixth-grade students). Both of these kinds of transactions and interactions need to be incorporated into our theories. An identity is also a theoretical construct.

The particular view of these constructs that will be discussed in this book is called identity theory, and it grows out of the perspective of structural symbolic interaction. Before discussing identities and their nature per se, we want to give a little background to put our understanding of identities in context.

Structural Symbolic Interaction

The term "structural symbolic interactionism" was coined by Stryker (1980 [2002]) to refer to a set of ideas about the nature of the individual and the relationship between the individual and society. This set of ideas draws upon the writings of a large number of scholars and thinkers including the Scottish Moral Philosophers, William James, Charles Cooley, W. I. Thomas, and George Herbert Mead (Stryker 1980 [2002]). Collectively, these people and other modern writers including Herbert Blumer, Manford Kuhn, George McCall, Morris Rosenberg, Sheldon Stryker, Ralph Turner, and Eugene Weinstein laid the groundwork for the scientific approach to identities and for the relationship between identities and society (social structure) that constitutes structural symbolic interactionism. Clearly, the intellectual debt of structural symbolic interactionism is large. In chapter 2, we more fully review the contributions of some of these people when we examine the roots of identity theory. In this introductory chapter, we will only provide a brief overview of some of the important points and assumptions that we draw on in the rest of the book. These points may be organized around three central concepts: the self, language, and interaction.

The Self

The self originates in the mind of persons and is that which characterizes an individual's consciousness of his or her own being or identity. The self has the ability to take itself as an object, to regard and evaluate itself, to take account of itself and plan accordingly, and to manipulate itself as an object in order to bring about future states. As McCall and Simmons (1978, p. 52) point out, "The individual achieves selfhood at that point at which he first begins to act toward himself in more or less the same fashion in which he acts toward other people." This reflexive behavior is the core of the self. The self is able to be both subject and object. We do not want to give the impression, however, that the self is a little "person" or *homunculus* residing inside of us that does these things. The self is rather an organized set of processes within us that accomplishes these outcomes. Our job is to understand that organization, how it occurs, and how it both maintains itself and changes over time.

According to Mead (1934), the "self" grows out of the mind as the latter interacts with its environment to solve the problem of sustaining the biological organism (person) that holds it. Mind, itself, arises and develops out of social interaction processes. Mind is the mechanism that controls the meanings that govern our responses to the environment. Mentality comes in, according to Mead, when the organism is able to point out meanings to others and to itself. The ability to pick out meanings and to indicate them both to the self and to others gives control to humans. This control is made possible by language, which encapsulates the meanings in the form of symbols. It is when one's self is encapsulated as a symbol to which one may respond, as to any other symbol, that self-control becomes possible and the "self" emerges.

The responses to the self as symbolized object are from the point of view of others with whom we interact (taking the role of the other toward ourselves), and this implies that our responses are like their response, and the meaning of the self is a shared meaning. Thus, paradoxically, as the "self" emerges as a distinct object, there is at the same time a merger of perspectives of the self and others and a becoming as one with the others with whom we interact. This becoming as one is implied in the shared meanings of the objects and symbols to which we respond in social interaction. It is implied in the fact that in using language, we communicate the same meanings to ourselves as to others. The self is both individual and social in its character. It works to control meanings to sustain itself, but many of those meanings including the meanings of the self are shared and form the basis of language communication, symbolic interaction and, ultimately, social structure.

Because the self emerges in social interaction within the context of a complex differentiated society,[2] because people occupy different positions within society, the self reflects this differentiation into components or what James (1890) called "multiple selves." Each of these smaller "selves" within the overall self is called an identity. Thus, self as father is an identity, as is self as colleague, self as storekeeper, self as student, and self as any of the other myriad of possibilities corresponding to the various roles one may play. Each of these is a different identity, and each may act as an agent instigating behavior within the different roles.

Identities are also important because they provide us with ties to others and to what is social in a situation. Part of their content consists of symbols and meanings pertaining to the self. In order to discuss these symbols and meanings, we need to turn to the second of the three central concepts: language.

Language, Signs, and Symbols

All organisms learn to respond to cues in their environment. Some stimuli come to stand for other stimuli. As in Pavlov's experiments, the sound of a bell (stimulus 2) came to stand for food powder sprinkled on the dog's tongue (stimulus 1) and led to the same response: salivation. A sign is a stimulus that calls up a response that is the same as or similar to the response previously evoked by some other stimulus. In the Pavlov experiments, the bell is a sign of food powder; the readings on a thermometer are a sign of the temperature; the needle on a car's gas gauge is a sign of the amount of fuel in the gas tank. Signs may also refer to other signs. For example, the word "toothache" refers to the signs one feels when a tooth decays to the point that it impinges on the nerve. A dictionary defines words in terms of other words.

Meaning is the response to a stimulus. In this, we are guided by the work of Osgood, Suci, and Tannenbaum (1957). One stimulus, for example, the word "fire," means the same thing as another stimulus, for example, an actual fire. The word "fire" leads to a set of responses that are a subset of responses previously elicited by the actual fire. Thus, in Pavlov's experiments, the bell came to have the same meaning as the food powder. What is important here is that meaning does not reside in objects. Meaning is a response to an object or stimulus, and meaning acts as a further stimulus to action. Meaning thus mediates much of our behavioral responses to various stimuli and allows us to get beyond the simple stimulus-response patterns that may characterize other animals.

A symbol derives its meaning from social consensus and is arbitrary, varying from one culture to another. Different symbols may have the same meaning (e.g., "sun" and "sol"), or the same symbol may have different meanings in different contexts (e.g., "sol" meaning an old French coin and "sol" meaning the sun as derived from Latin). Because the meanings of symbols are socially defined, those meanings are shared. Symbols are relative to social groups and language communities in which the same signs are interpreted in the same way by most persons. Symbols thus evoke the same meaning responses in different individuals.[3] Importantly, symbols evoke the same meaning in the person who uses them as in the person to whom they are directed. Words are our most important and most versatile symbols and provide a means of communication, which can be both subtle as well as complex.

Language is symbolic communication. Because each person is simultaneously a producer and hearer of language (having a self), a person may carry on communication with himself or herself in the form of thought, as chains of reasoning and as imagined possibilities dealing with both things present and things not present. In this case, the two partners of a conversation are both within ourselves—one talking, the other listening and responding. Out of this can grow future actual states or conditions that originally exist only symbolically. We can think about a dinner party. We can think about the things that need to be done in order to have a dinner party. We can think about the ordering and sequencing of the things that need to be done, and we can begin to do them. In this way, something that does not now exist (a dinner party) can come to exist. Thus, through the possibility of responding to oneself and one's own thoughts, plans can be made, action opportunities created, and the past remembered. Indeed, there is a tendency to symbolize virtually everything that is important to us, in order, through thought and interaction, to bring that which is symbolized under our control.

Interaction

To some extent in talking about language, we have already been discussing interaction because much of interaction involves language or symbolic communication. Because we are dealing with selves and symbols, most interaction is not between persons qua persons but between persons who are occupying named positions (statuses) in named groups or organizations while engaged in named patterns of behavior (roles).[4] The interaction is thus not between whole persons but between aspects of persons having to do with their roles in the groups or organizations: their identities.[5] As a father, one can talk with his daughters. As a husband, he talks with his wife. As a member of an organization, he talks with other members. As a friend, he talks with friends. In each of these cases, there are things that are not talked about because they are not relevant to that identity, and there are things that are more likely to be talked about.[6]

For now, we want to deal with the nature of interaction between identities, as they are positioned by statuses and roles in particular groups, organizations, or structures of one sort or another, including informal structures such as networks of friends. In doing this, we can take two different perspectives: agency and structure. With respect to the latter, we focus on the external, structural side and talk about taking on a role or playing a role. From this point of view, the structures in which the identities are embedded are relatively fixed, and identities (people) play out the parts (roles) that are given to them. District managers do the things that district managers are supposed to do. Variations across persons taking on the same identities are viewed as relatively minor, except insofar as they affect the success of the group, organization, or structure. A district manager who cannot increase sales may be replaced with another district manager who can increase sales. What is important is that the structure persists and develops according to its own principles.

However, we can also focus on the agency side. We can take the point of view of the identities that are engaging in the role behavior and talk about making or creating a role. In this case, the identities create the parts that they play out in the situation by making behavioral choices and decisions through negotiation and compromise, conflict and contention.[7] The identity of store manager uses the resources available in the situation—the money, telephone, computer, merchandise, and sales clerks—to create and enact the role of store manage. What is important from this perspective are not the structural "givens" or requirements, but how such things can be used and manipulated to accomplish what is necessary within those limitations. Individual variation is important here because it was through individual variation (and competition) that the current district manager (and not someone else) became district manager, and it is through such individual abilities that the current district manager will succeed or fail.

These are each perspectives, not arguable descriptions of fact. Both are true, but incomplete. From the structural perspective, *how* a district manager increases sales is not relevant. What is relevant from the structural perspective is *that* the district manager does increase sales. To the district manager, however, as the agent involved in the situation, *how* to increase sales is what is relevant.

The issue for the social theorist is to bring the two together in a meaningful way that allows us to move back and forth across levels (agents and structures) to understand how structures are the accomplishments of agents and also to understand how agents always act within structures they create. The agent as district manager is both agent (whole unit) and district manager (part of the structure). This hierarchical arrangement of parts and wholes has always been troublesome to social and behavioral scientists (e.g., Koestler 1969) who have generally opted to confine themselves to one level or another or to cross levels without examining the interface.

The concept of interaction is where these two perspectives meet. Moreover, it is in understanding interaction that we are forced to deal with the two levels of the individual and society. Signs, symbols, and language are key to this. When we examine social action generally, and interaction specifically, we see two different kinds of things going on: the use of symbols and the use of signs. Individuals use symbols (words, language, and the naming of things including the self) to engage in what Herbert Blumer (1962) called symbolic interaction to bring order out of the chaos of the world. In order to interact with others, we must first establish both who they are and who we are. Rachael is the "district manager." Joseph is a "store manager." In general, we do not know what to do with respect to others until we know their meanings for us and our meanings for them. This is the process of identifying the other. I know how to behave toward that person and have expectations about how that person will behave toward me only when I identify the other. Joseph identifies Rachael as the district manager and identifies himself as the store manager. He know what each of these categories of persons is supposed to do, how they relate to each other, who controls what, who reports to whom, and so on.

We must learn the identity of the others with whom we would interact. They must be labeled symbolically (named) and thus given an identity. We, too, must be identified or have an identity. The categories and classifications that are used for this purpose are provided by language and culture in which we are enmeshed. This helps solve another problem for the potential interactants, which is to come up with a set of meanings that is at least to some extent shared. By using the shared symbols, which have been learned, some consensus is provided. We already have common categories, concepts, and labels. In addition, we already have common reactions to these categories, concepts, and labels. Thus, Joseph is able to assume that Rachael also identifies herself as a district manager and that she identifies him as a store manager.

There is another use of the shared concepts and labels in addition to using them to label each other's identities. That is to provide what

W. I. Thomas (Thomas and Thomas 1928) called a "definition of the situation." To define the situation, we use the concepts to label the situation in which we find ourselves. Thus, situations also have meaning and are represented symbolically. Consider, for example, Joseph, who is in the office of the store that he manages. Rachael is currently going over the books for last week, during which Joseph had a successful sale. Having symbolically identified the situation, we can imagine the kind of interaction that might happen. We can imagine the kinds of feelings that Rachael, as the district manager, or Joseph, as the store manager, might have.

Notice that the terms "district manager," "store manager," "office," "going over the books," "sale," and so on serve to identify the persons (identities) and set up expectations about the nature of the interaction that might take place. Note also that these terms have little meaning by themselves. One must also know something about the structure of businesses as organizations, about the layout of stores, about the place of stores in society, and about a monetary economy and bookkeeping. Joseph, as the store manager, is not free to choose his behavior unconstrained by these contexts. Rachael, as district manager, is not free to choose her behavior unconstrained by the context. But by engaging in the behaviors that they do choose, they are contributing to the maintenance of that context. They are validating the symbols to which they both respond meaningfully. They are confirming the identities of "district manager" and "store manager." They are confirming the meanings of "store," "office," and "sale."

Nevertheless, they do choose the behaviors. As agents, they willfully take actions. And their actions may not fully confirm their identities or the identities of others or the meanings of the symbols that we use. Although the general picture is of two role identities doing what they must do, the details are in the eyes of the agents themselves who must choose what to do. Joseph, as store manager, may be concerned whether the sale went well enough. Did he make the right choices in his advertising? Should he have spent more on radio ads rather than on newspaper ads? Should he have sent out flyers? Could he have gotten the printing done more cheaply at another printer? In the interaction that will unfold in the next few minutes, there is much at stake. If the district manager says, "Congratulations, Joseph, you have done excellently. I think your use of the newspaper ads was especially helpful for this sale," the interaction can go one way. If, however, the district manager says, "Well, Joseph, that wasn't bad, but why did you spend so much in the newspapers rather than using the radio?" things could go a different way. The district manager has a choice, and that choice may be based on the effect she wishes to achieve—to put Joseph in his place and reduce his threat of becoming a district manager who may replace her or to bolster his ego and secure a stronger tie between Joseph and the company, making Joseph work harder to achieve more.

Indeed, Rachael may not make a full commitment to either line. Instead, she may find a way to feel out Joseph's potential reaction to each possibility before committing herself to either. In this way the interaction becomes tentative and negotiable. The precise meanings (reactions) are up for grabs (McCall and Simmons 1978). And in this way, the identities that each person has are also negotiated. Rachael may be district manager, but is she a supportive district manager or a hard-driving district manager? The social structure may not provide that detail, yet her style could come to help define the role for future district managers, so the impact is not all one way. It is not only that being a district manager makes her act in a certain way. Her actions also help define (the meaning of) what a district manager is and what a district manager does.

Two aspects of this narrative warrant comment. When we are dealing with the action choices of the agents, we see that they are guided by meanings. These include the meanings that each wishes to establish (it was an excellent sale or it was an OK sale; Rachael is a supportive district manager or she is a hard-driving district manager) and the meanings that are taken for granted (Joseph is the store manager, Rachael is the district manager, they are in the store office). The interaction consists of the use of symbols, language, and gestures to convey, negotiate, manipulate, and otherwise control meanings. The meanings that are being controlled are those that are being produced by the symbols given off by both of the interactants as well as those given off by symbolic objects in the environment, such as the books and other objects in the office, including those things that define the space as an office.

Not all of the action and interaction of the two identities in the situation involve symbols and the control of symbolic meanings. Some of the interaction involves the control of sign meanings through the control of various resources in the situation: things such as the books (which are actually records on a computer), the computer, the desk, a pad of paper and pencil for notes, a chair to sit down on, space to lay out notepaper and to write, heat to keep the office warm, light to see by, electricity to run the computer and operate the lights, the cups of coffee that keep us refreshed, and so on. Much of the physical activity is used to control these resources that sustain the interaction and allow the symbolic activity to take place. Symbolic activity always takes place in physical settings and is sustained by those physical settings.[8] We will discuss the use of signs in more detail in chapter 5.

Structural Symbolic Interaction: An Overview

The above discussion of self, language, and interaction can be summarized to form an outline of the structural symbolic interaction perspective. The following description is drawn from Stryker (1980 [2002]).

Symbols provide a shared view of the world by providing names for a large number of objects and categories that are relevant to social interaction. Along with the names, symbols provide shared meanings (responses) for the objects and categories named. Because the meanings (responses) to the objects and categories are shared, they also form the basis of expectations for the behavior of others. That is, because I know how I respond to some symbol, I will expect you to respond similarly.

These symbols are learned in interaction with others as one learns how to classify, divide, and name the world. Among the important things one learns to name and hence respond to are the "positions" in the ongoing patterns of interaction we call social structure. Because the named positions have the same meaning to everyone, these meanings form the basis of expectations for the behavior of those who occupy the positions. These shared expectations are held by the incumbents as well as by others, since they are all responding to the same set of symbols. In this way the incumbents also come to name themselves.

Since the "positions" are patterns of interaction, the names and the meanings conveyed are not isolated from other names and positions. Indeed each is defined relative to the others, and the meanings mutually support one another. Hence, for example, "husband" is meaningful only in relation to "wife." As the self is named in a position, an identity or agent is thereby formed in the set of meanings that must be maintained. The meanings also form the basis of the expected behaviors (role) associated with that position as it relates to other positions in the overall social structure.

The behaviors are also symbolic and convey meaning. Thus, as the behaviors initiated by the agent identities occur and proceed in interaction, there is a flow of symbols (action) and meanings (response). To the extent that these meanings are shared, such flow of symbols and meanings serves to validate and reinforce existing symbols and names in the situation. Because there is never perfect agreement between agents about the meanings of behaviors, the flow of symbols and meanings also can shift and alter existing names and meanings, so that, to some extent, they are constantly being negotiated. Commonality of meanings and understandings is always being developed and verified. Where the consensus is high, the resulting structure is more stable and rigid; when the consensus is low, the structure is more fluid and changing. What is important in the interaction is not the behaviors themselves but the meanings of the behaviors, and it was this that Blumer pointed to when he coined the term *symbolic interaction*. The fact that these occur within the structures of society and are highly dependent upon those structures (often being defined by them) is what Stryker pointed to when he coined the term *structural symbolic interaction*.

What we have, then, are agent identities that come into being with the emergence of structure, that is, named patterns of behaviors and expectations. At the same time, these identities produce the patterns of behaviors that are named and constitute the structures. The patterning of behaviors is really a patterning of symbols and meanings that produce and reproduce the structure of society in a tug-of-war between agents that seek to validate existing self-meanings and thereby (because of lack of perfect consensus) invalidate, to some extent, meanings being maintained by other agents. There is constant negotiation over meaning in the face of dissensus and the creation of meaning in the face of ambiguity. In this way identities both negotiate and create their roles—that is, the patterning of symbols and meanings they produce—as well as play out and maintain themselves through the display of self-validating meanings.

We have provided this brief overview of some of the principles of structural symbolic interaction as a way of summarizing many of the ideas we have been discussing. At the same time, we want to emphasize that there is more than is contained in this summary. More has to do with the nature of the agents carrying out the social action and interaction, as well as the nature of the setting of the interaction and the nature of the social structure that both arises out of the interaction and embeds that interaction. These are topics discussed in later chapters.

Overview of the Book

The next chapter presents the historical roots of identity theory in symbolic interactionist thought, and we revisit some of the ideas mentioned in this chapter to give a deeper understanding of the background of identity theory. Chapter 3 outlines identity theory in its more general formulation as viewed in the work of a number of contemporary researchers. Following that, chapter 4 presents the identity control model and the identity-verification process. In chapter 5, we extend the basic identity model from its symbolic interactionist origins to consider the role of resources that we touched on earlier in this chapter. Chapter 6 discusses the three different bases of identities that exist in roles, groups, and persons. Consideration of the multiple identities that people hold and that exist in situated interaction is the subject of chapter 7, while chapter 8 brings in the topic of emotion as it is understood in identity theory. Chapter 9 discusses identity change. In the final chapter, we discuss directions for future research on a number of theoretical and methodological fronts.

2

The Roots of Identity Theory

As pointed out in the last chapter, identity theory did not arise wholly new. It had its beginnings in two sets of ideas that originated prior to identity theory, and we will discuss those here. One set of ideas, *symbolic interactionism,* includes thoughts about what makes up identities as well as how they function. Stryker (1980 [2002]) traces the ideas of the symbolic interaction background of identity theory to the views of the nature of the self discussed by the Scottish moral philosophers (e.g., Ferguson 1792; Smith 1966 [1759]) and more recently to contributions of William James (1890), James Baldwin (1906), Charles Horton Cooley (1902; 1909), W. I. Thomas (1928), and George Herbert Mead (e.g., 1934). Each of these, and others, has added to the amalgam that is identity theory. The other set of ideas from which identity theory stems is *perceptual control theory* as developed primarily by William T. Powers (1973). This set of ideas concerns the nature of control systems and provides an understanding of "purpose" and "goals," which underlie all living things. These ideas are incorporated into identity theory as the basis for understanding how identities function.

In the present chapter, we review both symbolic interactionism and perceptual control theory. In looking at the ideas of symbolic interactionism, we pay particular attention to the work of Mead who laid the groundwork for much current thinking about the self. We present this not as a history of thought but as a consideration of ideas from a few writers (namely Mead, James, Cooley, and Stryker) that have made their way centrally into identity theory. In considering the more recent work on perceptual control developed by Powers (1973) that has been central to the more recent developments of identity theory, we choose to provide a conceptual outline of how control systems work on which we can build later without being too technical. The next chapter also provides some background to identity theory. In it, we will review the relationship between identity theory and its closely related cousins.

Symbolic Interactionism

George Herbert Mead

The term "symbolic interaction" was coined by Herbert Blumer (1962; 1969), in his exegesis of the thinking of Mead, to denote a perspective that focuses on the unique character of human interaction that centers on the shared use of symbols. Symbols, as we briefly discussed earlier and explain in more detail below, can be used to represent objects and events in the situation (including other symbols) even when the objects and events are not physically present. Words are symbols, for example, that are used to communicate ideas. Because Blumer's work mostly spelled out his interpretation of the work of George Herbert Mead, we start our exposition of symbolic interaction by looking at the contributions of Mead as the most fully developed and central components of symbolic interaction out of which identity theory has grown. This is by no means an outline of the writings of Mead. Rather, we include only those ideas that are directly pertinent to identity theory.

Mind and Self

Mead opens his book *Mind, Self, and Society* (1934) (derived from notes for lectures he gave in his courses at the University of Chicago) with a discussion of the mind, which develops in conjunction with the self as part of a social process. As we mentioned earlier in chapter 1, the mind/self in Mead's view is embedded in society and developed through communication and interaction with others. The mind adaptively operates to relate the person to his or her environment. Mead sees behavior as continuously adjusting to the environment, using the mind's ability for selective attention and perceptions (Meltzer 1972). Especially important in this process is the mind's ability to reflexively recognize the self and treat the self as an object much like any other object in the situation. This reflexivity of the mind/self is central to the symbolic interactionist perspective and identity theory.

This ability to recognize the self as an object allows the mind/self to think about and act on the self in the same way that the self can think about and act on any other part of the environment. For example, people may apply makeup to their faces (acting toward the self) or landscape their homes (acting toward something that may help define the self). Persons attend to those aspects of the environment that are relevant for their own behavior and goals. Indeed, having conscious goals for the self depends upon the ability to see the self and understand the status of the self in the environment. To move the self literally or figuratively from some point A to another point B, one has to perceive the self and recognize that one is at point A, and one has to see where point B is and see how to move the self to point B. Finally, one has to take action to carry out this movement and to recognize when one has arrived at point B. For example, if Tom wants to go from his office to his car, he has to recognize that he is currently in his office; he has to know where his car is parked; he has to see how he might negotiate his way from his office to where his car is parked; and finally, he has to actually move himself from his office to his car. In this way, by acting toward and on the self, Tom, or anyone, is able to accomplish his goals.

At the same time, Mead suggests, people not only act on themselves to achieve goals—for example, Tom moving himself from his office to his car—but also they adjust and change their environment as well as themselves and their behavior in order to achieve their goals. Tom may organize his office files for easy access to things he needs to do his job. He may also adjust his chair to put himself at what he perceives to be a comfortable distance from his computer monitor on his desk. Perception and action are intertwined and related through a mind that has socially developed to respond, not just to the environment, but also to the relationship between the person and the environment, adjusting each to meet the needs, goals, and desires of the person. This connection between perception and action or behavior is central to identity theory, as is the understanding that behavior is always in the pursuit of the goals of the person.

Mead's notion of the self as composed of an "I" and a "me" brings our attention to this connection between perception and action as guided by the mind. The "I" is the agent-actor aspect of the self that initiates action in order to bring about desired consequences or intentions. The "me" is the perceptive-observer aspect of the self that looks at the action, looks at the environment, looks at the relation between the two, and guides activity of the "I" to its intended end. The "me" is not just an individual's perceptions, however, as it also contains the social knowledge of the community or culture in which the individual lives, or what Mead refers to as the "generalized other," and the knowledge of the place of the person in the community. The "me" originates in the process of taking the role of the other (role-taking), in which one is able to perceive the world, including oneself, from the point of view of the other and their intentions. The "me" is social, embodying the meanings, understandings, and experiences of the community. In addition, the "me" is individual, knowing the needs of the self as well as the place of the self within the community. In this way the "me" is reflexive, being able to take the self into account as an object that is distinct from others, but as an object that has its definition and place in the community of others.

Mead gives the example of a person playing baseball. The actions of a baseball player are determined not only by the player's position on the team but also by the player's knowledge of all the positions in the team and their relationship to one another and to the player's position within that community or team. In addition, for smooth interaction and game play, the player must know the positions of the opposing team and the relationship among all of the positions on both teams. To have this understanding of the interrelationship among the positions, each player must take the role of the other (indeed, of the whole set of others) in relation to his or her own role and understand his or her own role from the point of view of the organized community of others. The second base player must know the roles of the pitcher and the first base player (among others) and how those players relate to the second base player.

Mead suggests that the "I" and the "me" are phases of the self. The "I" initiates the act that then comes under the direction, control, and guidance of the "me." This should not be understood as a series of steps, however. The "I" is continuously acting, and the "me" is continuously perceiving and guiding in order to both bring about and maintain the person in relationship to the environment and to others in the situation.

Being part of a culture, one comes to learn the concepts, the categories and classifications, and the meanings and expressions that are used by others in the culture to understand the world. Stryker (1980 [2002]) has noted this in his statement of the set of assumptions underlying the structural version of symbolic interactionism, which we discuss a little later. He states that behavior is dependent on a named and classified world. The names point to aspects of the environment and carry meaning in the form of expectations about those aspects of the environment that are shared with others. One learns how to classify and name objects and how to behave with respect to those objects and their names through interactions with others in the community. Among those class terms, Stryker suggests, are the names that are used to designate positions in the social structure such as teacher, student, truck driver, judge, police officer, and so on.

Signs and Symbols

Central to this process of naming things is the idea of shared meanings, which Mead discusses under the concepts of *signs* and *symbols*, which we discussed briefly in chapter 1. To understand how meanings might become shared, Mead suggests that imitation plays a large role. Imitation, he says, is possible when one observes another's reaction or response to some situational stimulus and that reaction has already been learned by the individual. That is, the observer already has the behavior or response as part of his or her behavioral repertoire—something he or she already has done and can do. When that stimulus, which calls forth the reaction in the other, also calls forth the same reaction in the observer, the observer sees this commonality and "understands" the other's reaction, since the observer is already familiar with the response. Because the reaction has already been learned by the individual, the meaning is understood. Moreover, because the response of the observer is also seen in the other, the observer understands that the response is shared. In this shared understanding of the commonality of responses to the stimulus lies the beginning of the symbol. In this case, we have what is known as a *natural sign* or simply a *sign*: a common reaction to some stimulus in the environment. As examples, the changing color of the leaves is a sign of autumn and the needle on the gas gauge pointed close to the "E" is a sign we need to stop and get gas.

We can take our understanding of the matter a step further when we consider the case in which the source of the stimulus is the person rather than the environment, and that stimulus calls forth a reaction shared both by the person and another. In this case, when the source of the stimulus is the person, we have a *conventional sign* or *symbol*, sometimes known as a *significant symbol*. This is a stimulus produced by a person that leads to a common response in both oneself and the other. The nature of this common response is arrived at by social convention. Language as used in communication is such a set of significant symbols, the meanings of which are shared by the user and the other. Symbolic interactionism has tended to focus primarily, or even solely, on symbols because it forms the basis of thought, language, communication, and interaction. As we will see in chapter 5, however, signs have a vitally important place as well, since they tie persons to resources and the natural world within the situation (Freese and Burke 1994). For now, common reactions to the symbols representing, for example, a judge or police officer allow us to understand the responses of others to these symbols because they are also our responses.

Gestures

Meaning, then, is a response to a conventional stimulus or symbol. The response may be observable behavior or internal, mindful behavior (thinking). The use of symbols allows thinking, language, communication, and interaction. With respect to language and communication, Mead sets forth the idea of the *gesture* as an important unit in communication and interaction. The gesture, Mead indicates, has meaning to the person who uses it and to the person to whom it is directed.

When Bill shakes a fist in Tom's face (the gesture), Tom assumes that Bill has not only a hostile attitude but also an idea behind it. That is, Bill, as the person making the gesture, understands the meaning of the gesture in terms of it being the beginning of an act that accomplishes Bill's purpose or goal. The gesture of the shaking of the fist also has a meaning to Tom, in whose face the fist is shaken. Tom understands the meaning of the shaking fist and understands the idea behind it—the attitude, the threat, and the intention of Bill. The meaning of the shaking fist is the idea behind it, an idea that is built up in the situation, but which draws upon the whole set of shared experiences. The gesture becomes a symbol when it calls up in Bill, the person making it, the same response as it calls up in Tom, the person to whom it is directed.

The gesture is the initial part of the act, but over time it comes to contain the meanings and implications of the complete act; it stands for and represents the complete act. The shaking fist may be the beginning of a complete aggressive act that aims to block and hurt another person. A complete act such as this includes the goals, outcomes, or intentions toward which the activity moves. Indeed, because the full set of meanings, intentions, and outcomes is contained in the gesture, one does not need to complete the entire act for communication to take place.[1] For humans to cooperate in interaction, there must be a process in which each acting individual ascertains the intention of the acts of the other and then makes a response on the basis of that intention. Thus, people must understand the lines of action of others and guide their own behavior to fit in with those lines of action.

Persons do not respond to the activities of others. Rather, they respond to the intentions of others as represented in the gestures. This is done through role-taking, that is, putting oneself in the position of the other to understand his or her intentions. Communication and interaction become a conversation of gestures between individuals to share and coordinate meanings and expectations. Each individual uses gestures (symbols) to indicate to the other the meanings and intentions *of* the self. In so doing, the individual also indicates those meanings and intentions *to* the self. Incidentally, Mead suggests that thinking occurs when the source and target of the gesture is the self—an internal conversation of gestures. By inhibiting overt external action, the individual is able to "think," that is, to complete the act "in the mind," trying out various approaches in imagination.

Mead suggests this happens in conjunction with problems that the individual encounters—problems primarily dealing with the interface between the individual and the physical and social environment in which the individual exists. By representing to oneself different possibilities and alternatives for future action in advance of overt behavior, the individual has a choice of actions to accomplish his or her goals in the best way possible in light of the problems presented. How often, for example, do we lie awake at night imagining some important interaction coming up, playing through in our mind all of the different ways it might go and how we might respond? Mind is thus symbolic in character, dealing with the hypothetical, the past, and the future as representations.

Planning and reasoning are processes of the mind. Objects, things, and processes in the environment thus take on a symbolic quality (especially those not present in the immediate situation) as they are represented in the mind, and their meanings and uses to solve a problem are worked out. Objects, things, processes, and other resources thus are understood in terms of their function for the individual—to sustain the individual, to help the individual meet goals, and to help the individual survive. Because these objects and resources are represented *symbolically*, the shared meanings and understandings are important for the individual in this context. However, as we indicated, Mead also considers nonshared or natural signs and sign meanings as stimuli in the situation. We shall see later how these become important within the context of identity theory.

William James

Although identity theory draws most heavily on the work of Mead, there are two important points from the work of James's writings (1890) that predate Mead and are important to identity theory. In addition to emphasizing that people are social and that habit plays an important role in human behavior beyond biology and instinct, James called attention to the complexity of the self with the recognition that people have multiple selves—as many different selves as there are different others that recognize the individual (James 1890, p. 294).

As we discussed in chapter 1, the structure of society is made of multiple positions that relate to one another: doctors, lawyers, truck drivers, teachers, students, and warehouse operators. James recognized that each person could occupy several positions and thus have multiple selves. One can be a teacher, a wife, a mother, a friend, a PTA member, and so on. Each position has its own meanings and expectations that are internalized as what we would now call an identity, but which James referred to collectively as multiple selves. Mary may be known by some as a teacher, by others as a wife, and by still others as a PTA member. James was one of the first to recognize this complexity of the self and its tie to the complexity of society. Each of these multiple selves we now recognize as different identities. Each "self," as we use the term, is therefore made up of the multiple identities a person has. We develop these ideas more fully in chapter 7.

The second idea we draw from James concerns his treatment of the feelings of self-esteem. James argues that self-esteem is a function of both our achievements and our aspirations (James 1890, p. 310). His often-repeated formula put it this way:

$$\text{SELF-ESTEEM} = \frac{\text{SUCCESSES}}{\text{PRETENSION}}$$

Thus, even if our achievements (successes in the formula) are high, our self-esteem will be low if our aspirations (pretensions in the formula) are higher still. Similarly, even modest achievements can boost one's self-esteem if aspirations are even more modest. James's formulation makes clear that the consequences of what we do, in this regard, are relative to our goals. Our goals set the standard for measuring our accomplishments. We discuss his ideas on self-esteem more fully in chapter 4.

Charles Horton Cooley

Cooley (1902) set forth a number of ideas that have come to be incorporated in the symbolic interaction perspective and in identity theory more specifically.

One of Cooley's strengths was his early recognition of the importance of senti-ments or emotions arising out of the way the self operates in interaction with others. For example, James (1890) understood self-esteem to arise out of the internal self-processes centering on one's aspirations and attainments, and Cooley recognized the importance of the relationship between oneself and others as central in the origins of sentiments. This relationship with others is suggested, for example, in Cooley's notion of a looking-glass self. As in a mir-ror, people see themselves reflected in the reactions of others to them. These are what are called *reflected appraisals* and constitute one of the main ways we come to understand who we are in identity theory. If others look puzzled, for example, Sally may realize she is not being clear. If another appears angry, Tom may realize he said or did something to upset the other. In addition, Cooley recognized that people imagine the other's response to that reflected view of who they are and have an emotional reaction such as pride or mor-tification to what they think others' reactions to them are (Cooley 1902). For example, based on another's reaction, Tom might think that the other per-ceives him as weak and might imagine the other is disappointed in him. Tom therefore may be very upset by that imagined assessment. These emotional responses thus come into being through the playing out in the mind of the actor the nature of their perceived relationship to the other in the situation.

Cooley (1902, p. 227 ff) continues this discussion of the emotional conse-quences of one's relationships to others in terms of having their self-views confirmed and shared by others in the community. To the extent that this does not happen—that is, to the extent that a person's self-views are not confirmed by others—Cooley suggests that person may become upset, turn bitter, feel cut off or anomic, and attempt to change things. As we will see in chapter 4, this idea, too, becomes central in identity theory.

Sheldon Stryker

To begin to understand what is meant by the term "identity," we turn to Sheldon Stryker since he is one of the originators of identity theory. For Stryker (1980 [2002], p. 60), a person has an identity or an "internalized positional designation" for each of the different positions or roles the person holds in society. Thus, if someone has the position of husband, he has a corresponding husband identity. If he holds the position of worker, he has a corresponding worker identity. As we will see later, for Burke (1980), these internalized designations are in the form of "meanings." For example, the husband identity is what it *means* to be a husband. It is the *content* as to how one sees oneself in a position.

In his outline of the structural aspects of the symbolic interaction frame-work, Stryker (1980 [2002]) presents a set of basic premises on which identity theory are based. Because of their centrality to identity theory, we present the main ones here. These premises are built primarily on the ideas of Mead but draw on other thinkers as well. Stryker's first assertion is that behavior is premised on a named or classified world. The names or class terms attached to aspects of the environment, both physical and social, carry meaning in the form of shared behavioral expectations that grow out of social interaction. From interaction with others, one learns how to classify objects one comes into contact with, and in that process also learns how one is expected to behave with reference to those objects (Stryker 1980 [2002], p. 53–54).

This statement succinctly describes the basic symbolic character of the world. It also makes clear that the meanings pertain to both physical and social objects. People respond to those physical and social objects, and their responses give them meaning. In this sense, meaning is a response to the socially defined objects that make up the world. That people share these responses lets people understand, predict, and come to expect the actions of others.

Stryker's second premise makes clear the way social structure fits into the structural symbolic paradigm: "Among the class terms learned in interaction are the symbols used to designate 'positions,' which are the relatively stable, morphological components of social structure. These positions carry the shared behavioral expectations that are conventionally labeled 'roles'" (Stryker 1980 [2002], p. 54). Roles such as teacher, judge, or truck driver are not just constructed or created anew in each situation. They exist and have existed before most of us were born. People perceive, react to, and label them within society. They are shared by members of the culture and only slowly change or evolve as their use may change. Once created, those labels/ categories such as judge or truck driver are present, shared, and used by all participants of the culture.

Stryker's third and fourth premises show how actors with identities fit into this view. The third proposition indicates that people in society name or label one another in terms of the positions they occupy, such as teacher or judge. When they do so, they invoke shared meanings and expectations with regard to one another's behavior as a teacher or judge, for example. The fourth proposition indicates that people, using the reflexive aspect of the self, also name themselves with respect to these positional designations. For example, not only do others name Mary as a teacher or Billy as a student, but also Mary names herself as teacher and Billy calls himself a student. In this way, Mary *is* a teacher and Billy *is* a student. It is these labels and the expectations and meanings attached to them that become internalized as the parts of the self that we call identities. People thus become a part of the social structure, occupying and identifying with the structural positions that are named in proposition two.

These self-labels define individuals in terms of their positions in society, and these positions in society are relational in the sense that they tie individuals together. For example, father is tied to son or daughter, teacher is tied to student, boy is tied to girl; the meanings and expectations for each position are related to the meanings and expectations for the other positions to which each is tied, as in Mead's example of the baseball team. This also implies that the meanings associated with each position are related to the meanings associated with other related positions. What it means to be a teacher is tied to what it means to be a student; what it means to be a boy is tied to what it means to be a girl. Because the meanings and expectations for each position and identity are tied to the meanings for a related position or identity (or a set of such), each person not only knows his or her own meanings and expectations but also knows the meanings and expectations of those of others in related positions. As a student, Billy knows what is expected of him, and that relates to what is expected of Mary as a teacher. This knowledge allows Billy to consider Mary's role in formulating his own behaviors and meanings in the classroom. Billy knows what his behavior may mean to the teacher, Mary, and he can choose those meanings that give his behavior credibility in defining himself as a student. In this way both teacher and student are able to interact with each other smoothly and are each able to achieve their goals and intentions.

In addition to the names, meanings, and expectations that are applied to persons who occupy particular positions in society, Stryker's (1980 [2002]) premises also recognize that interactive situations are also named. He suggests that when entering interactive situations, persons define situation by applying names to it, to the other participants in the interaction, to themselves, and to particular features within the situation, and use the resulting definition to organize their own behavior accordingly. If the situation is a funeral, we expect different behaviors than if the situation is a birthday party.

Overall, Stryker has laid out the symbolic interaction underpinnings of identities as well as the way in which identities and their symbolic underpinnings are tied into the larger structural aspects of society in terms of the roles that people play. As we will see, this provides a solid foundation on which identity theory is built.

Control Systems

In addition to the ideas and concepts derived from the symbolic interaction framework, identity theory also incorporates ideas about control systems that were developing in the middle of the twentieth century under the rubric of cybernetics. The work of Norbert Weiner brought these ideas to the fore with the founding of cybernetics as a field. The publication of his book on cybernetics (Weiner 1948) laid out the way in which "negative feedback" could be used to control the output of systems. The problem was to keep certain processes such as steam engines or electric motors from going too fast or too slow. The insight was to control the amount of steam or electricity going into the system (engine or motor) based on the output speed of the system. If the output was too fast, for example, this information was fed back to reduce the flow on the input side (steam or electricity). Conversely, if the output of the system was too slow, the information was fed back to increase the input. Too much output being used to reduce the input and too little output being used to increase the input is called negative feedback (from output to input). This idea of control through the use of negative feedback was picked up and used extensively in a number of fields to control the output of various mechanical and electrical systems.

The idea is illustrated in figure 2.1, in which a varying input (represented by the wavy line on the left) sent into the system (in the middle) becomes a steady controlled output (represented on the right by the less wavy line). As suggested above, this is accomplished by taking some of the output and feeding it back to the input in negative or inverted form (negative feedback). Thus, if the input rises above some set point or desired level of output, this is sensed in the output and the rise is reversed and subtracted from the input, thus in effect canceling the rise in the input quantity.[2] If the input lowers below the set point, this is sensed in the output and the lowering is reversed and added to the input, again canceling the lowering input. With proper tuning of the amount of feedback, the output is therefore maintained at the steady state of the set point. Motors are kept at constant rpm, flows at constant level, and so on.

What is not explicitly represented in the figure is the set point, sometimes called the reference or standard of the system. In these early models, the standard was generally seen to be in the hands of the designer/engineer who wants the motor to run at certain speed, for example. It was not viewed as an intrinsic part of the system itself. A control system of this sort is thus a system that controls its output through the appropriate use of feedback. It produces a constant output in spite of unstable and unpredictable inputs, and from this perspective is quite applicable to many engineering problems.

However, it was the work of William Powers (1973) that made the application of negative feedback to humans (and living systems) much clearer than the engineering perspective outlined above. Powers pointed out that it

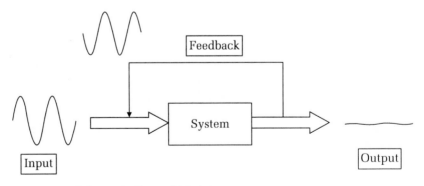

Figure 2.1. Cybernetic Control Model

is not the control of output or behavior that matters for persons. Rather, it is the control of perception or input to the system that is important. Humans maintain a steady and stable environment in the face of disturbances, not a steady output. Indeed, the output behavior of humans is quite variable, but the variation in behavior counteracts variability in the situation. Variability in the situation is introduced by factors that are not directly controlled, but which alter the situation. These factors are termed *disturbances*. By counteracting disturbances in the situation, what the person perceives is uniformity, constancy, and predictability.

Note that this idea is very similar to the perception-action coordination discussed by Mead that allows persons to adjust themselves and their environment to achieve their goals. By controlling their perceptions of the important aspects of the environment (rather than their behaviors in the situation), that is, by varying their actions to make their perceptions match a reference or set point (the goal), humans and other living systems achieve purpose or goals in the face of disturbances. This is the perceptual control model. People control their perceptions, not their behaviors. Indeed, people seem to use whatever behaviors accomplish the control of perceptions.

Imagine a person, Sarah, in an apartment in winter, and she perceives she is cold. She turns up the thermostat, which turns on the furnace, and the apartment gets warmer, and Sarah gets warmer. In that way, she returns her perception of how warm she is back to the set point at which she is comfortable. If that action of changing the thermostat did not result in turning on the furnace and making the apartment warmer, she may alter her behavior and call the landlord to fix the furnace or the thermostat. Or she may grab a blanket and wrap it around her. These varying actions all have the same end: make Sarah perceive that she is warm and comfortable. If it is too cold, she adds heat to keep her perceptions at a constant, comfortable level. If it gets colder, she may grab another blanket to achieve her goal of a comfortable temperature for her body.

The perceptual control model is the same control system discussed above and illustrated in figure 2.1 but rearranged and reconceptualized to include the set point or standard. Powers's perceptual control system is outlined in figure 2.2.

The loop represented by tracing the arrow from the situation through *perception,* to the *comparator,* on through the *error,* and *output* back to the situation in figure 2.2 corresponds to the feedback arrow of figure 2.1. The situation in figure 2.2 is equivalent to the output in figure 2.1. The wavy input of figure 2.1 is equivalent to the situation changing because of disturbances. Although the reversed feedback being added to the input in figure 2.1 stabilizes the output, a closer inspection shows that it also stabilizes the input just before it goes into the system, and it is that stabilized input that keeps the output stable. In figure 2.2, it is the output part of the "feedback loop" that acts on the situation to counteract the disturbances and maintain a constancy of the situation and hence the perceptions or input. The standard of

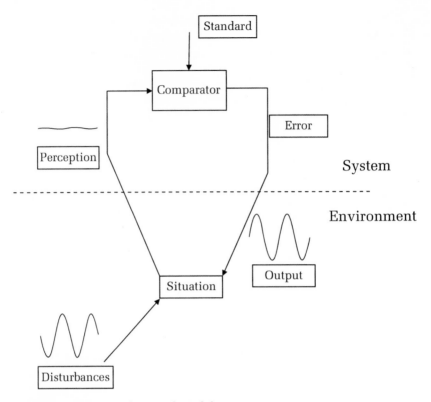

Figure 2.2. Perceptual Control Model

figure 2.2 corresponds to the set point implicit in figure 2.1. In figure 2.2, it is explicitly part of the system, and its source will be discussed later.

To illustrate the perceptual control system, imagine Sarah driving down the highway. One of her standards or goals is to drive in the middle of her traffic lane. She may also be attempting to maintain a certain speed, a certain distance from other traffic, and so on, but we ignore those other goals for a moment. As she is driving, trying to stay in the middle of her lane, she perceives her current position on the road. This is the perception. This perception of her current position is compared with her standard or goal of being in the middle of the lane. The comparator operates by comparing the perception with the standard, subtracting one from the other, representing the difference as an error. If the current position is in the middle of the lane, her perception and standard agree, the difference or error is zero, and no change in the output occurs; she continues to do as she has been doing. If she perceives that she is drifting to the right of the middle of the lane, perhaps as the result of a disturbance in the form of a gust of wind, her perception no longer matches her standard. A difference or error is registered, and her behavioral output is modified by taking action to steer the car to the left back toward the center of the lane. This reduces the error back toward zero and keeps her in the center of the lane. As Sarah becomes practiced at this, an observer will not perceive any drifting away from the center of the lane. Sarah's perception of her position is relatively constant.

Disturbances in the form of gusts of wind, turns in the road, and so on, all act to move the car away from the center of the lane. When that movement is perceived, an error is registered and counteraction to the disturbance in the form of changed output occurs, again reducing the error toward zero. In this way, Sarah maintains the standard of keeping her car in the middle of the lane. By varying the outputs (steering the car), a constant position is maintained in spite of the disturbances of wind, curves, and so on.

Now, it is quite possible for Sarah to have a different standard or to change her standard. For example, she may choose to stay in the right-hand side of the lane or between lanes, or she may choose to change her standard from staying in the center of the current lane to staying in the center of the lane to the left as she passes the car in front of her. These goals are achieved by the "purposive" actions of making one's perceptions match the standard that one holds.

The way in which these ideas about control are tied in to the ideas of symbolic interaction, meaning, and identities will be spelled out in some detail in chapter 4. Suffice it to say here, however, that the standard of the perceptual control model shown in figure 2.2 represents the set of meanings that define an identity of the person. The control system operates to maintain situational meanings consistent with the identity meanings of the standard in spite of disturbances to those situational meanings created by the interactions of others in the situation.

There is a conceptual connection between the "I" and the "me" as discussed by Mead and the perceptual control model. In the perceptual control model, output behavior is a function of the error term or difference between perceptions and identity standard. In the absence of any disturbance, the perceived self-relevant meanings in the situation (perceptions) are the same as the self-meanings in the identity standard, and behavioral output remains consistent with the identity (standard) meanings. This would be like the "I" acting in the situation producing behaviors that reflect the identity meanings of the person. On the other side, the perceptions of the self-acting in the situation (the reflexive aspect of the self) are like the "me." These perceptions are of the meanings produced and modified by the behavior of the self, and these meanings are understood by the self and others because one is part of the community of understanding—that is, the set of persons who share common reactions to the symbols. Sarah's "me" becomes known by both Sarah and others by seeing how Sarah actually comes across in the situation.

The mapping of perceptions to "me" and of output behavior to "I" is not perfect, however. The perceptual control model is a little more sophisticated. Identity theory makes a distinction between the reflexive perceptions of the self in the situation and the set of self-meanings that constitute the identity standard. Both of these seem to be part of the "me" in Mead's discussion, but the distinction is crucial in identity theory, as the standard defining the identity must be compared with the way the identity is coming across in the situation so that the activity can be coordinated to counteract disturbances and bring the perceptions into alignment with the standard. The guide for behavior, thus, is not the standard or "me" but the relationship between the standard and the current set of self-relevant meanings unfolding in the situation. Mead does talk about the goals of the act; but the mechanism by which these goals are attained, or by which one assesses progress toward the goals to make adjustments, is not spelled out by Mead. That kind of cybernetic model had not yet been discovered. Thus, it is not surprising that some adjustment of the theory must be made to accommodate this understanding.

In the perceptual control model, the output behavior is not just reflective of the self-meanings in the identity standard. It is a function of the relationship between the meanings of the perceptions and meanings of the standard. If how we are coming across in the situation is perceived as not consistent with who we are (the identity standard), behavior is changed until how we come across is consistent with the identity standard; the error or discrepancy is zero. This allows us to alter our behavior until it produces the meanings we intend (discrepancy is zero) and thus learn the local meanings in the situation and how to adjust them to fit with who we are.

Summary

We have briefly reviewed a number of ideas from earlier writers that have found their way into identity theory as central pillars. In the following chapters, we will see how these ideas play out within identity theory and within the close cousins of identity theory. Five key ideas discussed in this chapter are central among these. First is the importance of symbols and meaning for shaping our perceptions of the world and the objects and categories within it, allowing interaction, thinking, and planning. Second is the ability of the individual to take itself as an object of meaning both from its own perspective as well as from the perspective of others. The third idea is the gesture as containing meaning representing the intentions of the complete act of an actor that allows an understanding of intentions and goals of others and the self. The fourth idea is that the relationship between the individual and the situation is one of a dynamic control system containing an active agent part and a passive perceptive part that allows constant adjustment of the individual both to fit into its environment and to shape its environment to fit it. Last is the idea that the fit of the individual in its environment and with others in the situation has consequences for self-feelings and emotions of the individual, which feelings and emotions instigate and guide further action.

3

The Development of Identity Theory

The Symbolic Interaction Roots of Identity Theory

Historically, identity theory grew out of symbolic interaction (SI), particularly *structural* symbolic interaction (Stryker 1980 [2002]) as we have already mentioned. Specifically, structural symbolic interaction is a version of symbolic interaction that stands in stark contrast to the *traditional* approach to symbolic interaction. We will summarize how these two versions of SI are different since this has important implications for understanding the basis of identity theory.

Both versions of SI have the same intellectual heritage by drawing on the seminal work of the pragmatic philosopher George Herbert Mead (1934) and earlier intellectuals such as William James (1890) and Charles Horton Cooley (1902) as we discussed in the last chapter. Herbert Blumer (1969) coined the term "symbolic interactionism," and it was his ideas that led to the development of what we refer to as traditional symbolic interaction.

Although structural symbolic interaction and traditional symbolic interaction have many differences, which we shall review, we shall begin with one important commonality between the two. Most symbolic interactionists would agree that we can best understand social behavior by focusing on individuals' definitions and interpretations of themselves, others, and their situations. By identifying the meanings that actors' attributed to their surroundings, by getting "inside their head" and seeing the world from their perspective, we can understand why people do what they do (Meltzer, Petras, and Reynolds 1977). There is a strand in traditional SI that emphasizes the behavior of actors rather than their internal, subjective worlds (Couch, Saxton, and Katovich 1986). It takes seriously the pragmatic philosophers' theory of action. The focus is on how individuals' construct actions and how these actions are coordinated with others to accomplish individual and collective goals in interaction. This strand of symbolic interaction does not deny the fact that humans act on the basis of the meanings that things have for them. They simply choose to focus their attention on the actions of humans. In general, however, symbolic interactionists share the premise that we need to "get at" social actors' subjective world and understand their reality as they do. From this assumption, the traditional and structural versions of SI begin to diverge. The basis of this divergence is twofold. They differ as to the role of social structure in understanding self and social behavior, and they differ on the use of a prior theory and the development of theory to explain social psychological processes. We first turn to the role of social structure.

Substantively, the traditional version of SI has a tendency to neglect the relatively "fixed" nature of social structure in its analysis of social behavior. In the traditional version of SI, social structure (and society, more generally) is viewed as always in a state of flux, in the process of being created and recreated through the interpretations, definitions, and actions of individuals in situations. In situations, from the view of traditional SI, actors identify the things that need to be taken into account, they act on the basis of what it is they have identified, and they attempt to fit their lines of action with others in the situation to accomplish their goals. Individuals are free to define situations in any way they wish with the consequence that society is always thought to be in a state of flux with outcomes determined by negotiation, but with no overarching organization or structure from the view of the individual. If social structure exists at all, it is a temporary social order, which is assembled when actors greet one another and interact, disassembled upon actors parting, and assembled anew when actors meet again. As Stryker (2000, p. 27) has remarked on the traditional version of SI, "[It] tends to dissolve [social] structure in a solvent of subjective definitions, to view definitions as unanchored, open to any possibility, failing to recognize that some possibilities are more probable than others. On the premise that self reflects society, this view leads to seeing self as undifferentiated, unorganized, unstable, and ephemeral."

The structural version of SI examines the role of social structure in social life. Society is not continuously in a state of flux as the traditional version of SI would claim. Instead, it is viewed as stable and durable, as reflected in the patterned behavior within and between individuals. It is preexistent to the person; "in the beginning there is society" as Stryker (1997) titles one of his papers. We are born into a social world that is ongoing and organized, and we learn about this organization through socialization. Others (parents, educators, the media, and so forth) teach us what it is.

According to the structural version, we come to learn that within society there are an array of groups, networks, communities, and institutions that sometimes are distinct from one another and sometimes overlap in a competitive or cooperative manner. We navigate in and around these various crosscutting groupings depending upon our tastes, and they influence who we become. As Stryker and Vryan (2003, p. 22) argue,

> Social structures in general define boundaries, making it likely that those located within them will or will not have relations with particular kinds of others and interact with those others over particular kinds of issues with particular kinds of resources. Structures will also affect the likelihood that persons will or will not develop particular kinds of selves, learn particular kinds of motivations, and have particular symbolic resources for defining situations they enter.

Exposure to particular social structures helps shape individual goals. As Sewell (1992, p. 21) remarks: "Without a notion of heaven and hell a person cannot strive for admission into paradise; only in a modern capitalist economy can one attempt to make a killing on the futures market."

Social structure provides both limits and possibilities for actors' behavior. In chapter 1, we introduced the concepts of "agency" and "social structure" in order to set the foundation for understanding identities. We briefly revisit these concepts here to emphasize why we need to take into account the social structure, why we should not just give it "lip service." Because social actors have agency, that is, their actions are oriented to individually held goals (from proximal goals such as accomplishing a particular task in a situation to distal goals as in achieving one's moral objectives), individuals have the capacity to create social structures. Social structures emerge from individual actions as those individual actions are patterned across persons and over time. And, actors have the capacity to change social structures as well, thereby reorienting social behavior with the results that new patterns emerge. Social movements are a good example of a way that social action can mobilize social structural change, and movements such as the civil rights movement and the feminist movement have been effective in this change.

However, individual action also occurs in the context of social structures within which the individuals exist. On the one hand, social structures impose constraints on the agency of actors. For example, there is strong evidence on the intergenerational transmission of class position or the intergenerational transmission of aggression. On the other hand, social structures can provide resources and opportunity structures for actors such that they can overcome these constraints. For example, we take notice when the unexpected occurs, as when people become upwardly mobile actors in the class structure or when their experience of a violent upbringing becomes transformed into an adult life of nonviolence. Complexity is added to the picture when we see that although agency involves an individual accomplishing certain goals, if the goals are consistent with social structural arrangements, they are reinforcing not only for the person but also for the structures within which the interaction is embedded. If the individual's goals are in opposition to social structural arrangements, interaction may, on the one hand, become disruptive and destabilize the existing structures or, on the other hand, become squelched as the individual is prevented from obtaining his or her goals.

Considering the influence of the social structure makes us aware that individuals' outcomes are not completely orchestrated by their own or even others' actions as traditional symbolic interactionists would maintain. Structural arrangements persist according to their own principles and intrude into interaction, and they can constrain the actions of actors. Indeed, every situation has an implicit status hierarchy, a distribution of resources, a set of norms that shape and guide interaction and so forth, and this may constrain what actors can accomplish.

Structural symbolic interactionists grapple with how actors and social structure relate to one another. We think good sociological research is that which goes back and forth between the agency of individuals and the social structure in which their actions take place. Such work shows how structures are the accomplishments of actors, but it also demonstrates how actors are always acting within the structures they create and are thereby constrained. It is agents who are producing actions for their own goals, the patterns of which constitute social structure. But, social structural forces also act back on their creators guiding and limiting what individuals can do. Now we turn to the second difference between the traditional and structural versions of SI: the role of theory.

There are some traditional symbolic interactionists who agree with the Blumerian assumption that we cannot create theory or use *a priori* theory to explain social behavior, because we would be predicting social behavior and such prediction is impossible. They argue that there is no constancy or stability that exists, that can be studied, or from which we can develop theory. Within the traditional SI perspective, individuals are seen as actively and constantly constructing and reconstructing meanings and interpretations of themselves, others, and the interaction; coordinated lines of action are continuously being produced and reproduced, and social structure emerges in the situation rather than helping define and shape the situation. Because everything is in a state of flux, researchers are unable to obtain any reliable measures of their concepts or ideas. There is no stable reference point for measurement. If there is no reliable way by which to measure concepts, then a first step in building theory is not met. According to traditional SI, at best, what researchers can turn to are "sensitizing concepts" that provide them with some direction as to what and where to look when examining social action, recognizing that this direction may change as actors' meanings and lines of action shift and change in the situation. Further, *a priori* theory cannot be imported into one's study, because the local situation will be sufficiently unique (again, because of its constant construction and reconstruction by social actors), thereby rendering prior concepts from existing theories useless. All that social researchers can do is show, after the fact, what has developed in the situation. Essentially, the focus of traditional symbolic interactionists is on describing and understanding rather than explaining and predicting.

Many structural symbolic interactionists are committed to developing and testing predictive explanations of social behavior as are we. This commitment is rooted in Manford Kuhn's (1964) view of symbolic interaction, which stands in stark contrast to Blumer's position. Unlike Blumer, Kuhn was interested in universal predictions of human conduct. His development of "self theory" was an effort to develop a set of generalizations about the self. Kuhn saw individuals as having a stable, core self. As a way of measuring this stable reference point—the self—he developed the Twenty Statements Test (TST), which measured people's responses (allowing up to twenty answers) to the question, "Who am I?" This questionnaire was an important development by which symbolic interactionists could begin to examine internal processes in a quantifiable manner across people and situations.

Most structural symbolic interactionists maintain that there is sufficient constancy in social life to warrant the development of theoretical generalizations, which has been done with much success. Concepts can be measured; predictions about the self, action, and interaction can be developed and tested; theories can emerge from this testing; and further expansion and development of theories is possible with additional observations across place and time. Although there is change, there is enough stability to generate meaningful data that is sufficiently reliable and valid, which allows for generating and testing hypotheses, and which facilitates the growth of theory. In this way, the scientific procedure can be applied to an analysis of social life, and, as we will see, identity theory has been highly successful along these lines.

Introducing Identity Theory

Consistent with our focus, all of the theorists that we review below who have been instrumental in developing identity theory emphasize the social structural version rather than the traditional version of symbolic interaction. Sheldon Stryker emphasizes this approach the most, and Peter Burke probably emphasizes it the least. Nevertheless, all share the assumption that society is patterned and organized, and the self emerges within the context of a complex, organized society. If society is organized, so too must the self be organized. This reflects that dictum that the "self reflects society" (Stryker 1980 [2002]). This idea follows from James's (1890) notion that there are as many selves as there are different positions that one holds in society and as there are different groups who respond to the self.

In identity theory, different theorists focus on different aspects of one's identity. For this reason, we can say that identity theory has slightly different emphases (Stryker and Burke 2000). In the work of Stryker and his colleagues (Serpe 1987; Serpe and Stryker 1987; Stryker 1980 [2002]; Stryker and Serpe 1982; 1994), the focus is on how the social structure influences one's identity and behavior. Peggy Thoits's (1983; 1991; 1995) research also has this emphasis. The work of Burke and his associates (Burke 1980; Burke 1991; 2004a; Burke and Reitzes 1981; 1991; Burke and Stets 1999; Cast, Stets, and Burke 1999; Stets and Burke 2000) emphasizes the internal dynamics within the self that influence behavior. A third emphasis is in the work of George McCall and J. L. Simmons (McCall 2003; McCall and Simmons1978). Here the focus is on how identities are maintained in face-to-face interaction. Though a clear program of research has not come out of McCall and Simmons's work, they do make important theoretical contributions to understanding identities that are important to review. Below, we provide more detail on each of these orientations. Before reviewing these major emphases in identity theory, we'd like to briefly discuss the history of the idea of identity from some of the earliest theorists.

Erik Erikson (1950) was one of the first to bring this concept into the social sciences, though his usage of the term corresponded more to what we would call the self-concept, a more global representation of what Rosenberg (1979) described as all that one knows, thinks, and feels about oneself and who one is. Nelson Foote (1951) was perhaps the first to use the term "identity" close to the way it is used in identity theory. For Foote, the concept of identity gave motivation to the rather sterile concept of role. He recognized that roles prescribe relationships and behaviors, that there are expectations associated with the role positions. But the energy, motivation, and drive that make roles actually work require that individuals identify with, internalize, and become the role. The term "identity" thus describes this part of the individual who takes on and becomes the police officer or the quarterback or the mayor. It was this view of identity that McCall and Simmons (1978) used in their discussion of role identities. These were defined as "the character and the role that an individual devises for himself as an occupant of a particular social position" (p. 65). McCall and Simmons suggest that these are not idle musings, however, but serve as important influences on daily life and are a primary source of plans of action. There is motivational drive involved.

There is another side to identity that Greg Stone (1962) made clear. It is not simply the case that an identity involves an identification with and internalization of some position such as police officer by an individual. It is also the case that others identify the person as a police officer. Stone suggests that "a person's identity is established when others place him as a social object by assigning him the same words of identity that he appropriates for himself" (p. 93). For Stone, "appearance" establishes and maintains one's identity. By dressing a certain way, one announces to oneself and to the audience the identity that is being enacted such as one's age, gender, occupation, and so forth. And as one's position changes in and out of social relationships and in and out of social positions, one's appearance and identity to which it refers also changes. Stone's emphasis on appearance and performance of one's identity in interaction is a theme that continued to be discussed in McCall and Simmons, Stryker, and Burke's work. We now turn to these contemporary theorists in more detail.

The Interactional Emphasis: George McCall and J. L. Simmons

McCall and Simmons (1978) are among the early originators of modern work in identity theory. In their interactional focus, we see the influence of Kuhn's self theory (Kuhn and McPartland 1954) and George Homans's (1974) exchange theory, among others. Unlike some who see the self as a study unto itself, McCall and Simmons are interested in how the self influences behavior. Further, since behavior emerges in interaction, they take seriously aspects of exchange such as negotiation and bargaining and rewards and costs that facilitate or impede action.

For McCall and Simmons, their central concept is a role identity. A role identity is one's "imaginative view of himself as he likes to think of himself being and acting as an occupant"of a particular social position (McCall and Simmons 1978, p. 65). McCall and Simmons remark that role identities have a *conventional* dimension (the *role* of role identities), which includes the cultural expectations tied to social positions in the social structure that actors try to meet, and they have an *idiosyncratic* dimension (the *identity* of role identities), which involves the distinctive interpretations that individuals bring to their roles. For example, a professor identity may entail meanings of one as an educator and researcher. These are the conventional dimensions of the professor identity. Some may add to this an idiosyncratic dimension such as "friend to students" or "protector of students." Either one of these is more distinctive meanings not typically found in the professor identity. Nevertheless, some may take on these meanings, and their behavior as professor will be slightly different than if they were guided completely by conventional meanings. McCall and Simmons point out that individuals can be at one extreme or the other on these dimensions. For example, they can rigidly adhere to the culturally defined behaviors attached to roles, or they can adopt unique behaviors such that they become unrecognizable to others, and others may perceive them as eccentric, even mentally disturbed. However, most individuals fall somewhere between the two extremes.

In their conceptualization of role identities, McCall and Simmons are more likely than other identity researchers in the structural SI tradition to discuss the idiosyncratic and idealized dimension of identities—to see identities as improvised and negotiated rather than as normative and conventional. In an effort to maintain an idealized conception of themselves—to legitimate their role identities—McCall and Simmons indicate that individuals enact *role performances*. This is the behavior (real or imagined) that they enact and that is guided by their role identity. Imagined behavior is what persons fantasize would maintain their role identity. In imagining, people provide themselves with varying amounts of self-support, that is, self-confirming feedback that the behavior they would enact would fit their view of their identity. However, behavior that is portrayed in people's imagination only partially legitimates an identity claim. An identity is also legitimated by behavior in the presence of others. When roles are performed in front of an audience, others evaluate persons' identity performances and confirm or disconfirm their idiosyncratic imaginations of themselves as well as their conventional and normative views.

McCall and Simmons maintain that individuals typically claim more than one role identity. They conceptualize individuals' multiple role identities as organized into a hierarchy within the self. They are primarily concerned with what they label a *prominence* hierarchy of identities. This hierarchy entails how individuals like to see themselves given their ideals, desires, or what is central or important to them. Perhaps what is central to them is being a good parent or professor or friend; thus they would claim the parent identity or professor identity or friend identity. The higher the identity in the prominence hierarchy, the more important it is. Where an identity appears in the prominence hierarchy depends upon several factors. First is how much individuals get *support* for the identity they are claiming in a situation. The more those individuals generate self-support and experience support from others for an identity they are claiming, the higher that identity in the prominence hierarchy.

Another factor influencing the placement of an identity in the prominence hierarchy is how *committed* individuals are to the role identity. If persons are invested in the identity that they are claiming, such that they derive a great deal of esteem or positive feelings when they live up to the view they have of the identity, then that identity is prominent to them. Still another factor influencing placement of an identity in the prominence hierarchy is the *rewards* individuals receive from the identity, both *extrinsic* and *intrinsic*. Extrinsic rewards include resources such as money, valued items, favors, and prestige that individuals obtain from others for an identity that they claim. Intrinsic rewards are the gratifications that individuals experience, internally, for the performance of a role. These may include a sense of efficacy or feeling of competence while enacting a particular behavior or following from the behavior. The more the extrinsic and intrinsic rewards associated with a particular identity, the higher that identity in the prominence hierarchy.

The above three factors, then—support, commitment, and rewards—influence the prominence hierarchy, or what McCall and Simmons sometimes label the *ideal* self. Which factor weighs more heavily into the ideal self is assumed to vary from person to person. For some it may be support from others, while for others it may be the internal and external gratification. Generally, the prominence hierarchy reflects persons' priorities, which in turn serve to guide their actions across situations and over time. However, the prominence hierarchy is not the only determinant of behavior, because prominent identities are not always activated in situations. Sometimes, less prominent identities get activated in a situation because of norms or pressures from others. For example, at a party, one might want to enact behavior associated with the professor identity such as instructing a student at the party about a way to collect his data for his dissertation, but the norm in the situation may be to behave along lines associated with the partygoer identity as in keeping discussions to topics that are not work related. Consequently, McCall and Simmons identify a second hierarchy of identities: a *salience* hierarchy.

The salience hierarchy of identities reflects the situational self rather than the ideal self. It is the self that responds to the expectations of the situation rather than to the desires of the self. It is the identity that is perceived as most advantageous to adopt in a situation in terms of getting support. Although the salience hierarchy is rather fluid as role identities become temporarily activated in different situations, the prominence hierarchy is more enduring and stable. Several factors influence the salience of an identity in a situation: *prominence, support, rewards,* and the *perceived opportunity structure.* McCall and Simmons maintain that the degree of prominence of the role identity is the most significant factor. The weight of the other factors in influencing the salience hierarchy varies from person to person.

The more prominent a role identity, the more likely it will be invoked in a situation. The second factor is how much individuals *need support* for a particular identity. According to McCall and Simmons, if support for an identity has recently been *less* than expected, particularly from an audience that is important to him or her, he or she will focus attention on another identity that has received prior support. The person will not seek to maintain a previously nonsupported identity, because he or she doesn't want to risk the identity not being supported again. Thus, he or she will disinvest in a threatened identity and reinvest in an alternative, nonthreatened identity. For example, if the professor identity was not supported at a party but the parent identity was supported, the parent identity may be more likely to be activated in the future when a social event emerges. Looked at another way, an identity that has received prior support and in which the support is at expected levels or higher than expected levels will be the identity in which persons will continue to activate in a situation.

The third factor that determines the placement of an identity in the salience hierarchy is a person's need for the kinds and amounts of *intrinsic rewards* (for example, esteem or physical gratification) and *extrinsic rewards* (for example, material possessions or power) gained through performance of an identity. Unlike the above in which expected or higher-than-expected levels of support for an identity increases the likelihood that individuals will continue to seek support for that identity, when persons' receive *less* than expected or *more* than expected intrinsic or extrinsic rewards for an identity, they will be more likely to enact that identity in the future. In receiving less than the expected rewards for an identity, persons experience relative deprivation; the more they are deprived, the more they desire the rewards that are tied to the identity. In receiving more than the expected rewards, individuals experience relative enhancement; and the more they obtain an excess of rewards, the more they will come to expect the surplus of rewards that are associated with a particular identity.

The final factor associated with the placement of an identity in the salience hierarchy is the *perceived opportunity structure* in the situation. Opportunity involves the amount of profit (rewards-costs) individuals will experience for playing out a particular identity in a situation. It is important to emphasize that reward/cost calculations are subjective; they are from the point of view of the actor in terms of what role identity is prominent, needs support, and is rewarding to the actor. A person may think that the playing-out of a particular identity by another actor in a situation is not profitable from the person's perspective. However, the person needs to take the role of the other actor, for it is that actor's role identity that is important, not the person's role identity.

McCall and Simmons discuss the fact that individuals may not accurately assess the opportunity structures available. There may be a significant difference between what individuals perceive to be the costs and rewards for enacting a particular identity and what actually exists in a situation. For example, a person may not see the opportunity for profit in a situation as when a first-time mother sees no advantage to performing well in the worker identity at her job because she sorely misses her newborn and prefers spending the time with her child. So she may spend her time at work socializing with others and talking about her newborn, planning activities for her child, and so on. In this sense, she underestimates the rewards such as a salary advance for engaging in behavior associated with the worker identity. Alternatively, individuals may overestimate the rewards that may accrue for the enactment of a role identity. For instance, a person who invests in the worker identity may find himself the recipient of a low salary. Persons may also overestimate or underestimate the costs associated with performing a certain role identity. Indeed, a young lawyer may underestimate the costs associated with becoming a partner in a firm, or a new parent may underestimate the costs associated with having a child. Finally, persons may miscalculate the nature of the costs and rewards; the costs and rewards may be of a different kind from that which was anticipated. For example, rather than a behavior associated with an identity being costly in terms of physical energy, it may be costly in terms of emotional energy. Thus, a therapist may tire easily not because she is putting in long hours at the office but because her clients' problems are emotionally taxing. And although one may expect material rewards such as money for enacting an identity, he or she may only receive social rewards such as praise and admiration.

For successful enactment of a role identity in a situation, McCall and Simmons highlight the importance of negotiation with others in the situation. Specifically, enacting an identity in an interaction is always done in relation to a corresponding counteridentity of another as in the case of a husband supporting his wife, a mother instructing her child, or a professor teaching a student. However, one's own expectations (whether conventional or idiosyncratic) as to how to act based on the content of a role identity (as its held for himself or herself) in a situation may differ from the expectations others associate with that role identity. For example, one may enact a role behavior that others have not seen before because the content of the role identity is more idiosyncratic. Another in the situation may rely on the conventional expectations associated with that role behavior because the content of the role identity (as he or she views it) is more conventional than idiosyncratic. For example, some professors may go out for a beer with their students after class while other professors may see this as unprofessional and inappropriate. A compromise is needed between disparate views.

Aside from the possible conflict in the meaning of identities and their corresponding behavior, each actor in an interaction has a view of his or her own identity as it relates to the identity of the other, and both actors need to enact a behavior that interrelates with the other. McCall and Simmons indicate that this requires a certain degree of coordination between individuals; and when conflict emerges, negotiation and compromises must follow so that there is support for each person's behavior and the interaction can proceed smoothly. When interaction does run smoothly, it aids in the development of durable relationships, which helps stabilize persons' prominence hierarchies (salience hierarchies in McCall and Simmons's view are transitory and unstable, by nature). Essentially, people can come to settle on what is central or important to them if they have positive interactions and strong ties with others. This is not to say that individuals' prominence hierarchy does not change as some priorities change over time and relationships end and others emerge.

Sometimes an identity is threatened in a situation as when others do not support one's role performance (behavior). Here, the role identity is not being legitimated. Under these conditions, individuals will experience negative emotions, which may prompt them to use any one of the negative emotions in a series of what McCall and Simmons (1978, p. 92) label "mechanisms of legitimation" to cope with the negative feeling. One mechanism is *short-term credit* in which an identity that is currently not being supported is temporarily accepted by others because it was supported in the past. Essentially, actors draw upon a line of credit they have earned from prior identity support to "ride out" a current, unsuccessful role performance. Here we might have a physician who is having difficulty diagnosing a patient's health problems. He might ask his patient to trust him until he figures out what might be the problem. Perhaps he might remind his patient that he has served her well in the past. If the physician still can't make sense out of what the symptoms represent, he might send her to a specialist. He still hopes the patient will call upon him when she experiences additional ailments even though he has not found a diagnosis for her current ailment.

Another mechanism is *selective perception* in which actors attend to cues that they think support an identity of theirs, and they do not attend to cues that do not support their identity. In the above example, a physician may focus on the patient's positive nonverbal cues such as smiling, nodding her head, and showing a comfortable and relaxed posture, but he may ignore her verbal cues such as complaints that the medication he prescribed was ineffective in eliminating her symptoms or that he is unavailable for consultation when she needs it. Closely related to this is *selective interpretation* in which actors interpret cues as supportive of their identity when these cues are not supportive. So although the patient may voice her complaints to the physician, the physician may not interpret these as complaints. Instead, he may think that she is simply demonstrating how much she trusts him; otherwise, she would not be open and honest on her thoughts and feelings.

Other strategies to manage negative emotions when an identity is threatened include *blaming others* in the situation for not confirming an identity, criticizing them, and even sanctioning them for their lack of support. Here a physician may reprimand a patient for any criticism of him and inform the patient that she is no expert. One may also *disavow* an unsuccessful role performance as not what the person intended. So a physician may inform the patient that it was not his intention to prescribe the medication that was ineffective; rather his intention was to prescribe an alternative. Still yet, one might *switch identities* and in so doing, the alternative identity can be confirmed. Or the person can simply *withdraw* from the interaction. Essentially, these mechanisms help individuals avoid the pain associated with disconfirmed identities.

McCall and Simmons's work has provided identity researchers with a theoretically rich and fruitful way of understanding the self and other in interaction. Their focus on how actors identify themselves in terms of taking on particular roles, and the implications of this identification for self-other interactions, has led to important contributions in identity theory. Recently, McCall (2003) has called for an expansion of self-identification by arguing that we need to investigate actors' self-disidentifications, that is, who people claim *they are not.* Rather than answering the question, "Who am I?" following Manford Kuhn's TST, he indicates that we should also answer the question, "Who am I Not?" McCall proposes that self-identification and self-disidentification can be regarded as the positive and negative poles of identity: the "Me" and "Not-Me." In a pilot study examining these poles, he finds some interesting differences. For example, he finds that the "Me" is framed more in terms of roles and statuses, for example, "I am a student" or "I am a Catholic," while the "Not-Me" is framed more in terms of characteristics and dispositions, for example, "I am not dishonest" or "I am not a wimp." An important issue he raises for future research is how, over time, what is "Me" can become "Not-Me" and correspondingly, what is "Not-Me" can transform into "Me." Although these identity changes can be brought about by expected role transitions throughout the life cycle, they may also occur unexpectedly. Conceptualizing identity change as a movement between the positive and negative poles of identity serves as fertile ground for the theoretical development of identity theory.

The Structural Emphasis: Sheldon Stryker

Stryker is another early originator of contemporary work in identity theory. His structural emphasis in identity theory is rooted in bringing together ideas from role theory and Mead's social psychology. The precursors of role theory such as Georg Simmel (Wolff 1950) and Ralph Linton (1936) brought to our attention the idea that society can be conceptualized as a structure of positions, and these positions carry with them expectations for behavior (roles). Viewing society as organized and patterned and merging these ideas with Mead's (1934) ideas on the self and action serve as the foundation for a structural version of identity theory.

Like that of McCall and Simmons, Stryker's key concept has been a role identity, but he has focused more on the normative, conventional aspect of role identities rather than the idiosyncratic aspect that McCall and Simmons address. In this way, he takes as a starting point the meanings of role identities that are largely shared among individuals. For example, the parent identity includes meanings of caregiver, teacher, and moral guider that most people would agree with, and parents would behave according to these meanings. Stryker is also less concerned than McCall and Simmons with how identities get negotiated in interaction. Instead, he is more concerned with how the social structure affects the self and one's identity and, in turn, behavior. However, like McCall and Simmons, Stryker shares the idea that individuals typically claim more than one role identity, and given individuals' multiple role identities, these identities can be conceptualized as organized into a hierarchy within the self.

As Stryker (Stryker and Burke 2000) has recently reiterated, society is made up of an enduring pattern of interactions and relationships that are differentiated yet organized. These interactions and relationships exist within groups, organizations, communities, and institutions. Persons live their lives in small networks of social relationships by playing out roles that support their membership in these networks. The probability of entering some networks (and not others) is influenced by the larger social structure within which the networks are embedded that makes available some networks (and not others) for individuals. Given the different positions persons may hold in different social networks and the corresponding roles and expectations associated with those roles, Stryker became interested in how persons choose one role behavior over another in a particular situation. This led him to look at the self for an answer.

For Stryker, people's role choices are a function of the identities they claim in a situation. Identities are persons' internalized role expectations in the sense that individuals take these expectations to be their own, as part of who they are. For each role a person plays out in a social network, there is a corresponding identity attached to it. Thus, the role of father, colleague, or friend embeds individuals into the network of family, the academy, and friends, and there is a corresponding father identity, colleague identity, and friend identity attached to each role, respectively. The content of these various identities—these role expectations—becomes incorporated into individuals' self-views.

If people play out different roles in different networks, Stryker reasoned that the corresponding role identities must be organized in some fashion such that some role identities are more likely to be invoked in a situation than other role identities. Thus, Stryker conceptualized persons' role identities as organized in what he termed a salience hierarchy (Stryker 1980 [2002]). A more salient identity (near the top of the hierarchy) is one that has a higher probability of being activated across different situations. If it has a greater chance of being activated across a variety of settings, then the behaviors associated with that identity that are in accord with the role expectations will be more likely to be enacted. Thus, the salience hierarchy identifies how social actors will likely behave in a situation.

Stryker's approach to conceptualizing identities is somewhat different from McCall and Simmons's approach. Recall that for McCall and Simmons, the salience hierarchy—the situational self—is "the person's own preferences as to the subset of role identities he will enact in a given situation" (McCall and Simmons 1978, p. 84). Essentially, the salience hierarchy helps predict a person's behavior in the short run. Longer-run predictions, according to McCall and Simmons, are determined by the prominence hierarchy—the ideal self—the relatively enduring aspect of the self that focuses on what is important to the self. More prominent identities influence which identities individuals prefer to enact in a specific situation. In this way, the prominence hierarchy influences the salience hierarchy.

For Stryker, the salience hierarchy—the readiness to act out an identity across situations—directly influences the choices people make among behavioral options. Thus, rather than the salience hierarchy predicting short-run behaviors as McCall and Simmons would argue, it predicts longer-run behaviors. In this sense, Stryker's salience hierarchy has the same effect as McCall and Simmons's prominence hierarchy; it captures the more enduring rather than fleeting source of behavior. However, McCall and Simmons's prominence hierarchy is different from Stryker's salience hierarchy in that the former assume that individuals are aware of their prominence hierarchy, that is, persons are self-aware of more important identities compared to less important identities. For Stryker, people may not be aware of how salient an identity is in their hierarchy, but their behavior would inform them as to its ranking in their hierarchy (Stryker and Serpe 1994). Additionally, each hierarchy carries different meanings (what is important, or the prominence hierarchy, compared to what one is ready to enact, or the salience hierarchy). Thus, identity prominence and identity salience should be kept distinct. Future work will want to investigate whether it is fruitful in the development of identity theory to establish a causal ordering between identity prominence (importance) and identity salience (probability of enacting the identity).

Stryker (1980 [2002]) maintains that one important factor that influences the salience of an identity is the degree of commitment one has to the identity. Broadly speaking, commitment is equated with the costs the person incurs for not playing out a role based on an identity (Stryker 1980 [2002]). If the costs for giving up the identity are high, then commitment to the identity is high. Costs are examined along two dimensions: the number of ties and the strength of the ties to others in one's social networks based on an identity.

The above two dimensions have been labeled the quantitative and qualitative aspects (Stryker and Serpe 1982; 1994) or interactional and affective components (Serpe 1987; Stryker 1987) of commitment, respectively. In the former, reflecting the individual's ties to the social structure, commitment is the number of persons that one is related to through an identity. The greater the number of persons to whom one is connected through having a particular identity, the greater is the commitment to that identity. Regarding the qualitative or affective dimension of commitment, the stronger or the deeper the ties to others based on a particular identity, the higher the commitment to that identity. Stryker (1968; 1980 [2002]) suggests that the greater the commitment to an identity, the higher the identity in the salience hierarchy.

Once again, the relevance of social structure in understanding the self is made clear in Stryker's conceptualization. Because people live their lives in social relationships, commitment takes these ties into account when explaining which identities persons are likely to invoke in a situation. For example, if a man's social network in terms of the number of others and the importance of those others is largely based on him occupying a particular role, such as father, then the father identity is likely to be invoked across various different situations. He'll enact the father identity not only at home but also at work (by frequently talking about his children and displaying many pictures of them in his office), at social gatherings (again, discussing his children often), and so forth.

Empirical research strongly supports the link among commitment, identity salience, and the enactment of behavior that is consistent with salient identities. For example, Stryker and Serpe (1982) examine the religious role identity. Their six-item commitment scale measures the extensiveness and intensiveness of relations with others in life based on being in the religious role. For example, "In thinking of the people who are important to you, how many would you lose contact with if you did not do the religious activities you do?" (Extensiveness), or, "Of the people you know through your religious activities, how many are close friends?" (Intensiveness). The salience of the religious identity is measured by asking respondents to rank the religious role in relation to other roles they may assume such as parent, spouse, and worker. Their measure of behavior is time in the religious role. Respondents are asked how many hours in an average week they spend doing things related to religious activities. Stryker and Serpe find that those persons with many relationships based on religion (high commitment) have more salient religious identities that are associated with more time spent in religious activities.

In another study, Callero (1985) examines the blood-donor role identity. In separate measures of the salience of the blood-donor role identity (in relation to other identities one might claim), commitment to the blood-donor identity (borrowing Stryker and Serpe's 1982 commitment scale), and behavioral measure of the identity (number of blood donations given in a six-month period), Callero reaches similar conclusions to that of Stryker and Serpe. The more one has relationships premised on the blood-donor identity, the higher the blood-donor role identity is in one's identity salience hierarchy, and the more this salient role identity is related to donating blood.

In still another study, Nuttbrock and Freudiger (1991) investigate the salience of the mother identity among first-time mothers. They find that a more salient mother identity or the tendency for women to invoke the mother identity at school, at work, and with friends by talking about their child and showing pictures of their child influences behaviors consistent with the mother identity. Specifically, women with a more salient mother identity are more likely to accept the burdens of motherhood, that is, per- form the parenting role without help from others such as their husband, and they are more likely to make sacrifices for their child including spending the necessary time and energy with the child.

Nuttbrock and Freudiger (1991), along with McCall and Simmons (1978), maintain that there is a causal ordering between identity prominence and identity salience, with an important identity influencing the salience of the identity. Some earlier work didn't even maintain a distinction between identity prominence and identity salience and instead merged the two con- cepts both conceptually and empirically (see the discussion on this point by Stryker and Serpe 1994). Others have argued that we should not assume a causal ordering between identity importance and identity salience (Ellestad and Stets 1998; Stryker and Serpe 1994). Here, there is simply an association between the two processes. Not only is it possible that enacting an identity based on it being salient in one's hierarchy of identities could reflect the importance of that identity to the person, but also the importance of the identity could guide the invocation of the identity in the situation. Since there is no empirical evidence, to date, that verifies a causal ordering, we prefer not to identify one.

The Perceptual Control Emphasis: Peter J. Burke

While Sheldon Stryker focuses on the hierarchical arrangement of identities and how identities are tied to the social structure, Peter Burke's work focuses more on the internal dynamics that operate for any one identity (Stryker and Burke 2000). In early work, Burke (1980; Burke and Reitzes 1981; Burke and Tully 1977) argued that identity and behavior are linked through a common system of meaning. When we try to understand a person's behavior, the meaning that the behavior evokes should correspond to the meaning that is held in one's identity. For example, if a person has a student identity that contains the meaning of being "academic," then we should find that the person regularly attends class, take notes, passes exams, and finishes courses (Burke and Reitzes 1981; Reitzes and Burke 1980). However, if a person has a student identity that contains the meaning of being "social" rather than "academic," then we should expect this person to spend much of his time socializing with his friends, attending parties and other social events, and so forth. Essentially, the meaning of one's identity has implications for how one will behave, and one's behavior confirms the meanings in one's identity. For Burke, meaning is critical to understanding an identity. We discuss the role of meaning in identity theory in more detail in chapter 5. Here, we briefly review the major points.

Essentially, tied to each identity is a set of meanings that persons attribute to themselves when they are playing out or claim an identity. The meanings associated with the identity come to be known to the person through interaction with others in the situation in which others respond to the individual as if the person had these set of meanings. Thus, self-meanings develop from the reactions of others; and over time, a person responds to him or her self in the same way that others respond to the person, such that self-meanings become significant or shared by all (Burke 1980).

Drawing on the work of Osgood, Suci, and Tannenbaum (1957), Burke and Tully (1977) developed a method for the measurement of identity meanings that people claim for themselves. As we will discuss in more detail in chapter 5, to identify the self-meanings associated with an identity, a semantic differential framework is used in which respondents are given a set of bipolar adjectives. They respond to themselves as objects along the bipolar dimensions such as good and bad, powerful and powerless, or active and passive to help locate their identity meanings. Since any identity contains a set of multiple meanings (Burke and Tully 1977), multiple bipolar dimensions are provided for any one identity to which one can respond. For example, the gender identity of femininity includes being "noncompetitive" (competitive–not at all competitive dimension), "passive" (very active–very passive dimension) and "feelings easily hurt" (feelings not easily hurt–feelings easily hurt dimension) (Burke, Stets, and Pirog-Good 1988; Stets and Burke 1996). The Burke-Tully procedure uses the meanings of the people in a particular subpopulation to formulate a particular identity rather than meanings from another source, such as the researcher's own intuitive feeling or another population. The semantic differential method has been used to investigate the meanings associated with a variety of identities such as gender identity (Burke and Cast 1997; Burke, Stets, and Pirog-Good 1988;

Stets and Burke 1996), the student identity (Reitzes and Burke 1980), the old age identity (Mutran and Burke 1979b), the environment identity (Stets and Biga 2003), and the moral identity (Stets and Carter 2006).

From the above measurement of meaning, we've come to understand some of the primary meanings of people's identities within our culture. For example, we find that the student identity is comprised of multiple meanings including being academically responsible, intellectually curious, sociable, and personally assertive. The environment identity can be understood in terms of individuals holding either meanings of anthropocentrism (humans are independent and separate from the environment) or ecocentrism (humans are interdependent with the environment and should care for the physical world). The moral identity involves meanings of care and justice. What is important about the measurement of identities is that the meanings that individuals have for their identities affect how they will behave. For instance, those with a more feminine gender identity would be less likely to be a leader in a group, and those with an environment identity of ecocentrism would be more likely to recycle. Thus, when we identify the meanings of an identity for an individual, we can predict the meanings of the person's behavior.

More recent conceptions of identity since Burke's early work on meaning expand on the notion of a correspondence of meaning between identity and behavior and incorporate the idea of a perceptual control system, a cybernetic model, based on the work of Powers (1973), which we discuss in more detail in the next chapter. This is where the internal dynamics of identities are most clearly seen (Burke 1991; 1996; Burke and Cast 1997; Riley and Burke 1995; Tsushima and Burke 1999). In the next chapter, we discuss in detail how identities operate within the perceptual control system. For now, we highlight the critical features of the cybernetic model of the identity process.

Since an identity is a set of meanings attached to the self, this set of meanings serves as a standard or reference for a person. When an identity is activated in a situation, a feedback loop is established. This loop has four components: (1) the identity standard (the self-meanings of an identity), (2) perceptual input of self-relevant meanings from the situation including how one sees oneself and the meaningful feedback that the self obtains from others (reflected appraisals), (3) a process that compares the perceptual input with the identity standard (the comparator), and (4) output to the environment (meaningful behavior) that is a function of the comparison (difference) of perceptions of self-meanings from the situation with actual self-meanings held in the identity standard. The system works by modifying outputs (behavior) to the social situation in attempts to change the input to match the internal standard. In this sense, the identity system can be thought of as having a goal of matching the situational inputs (perceptions) to the internal standards. What this system attempts to control is the perceptual input (to match the standard). When perceptions are congruent with the standard, identity-verification exists.

In the cybernetic identity model, behavior is the result of the relation between perceived meanings of the self in a situation and internal self-meanings held in the identity standard. Behavior is goal-directed in that there is an attempt to change the situation in order to bring perceived situational self-meanings in line with the meanings held in the identity standard. When perceived self-in-situation meanings match self-meanings in the identity standard, the meanings of the behaviors correspond to these meanings and there is verification of the identity. However, if the perceived self-in-situation meanings fail to match, distress is felt and behavior is altered to counteract the situational meanings in an attempt to accomplish identity-verification. Thus, for example, if one views herself as strong and sees that others agree, she will continue to act as she has (strongly). But if she sees that others appear to view her as weak, she will experience distress, and she will increase the "strength" of her performance in an effort to restore perceptions of herself as strong as seen in the reflected appraisals.

The cybernetic nature of identities posited by Burke has led to a view of the nature of commitment that is slightly different from the view outlined earlier by Stryker. In this slightly different view, commitment to an identity is the sum total of the pressure to keep perceptions of self-in-situation meanings in line with the self-meanings held in the identity standard (Burke and Reitzes 1991). One is more committed to an identity when one strives harder to maintain a match between perceived self-in-situation meaning and the meaning held in the identity standard. Commitment thus moderates the link between identity and behavior making it stronger (high commitment) or weaker (low commitment). This does not negate the importance of the structural side shown in ties to role partners (Stryker and Serpe 1982; 1994), but it shows how those ties as well as other factors, such as rewards and praise one might receive for being in the role, bring about commitment as defined by Burke and Reitzes (1991) in terms of the strength of the identity-verification response. The structural connection is maintained. For example, Burke and Reitzes show that those who are highly committed to a student identity (by having more ties to others as well as by receiving rewards for having the identity) have a stronger link between identity meanings (for example "academic responsibility") and behavior meanings (for example, time in the student role or grade point average) than those with lower levels of commitment.

More generally, research has been accumulating on understanding identities using the identity control model. For example, research has examined the emotional reactions to identity-nonverification. Even though we discuss the role of emotion more fully in identity theory in chapter 8, we briefly mention a few pertinent studies in this regard. Using a sample of newly married couples, Burke and Harrod (2005) find that, compared to partners who experience spousal identity-verification, those who experience spousal identity-nonverification report negative emotions. This is true whether the identity meanings of the spouse in the situation are overly positive or overly negative compared to their identity standard for such meanings.

However, in a series of laboratory studies on the worker identity, Stets (2003; 2005) finds that identity-nonverification that is overly negative (workers are underevaluated relative to their worker identity) leads to negative emotions, while identity-nonverification that is overly positive (workers are overevaluated relative to their worker standard) leads to positive emotions. Stets argues that her results might be due to individuals in the laboratory responding automatically to positive feedback rather than processing the feedback more deeply, which may be more likely to occur in marriage.

Researchers have also examined who is more likely to experience identity-verification. For example, using a sample of Los Angeles County residents, Stets and Harrod (2004) find that individuals with higher status characteristics—for example whites (compared to nonwhites), males (compared to females), older individuals (compared to younger individuals), and the more educated (compared to the less educated)—are more likely to experience identity-verification across multiple identities. This helps us see one of the ways in which the external social structure (one's position in terms of status) impinges on internal processes (the identity-verification process), thereby linking the structural emphasis (of Stryker) in identity theory with the perceptual control emphasis (of Burke).

Still other research takes into account interaction in dyads and groups and includes the idea that in many social settings there are multiple persons, each with their own identities, all seeking to have their own identities confirmed in the situation. As an illustration, Cast and her colleagues (Cast, Stets, and Burke 1999) find that in newly formed marriages, spouses with higher status (in terms of a higher education and occupational status) than their spouse are more likely than their lower-status spouses to influence their partner's view of them (the higher-status spouses). The higher-status spouses also are more likely to influence their partner's self-view. In this way, higher-status actors are more likely to have their identities verified than lower-status actors. Cast and her associates' emphasis on the status of the actors and how each influences (or fails to influence) the other's view shows us how the structural emphasis (of Stryker) in identity theory and the interactional emphasis (of McCall and Simmons) of identity theory can be merged into the perception control emphasis (of Burke).

Summary of Identity Theory

Figure 3.1 offers a "road map" on the development of identity theory. It highlights the important points regarding the roots of identity theory and the current emphases in identity theory that we have discussed. Notice the arrow going from the structural version of symbolic interaction to identity theory. The traditional version of symbolic interaction has contributed less to identity theory.

In chapter 7, the reader will discover that in the perceptual emphasis in identity theory, identities also are conceptualized as hierarchically arranged

Roots of Identity Theory

Traditional Symbolic Interaction	Structural Symbolic Interaction
Focuses on actors' meanings	Focuses on actors' meanings
Social structure is always in a state of flux	Social structure is stable, patterned, and organized
Constant creation and re-creation of selves, action, and society makes us unable to use a priori theory or develop theory	Stability and constancy of selves, action, and society makes us able to use a priori theory and develop theory

Current Emphases in Identity Theory

Interactional Emphasis	Structural Emphasis	Perceptual Emphasis
McCall and Simmons	Stryker	Burke
Highlights the idiosyncratic dimension of identities	Highlights the conventional dimension of identities	Highlights the meaning dimension of identities
Salience Hierarchy	Salience Hierarchy	Perceptual Control Model
Prominence	Commitment	Identity Standard
Support	Quantitative	Perceptual Input
Rewards	Qualitative	Comparator
Perceived Opportunity		Behavior
Structure		
Prominence Hierarchy		
Support		
Commitment		
Rewards		

Figure 3.1. Development of Identity Theory

but in a control system of identities rather than in a salience or prominence hierarchy. Identities higher in the control system hierarchy are conceptualized as more abstract such as one's moral identity, and they influence identities lower in the hierarchy such as the parent identity or friend identity. The relationship between identities at higher and lower levels in the control system of identities delves into the area of multiple identities, which we discuss in more detail in chapter 7.

One can compare the interactional, structural, and perceptual emphases in identity theory by discussing how each explains identity performances or identity behavior. For McCall and Simmons, identity performances are a result of actors attempting to interrelate their identities with those of others in a situation. Every identity is played out in relation to a complementary identity; for example, the identity of doctor is played out in relation to the identity of patient, or the identity of salesclerk is performed vis-à-vis the identity of customer. When conflict between two identities emerges—as when a patient tells her physician that she is not listening to the patient's symptoms or a customer complains that a salesclerk is not "helping" her—negotiation strategies and compromises are employed so that each actor's identity claim can be confirmed and interaction can proceed smoothly. So the physician or salesclerk may apologize for her inattentiveness and work harder to help or listen.

For Stryker, identity performances or behavior is a function of how salient an identity is in one's overall hierarchy of identities; a more salient identity is more likely to be invoked in a situation. For example, if the physician identity is salient to an individual, she will be more likely to "call it up" outside of work, as in talking about medicine and perhaps even "treating" others while at home or at a social event. One important factor that influences the salience of an identity is how committed one is to the identity. Greater commitment to an identity is a function of being tied to a larger social network that is premised on the identity and having stronger ties in that network. So if a physician can name most of her friends as physicians as well, and she has a close relationship with these friends, then the physician identity is likely to be salient for her.

For Burke, identity behavior is a function of the relationship between perceived meanings of the self in a situation and identity-standard meanings. When perceived self-in-situation meanings match identity-standard meanings, identity-verification exists, and the meanings of behavior are consistent with the meanings of the identity standard. When self-in-situation meanings do not match identity-standard meanings, behavior is modified to restore meanings of the self in the situation to correspond with identity-standard meanings, thereby moving the self from a state of identity-nonverification to identity-verification. For instance, if at a doctor's appointment, a physician gets feedback from his patient that he is not a good plastic surgeon because the liposuction that he recently performed did not remove all of the cellulite on the patient's legs, the physician is not being verified in his role identity.

The physician may respond in a variety of ways: he may disagree with the patient and show her how what she sees is not additional cellulite, he may agree with her and offer to perform another surgery to remove the remaining cellulite, or he may have some other response. Essentially, the responses are designed to move the physician from being in a nonverifying state to a verifying state.

The development of identity theory can be enhanced by merging Stryker's ideas about identities at the social structural level with McCall and Simmons's views at the interactive level and Burke's conceptualization at the individual level. For example, in the above example of the woman responding in a manner in order to accomplish identity-verification, it would be valuable to identify the various ways in which individuals respond to identity-nonverification and the conditions under which this response occurs. McCall and Simmons provide a host of ways in which individuals can respond to disconfirmed identities such as using "short-term credit" to "ride out" an unsuccessful role performance, blaming others, or withdrawing from the interaction. These "mechanisms of legitimation"—as they label them—can be incorporated into the identity control model. However, we still have not identified the conditions under which they will occur. Relying on Stryker's structural emphasis in identity theory, we might predict that those who have a more salient physician identity (that is, their network of social relationships involves others claiming the physician identity as well and their ties with these others are relatively strong) and who have greater commitment to that identity may be more likely to initially blame others for their nonverification. They might assume that others are not knowledgeable or skilled in their role identity and thus are not competent to evaluate them. The above illustrates how we might borrow ideas from the different emphases in identity theory in order to better predict social behavior.

By considering the macro, meso, and micro levels of identity theory simultaneously, we can expand identity theory beyond its current boundaries. By encouraging different theorists working within identity theory to look outside of their current conceptual borders and consider the influence of other pertinent sociological processes raised by identity theorists at other levels of analysis, we are in a position of developing a more general theory of identities. Essentially, there is still much to be done in identity theory, and one avenue for the future is working across the different emphases in identity theory, which, up to this point, have remained distinct in theory development and empirical testing.

Affinities to Identity Theory

Identity theory is not alone in dealing with these issues. We turn to two theories that have much in common with identity theory. One is in sociology: affect control theory (Heise 1979; MacKinnon 1994; Smith-Lovin and Heise 1988); and the other is in psychology: self-verification theory (Swann, Rentfrow, and Guinn 2003). Affect control theory shares with identity theory its roots in structural symbolic interaction. Further, like Burke's perceptual control emphasis, affect control theorists share the idea that the best way to model the identity process is through a cybernetic model. Self-verification theory shares with identity theory the assumption that people desire to confirm what they already believe about themselves and that persons will seek to maintain their self-views in the face of resistance. We discuss each theory in more detail below so that the reader may get a better sense of the similarities between the theories.

Affect Control Theory

David Heise, the originator of affect control theory, was initially influenced by the psycholinguistic measurement of meaning (Osgood, Suci, and Tannenbaum 1957) and the social psychology of impression formation, a largely cognitive activity. To begin, affect control theorists are interested in the definition of events and the affective reaction people have to these events. To arrive at definitions of events, they consider the actor in a situation, his or her behavior, the objects of one's actions, and the setting. For example, an event might be, "A judge (actor) reprimands (behavior) the prosecutor (object) in the courtroom (setting)."

In order to identify people's affective reaction to events, affect control theorists turn to Osgood and his colleagues who maintained that individuals universally respond to meaning along three primary dimensions: evaluation (the assessment of good/bad or nice/awful), potency (the level of something being powerful/powerless or big/little), and activity (how fast/slow, young/old, or noisy/quiet something is). These are called the evaluation/potency/activity (EPA) dimensions of meaning. Affect control theorists apply the EPA dimensions of meaning to each feature of an event. Thus, there would be EPA ratings for the actor, the behavior, the object, and the setting (ABOS), which are viewed as the primary elements of interaction.

In order to assess the average person's affective reactions to each of the ABOS dimensions, Heise and his collaborators draw samples of individuals and ask them to provide an evaluation/potency/activity profile for concepts related to a variety of actors, behaviors, others, objects, and settings. For each concept, respondents use a scale that usually ranges from +4 to −4 in order to assess evaluation, potency, and activity. Zero is neutral on each of the dimensions—being neither good nor bad, strong nor weak, active nor passive. For example, in a sample of Canadian university females, the EPA profile of the actor, mother, is 2.7, 1.6, and 1.0; thus, on average, mothers are seen as very good, somewhat powerful, and slightly active (MacKinnon 1994). EPA profiles of actors, behaviors, objects, and situations comprise fundamental sentiments in affect control theory. This is the culturally established EPA meanings of every element related to an event.

When different actors, behaviors, objects, and situations are combined into events, they create transient impressions or transient feelings. For example, "a mother screamed at her child" generates transient feelings that are negative for both the mother and the child. Ordinarily, mother and child might have EPA profiles that are, on the average, positive, but when the act of "screaming" occurs, it may change the sentiment of the actor (here, the mother) because she is doing a bad thing (screaming) as well as change the sentiment of the object (the child) who may have done a bad thing. Alternatively, "a mother hugging her child" generates transient feelings that are positive for both the mother and the child. The act of hugging is positive, and this behavior would enhance rather than diminish the positive sentiments attached to the mother (as the actor) and the child (as the object). Affect control theorists create impression formation equations that predict what transient feeling is likely to be experienced given different configurations of actors, behaviors, objects, and situations in events. The predictions take into account how behaviors and even settings can change existing fundamental sentiments. The reason affect control theorists use the term "transient impressions," or "transient feelings," is to recognize that once an event occurs, the feelings that it generates quickly can change as new events subsequently emerge.

Affect control theorists maintain that individuals attempt to experience events in which the transient feelings confirm fundamental sentiments. A discrepancy between fundamental sentiments and transient impressions is a deflection. When this occurs, something has to be done to bring the two into alignment. Either other behaviors are activated in order to restore fundamental sentiments or the event is reinterpreted. For example, in the above example, a restorative act for the event involving the mother screaming at her child may involve the mother apologizing to the child. Alternatively, the event could be reinterpreted if the modifier of "abusive" was included as a descriptive of the mother (thus changing her identity), or if, alternatively, rather than committing a bad act, the child committed a good act such as taking his first steps and the mother is "screaming" out of elation.

Identities take on significance for affect control theorists because individuals can take on roles and therefore claim role identities. Individuals can claim role identities as "observers" to events or as "actors" in events. The role identity meanings are understood along the EPA dimension as well. When affect control theorists focus on the identities of actors in events, the overlap with identity theory is most clearly seen (Smith-Lovin and Robinson 2006).

Theorists in both identity theory and affect control theory assume that in situations, actors try to maintain identity meanings, and that in situations, these meanings are often disturbed by the actions of others. In response, actors will emotionally react and be motivated to restore perceptions. This is the basic control system approach which both traditions share (Smith-Lovin and Robinson 2006). However, while in identity theory, actors are trying to maintain their self-meanings held in their identity standard, in affect control theory, actors are trying to maintain meanings of all elements in the event: actor meanings, behavior meanings, object meanings, and situation meanings (ABOS meanings). In this way, while the control system in identity theory refers to the self, the control system in affect control theory refers to events.

Another difference between identity theory and control theory is in the nature of meaning (Smith-Lovin and Robinson 2006). While both Heise and Burke turned to Osgood and his collaborators as a guide for measuring meaning, Heise became interested in measuring meaning at the cultural level, and Burke became interested in measuring meaning at the individual level. In measuring meaning at the cultural level, Heise uses the EPA dimensions of meaning and applies them along the ABOS dimensions. Burke uses the semantic differential framework described above (and discussed in more detail in chapter 5) to measure individuals' identity meanings. For Burke, other elements in the situation are left unmeasured, but they are nevertheless relevant in maintaining congruence between self-in-situation meanings and identity-standard meanings. We point out that although Heise's approach allows us to understand cultural meanings, those meanings may not predict behavior for an individual in a specific situation. This is where Burke's measurement procedure may garner more power. By drawing upon an actor's own set of meanings, which are both cultural and idiosyncratic, in nature, we may be in a better position of predicting the actor's behavior.

Self-Verification Theory

Self-verification theory has been developed and extensively tested by William Swann, Jr. and his students (Swann 1990; 2005; Swann, Griffin, Predmore, and Gaines 1987; Swann and Hill 1982; Swann, Rentfrow, and Guinn 2003). The theory does not specifically address identities; rather, it deals with the self more globally. However, in specific studies, Swann investigates individuals' self-meanings when persons are in specific situations or roles. In this sense, it could be argued that he is studying identities.

In brief, self-verification theory assumes that people are motivated to verify or confirm currently held persistent self-views. People want to confirm their view of themselves as a means of bolstering the perception that their world is predictable and controllable. This desire for prediction and control is central to the theory. In people's efforts to exert control over situations, they turn to their self-view as a guide. Indeed as identity theorists have argued, self-verification provides an emotional anchor that leaves one less vulnerable when encountering life's events. When a person knows who he or she is, others also will come to know and support the person, and this helps keep the person on an even keel (Cast and Burke 2002).

To facilitate self-verification, or people's desires to confirm what they already believe about themselves, Swann suggested that individuals employ various strategies in interaction with others (Swann 1987). For example, individuals may engage in selective interaction, that is, choose to interact with others who confirm their identities and avoid those who do not (Swann, Pelham, and Krull 1989). Alternatively, they may display identity cues or lay claim to an identity by looking the part, for example, dressing a certain way or using a particular speech style so that others recognize their identity and behave appropriately, thereby confirming their identity. Individuals may also use interpersonal prompts, that is, interaction strategies that get others to behave toward them in a manner that is congruent with their identity (Swann 1987). If one receives disconfirming reactions from others, then interpersonal prompts may be used to counteract this disconfirmation. For example, Swann and Hill (1982) found that persons who thought of themselves as dominant reacted in an even more dominant fashion if they received feedback that they were submissive. And self-designated submissive persons acted in an even more submissive fashion when they received feedback suggesting they were dominant.

The above strategies imply that individuals create a verification context for themselves. This is an important assumption in identity theory as well (Burke and Stets 1999). People seek ways to establish and maintain social situations and relationships in which their identities are verified. According to identity theorists, these are self-verification contexts (Burke and Stets 1999). When one appears predictable in the eyes of others, this predictability, in turn, stabilizes the way that others respond to the self. And the stable way that others respond to the self further stabilizes one's own self-views. Ultimately, individuals are dependent upon others to provide a steady supply of self-verifying feedback, and in so doing, a self-verifying environment develops.

What is interesting about self-verification theory is that it suggests that people prefer self-confirming feedback even when the self-view that is being confirmed is not a positive self-view. Although it seems counterintuitive that people will find negative feedback just as reinforcing as positive feedback, many empirical studies support this finding (Swann 2005; Swann, Rentfrow, and Guinn 2003 for reviews of this work). Individuals prefer others who verify not simply their favorable self-views but also their unfavorable self-views. This is especially true when individuals are given the time to access their self-views and compare the fit between their self-views and the feedback from others. If these mental resources are not made available to individuals, they will seek out others who enhance them rather than confirm their negative self-views.

In identity theory, the assumption is made that individuals desire to verify who they are even if that identity is negative (Burke and Harrod 2005).

There is nothing in identity theory that maintains that identity-verification only operates for positive identities. In the same way that people with positive self-views seek out positive feedback and positive interaction partners, people with negative self-views seeks negative feedback and negative interaction partners.

Research Given the Affinities

Researchers are beginning to look across identity theory, affect control theory, and self-verification theory and see where there may be some common ground. For example, in trying to understand individuals' emotional reactions to verifying and nonverifying feedback in a laboratory setting, Stets (2005) turns to insights from both affect control theory and self-verification theory. As another example, although Swann has typically discussed self-verification strivings in terms of individuals' self-views rather than identities per se, he recently argued that the self-verification motive operates for social identities (Pinel and Swann 2000). This opens the door to the identity-verification process operating for other bases of identities such as role identities and person identities, which we will discuss in greater detail in chapter 6. Perhaps a more striking example of looking across theories is recent work by affect control theorists Smith-Lovin and Robinson (2006), in which they compare both the similarities and differences between affect control theory and the perceptual control emphasis in identity theory. In comparing the two, they develop research questions on empirically testable differences that might prompt further research and advances in each theory.

In chapter 10, we discuss future directions in identity theory. One direction is linking identity theory with other theories in the discipline in order to broaden the scope of identity theory. This link is easier when theories share common ideas. Affect control theory and self-verification theory are two theories that are closer to identity theory than others that we shall discuss.

4

Identities and Their Operation

As indicated in the previous chapter, identity theory is that part of structural symbolic interaction that deals most directly with the agent of action—an identity. In this chapter, we will identify and discuss the component parts of identities and examine our current understandings about the way in which identities work. In doing this, we will see that identities have both cognitive as well as affective or emotional component processes; and although the former have received much more attention than the latter, that situation is changing in current research. As Damasio (1994) has so clearly demonstrated, human agency depends on emotional processes to carry out what might initially appear to be purely cognitive tasks such as reasoning and decision-making. As we go through our understanding of identities and the processes involved, we will try to make clear the points at which emotional as well as cognitive processes may play a role.

In addition to having both cognitive and emotional processes, identities also function at both conscious and unconscious levels. It is clear that much of what we do, we do so deliberately and with conscious awareness. We choose our words carefully to reflect the meanings we intend, and we attend carefully to the words and symbols used by others. However, we may also process symbols automatically (Fazio, Sanbonmatsu, Powell, and Kardes 1986) and habitually (Charng, Piliavin, and Callero 1988; Piliavin 1991), without conscious thought, as we become more familiar with particular situations. Such automatic processing is not necessarily different; only our attention is not focused on those automatic processes as they occur. Thus, as we go through the model, we are not suggesting that people are necessarily aware of and consciously controlling their identity processes, only that control is present, whether conscious and deliberate, or habitual and without much thought.

The Components

An identity is composed of four basic components: an *input*, an *identity standard*, a *comparator,* and an *output*. Each of these components is a process dealing with meanings within the environment and within the self. These processes are interconnected in a cyclic arrangement, as displayed in figure 4.1. They operate in a homeostatic and conservative fashion to maintain perceived self-meanings within a certain range, much as a thermostat operates to maintain temperatures within a certain range. In this chapter, we first describe the basic components and processes of identities that are oriented toward the management of meanings; those that are contained in the perceptions of the situation and those that are contained in the standard. In this initial description, we will present a very basic and somewhat oversimplified version of the model in order to make clear its key parts and functioning. We will deal with the more complex view in later chapters.

The four key components of the identity process are organized into a *control system* that operates to *control the input* to the system. Just as a thermostat operates to control the temperature it "perceives," an identity controls

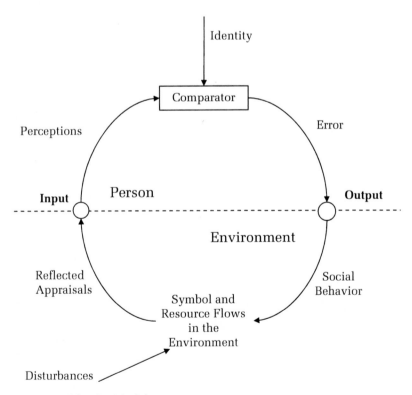

Figure 4.1. Identity Model

the meanings it perceives. One can observe that a thermostat controls the perceived temperature and not the furnace by the following simple experiment. If one holds a lighted match near the thermostat, the furnace does not come on, even in a cold house. It does not come on because the thermostat perceives the heat from the match and is "satisfied" that the temperature is OK and not in need of further heating. The identity process operates in the same fashion. Outputs are altered in order to make the input perceptions of meaning correspond with the meanings of the identity standard.

The Identity Standard

Each identity contains a set of meanings, which may be viewed as defining the character of the identity. This set of meanings is the *identity standard*. With respect to gender identity, for example, people may be characterized as more masculine or more feminine. Clearly, the character of masculinity and femininity—that is, what it means to be male or female—varies from one society to another and even across individuals within a society. Yet, individuals with particular gender identities, who see themselves as more or less feminine or masculine, may be arrayed along some dimension of meaning that distinguishes masculine from feminine (Burke and Cast 1997; Burke and Tully 1977). In finding the location of an individual's gender identity on that array, we are discovering what it means to that individual to be male or female in his or her own culture. Again, this set of meanings is the identity standard. A stereotypical male in our culture might say, "As a man, I am strong, resourceful, independent, and assertive." A stereotypical female in our culture might say, "As a woman, I am supportive, warm, affectionate, and tender." Another person might say, "As a man I am warm, supportive, independent, and resourceful." The cumulated meanings of each of these adjectives (and all the others that might apply) help us locate the individual along a continuum ranging from very stereotypically masculine to very stereotypically feminine, covering all the points in between.

For each of these persons, with respect to their gender identity, there is a fairly stable set of meanings that characterizes who they are (Burke and Cast 1997). Identity theory suggests that these meanings define the identity standard and serve as a point of reference in the processes to be discussed below. The meanings that define the identity standard are stored in memory and are accessible to the comparator. For each of the many identities that a person holds, there is a separate standard containing the meanings that define the identity in question. A college student might be characterized with respect to her college student identity in terms of different sets of meanings. For example, she might be characterized with meanings having to do with academic involvement, intellectualism, sociability, and personal assertiveness.[1] At the same time, with respect to her gender identity, she may be characterized in terms of meanings having to do with masculinity and femininity. Still further, with respect to a friend identity, she may be characterized in terms of meanings having to do with support, trust, loyalty, and other relevant dimensions.

Two important questions that we will discuss later concern how particular dimensions of meaning become relevant for any particular identity and how a person comes to view himself or herself as being located at some point along that dimension. For example, with respect to the first question, how does the dimension of strong–weak come to be an important dimension of meaning for gender identity, while degree of sociability might be an important dimension of meaning for a college student identity? And with respect to the second question to be considered later, how is it that one particular male's gender identity, on the strong–weak dimension, is only "moderately strong," while another's is "very strong;" or why is it that the meanings of one college student's identity is "very sociable" while another's is "rather unsociable"? We will take these questions up at a later point when we have better tools at our disposal. For now, we assume the dimensions of meaning for a particular identity are given, and we assume that each person is located at some particular point along that dimension. Strong–weak is a particular dimension relevant to gender identity in our culture, and individuals are located at points along that dimension.

For the time being, it is sufficient for our purposes to note that *meaning* is what is contained in the identity standard. It is not necessarily one meaning but perhaps several meanings or even a very large number of meanings that are contained in the identity standard. It may help to think of all the relevant meanings as a set.[2] For example, as we indicated with respect to the college student identity, four different meanings have been found to be important: academic ability, intellectualism, sociability, and assertiveness. We can represent these four dimensions in a single set of meanings. Such a set of meanings may include denotative and connotative meanings, as well as emotional meanings and meanings not yet measured.

The Inputs

Perceptions are central to the identity process. It is our perceptions that we are trying to control, as shown in figure 4.1. Our perceptions tell us about our environment; our perceptions are our only source of information about what is happening around us. We often think of ourselves as trying to control our environment, trying to manipulate physical and social objects, trying to interact with others. We pick up a pen or pencil, we put groceries into our shopping basket, and we use words to communicate with others to share, instruct, and love. However, a little thought can convince us that we know of these things because we see them, we hear them, and we feel them. In short, we perceive them, and ultimately, it is only our perceptions that we have. We know we have picked up the pencil because we can feel it and see it. However, to put this in another way, we move, reach, and grasp until we see and feel that we have the pencil. If we perceive that it is slipping from our grasp, we make adjustments to our grip until we perceive that we have it firmly. Our perceptions can be fooled, just as our example of a match held near the thermostat fools the thermostat into "thinking" that it is warmer than in fact it is.

This difference between controlling the environment and controlling our perceptions is a subtle one, and a first reaction is often to ask what difference it makes to think about the process one way or the other. If we assume that our perceptions of the environment are generally accurate and certainly correctable, then, in general, it doesn't seem to make any difference. The importance of the distinction lies not in the perception itself, but in what we do with it. Within the identity model, the perceptions are compared with the identity standard, with the goal of matching the perception to the standard. Only when the perception matches the standard have we accomplished our goal, so to speak. The standard is thus, as we indicated, a goal for the perceptions. The importance of this is not that we *change* the environment, but that the consequences of what we do are only known to us in our perceptions. Since the standard is ours, only we can tell when our perception matches the standard.

As an analogy, we can watch a person drive a car. We can see that person move the steering wheel in response to what we assume is a variety of disturbances that disrupt the car from staying where the driver wants it; disturbances such as the wind, variations in the roadbed, slippage in the steering mechanism, and so on. We know that this is what is happening (if we have driven). However, we do not have the perceptions that the driver has, and we do not know exactly the standard for the position of the car that the driver has, so we cannot see the link between what is happening in the environment (where the disturbances are created) and the steering motions made. The steering motions keep the vehicle where the driver wants the car to be positioned (her standard), but we do not see what has caused the steering motions; only the driver has these perceptions, is comparing them to her standard for where the car should be, and is responding to that comparison with the steering motions.

When it comes to identities, perceptions are the inputs to identities, in particular, perceptions are meanings in the situation that are relevant to the identity.[3] By identity-relevant meanings, we mean responses to those stimuli in the situation that might be characterized as having been "tagged" or "marked" as implying something about the identity of the perceiver.[4] If we go back to our example of gender identity, Tom's identity standard provides a criterion that tells him how masculine he really is in his "true" self. It defines Tom with respect to that particular identity. Tom's perceptions of the situation tell him how masculine he seems to be in the current situation. Perhaps in this particular situation Tom perceives that he is acting in a somewhat feminine fashion. These perceptions form the input to the identity process.

What, specifically, is it one perceives? Just as we cannot tell exactly what the driver of the automobile perceives, we cannot know exactly what other people perceive with respect to their identity without some kind of test. It may be perceptions of their own behavior, it may be perceptions of the behavior of others in the form of overt actions or in the form of expressions given off, or it may be combinations of these things and other things as well.[5] Irrespective of the source or content of the perceptions, they exist continuously. They are input to the identity process and compared with other meanings already "stored" in the identity as the identity standard. In the current example, Tom's perceptions may include observations of his own behavior, which may strike him as somewhat feminine. It may also include others' reactions to that behavior, both verbal and nonverbal, which tell him that he is behaving in a somewhat feminine manner. While all of this is going on, these perceptions are continuously fed into the comparator.

The Comparator

The third component of the identity system is the comparator, which does nothing more than compare the input perceptions of meanings relevant to the identity with the memory meanings of the identity standard. It then produces an "error signal," which is the difference between the input and the standard. The flow of meanings from the input and the standard into the comparator is shown in figure 4.1 along with the output of the comparator. Continuing with the above example of gender identity, Tom's perceptions of the situation tell him that he is acting in a somewhat feminine fashion. The identity standard is a ruler for measuring his input perceptions, telling him, in this instance, that he is acting more feminine than his standard for himself as a male. To think numerically, Tom is acting "6" in terms of femininity, while his standard may be "4."[6] The comparator makes this comparison and outputs the difference (in this case, subtracting the perception from the standard gives "−2") as an "error signal," indicating that his perceptions are not in accord with the standard. In this case, Tom's perceptions are higher (or more feminine) than the standard. The error signal ultimately affects the patterns and sequences of his verbal and nonverbal behavior, which, in turn, alters the meanings of the behavior in the situation.

The Outputs

The last component of the identity system is the output to the situation or environment. The output is behavior in the situation, which behavior is based on the error signal from the comparator. The error signal indicates the magnitude and direction of the difference between the input perceptions and the identity standard along some dimension of meaning—in this case, masculine/feminine. Output, in the form of meaningful behavior, is produced in the environment, just as input comes from the environment. The effect of the output behavior is to alter the environment from what it was. Specifically, it alters the symbolic character of the environment. With the symbols changed, everyone in the environment, oneself included, will have changed perceptions, which perceptions feed back up into the identity in a continuing cycle. The meanings are altered.

Returning, once again, to the above example of Tom's gender identity, if Tom perceives himself to be acting more feminine (+6) than his gender identity standard (+4), the output (−2) tells him to lower the degree of femininity in the meanings of his actions, perhaps by becoming more forceful in the situation. Taking this action will result in his changing the symbols in the situation. Because of that, Tom will perceive less femininity in his actions, and, because symbols are shared, others will see less femininity in his actions. If Tom has changed his behavior just right, he will see the degree of femininity of his behavior as +4, which will match his identity standard. At that point, the error will be zero, and he will not change his behavior patterns further. However, if Tom's actions are not just right, he may perceive the femininity of his behavior as +5 or +3, for example. In either case, his new perceptions still do not match his gender identity standard, and an error signal of −1 or +1 will result, causing him to modify his behavior further.

Clearly, according to this model, the actual behaviors themselves are not relevant. Rather, the meaning or symbolic value of the behavior is relevant, inasmuch as it changes the meanings in the situation (Burke and Reitzes 1981). Thus, for Tom to change the level of masculinity or femininity of his behavior, he has to know what the meanings of various behaviors are and to choose those behaviors that move meanings in the correct direction, given the current situational meanings and his gender identity standard. The arbitrariness of the link between meaning and behavior means that as one moves from one culture or subculture to another, one may have to change his behavior to maintain his appearance of having a certain degree of masculinity. These are different ways of obtaining the same effect. Behaviors that might be taken as more feminine in one context may be seen as more masculine in another context. One has to experiment a bit to find the behaviors that result in the desired level of perceived masculinity.

The Processes

Notice that in looking at the parts of the identity process, we were tracing the flow of meanings from the environment where they were perceived[7] to the comparator where they were compared with other meanings (the identity standard). From there we trace them to the output of behavior that had meaning and back to the situation where the behavior altered the meanings available in the situation, so that new perceptions are input to the comparator as the cycle continues. Three aspects of this description warrant comment. First, we are dealing with a *continuous loop* or cycle that is never ending. Second, we are dealing with *meaning* as the signal that flows through the cycle. Third, the cycle or loop of meaning is organized as a control system.

The fact that there is a continuous loop of meaning tells us that perceptions of meaning are continuously coming into the comparator while meaningful behaviors are continuously output to the environment. Action does not stop while perception occurs, and perception does not stop while action occurs. As a male, Tom is constantly monitoring his environment and perceiving indications (symbols and signs) about the degree of his masculinity/ femininity being manifest in the situation. Such manifestations occur in his own behavior (which is constantly being produced and which has meaning for him and for others in the situation) as well as in the behavior of others (which also has meaning for him and them).

As a control system, identity processes are organized to maintain the inputs as close to the identity standard as possible, counteracting any disturbances that occur in the environment. Because identities deal with meanings, it is the *meanings* that are being input to the identity system (i.e., perceived) and being controlled (or disturbed). Thus, as Tom monitors input perceptions (the self-meanings of his masculinity), these are being compared to his identity standard (gender). The output of the comparator, on which Tom's behavior with its attendant meanings is based, is a function of the degree of match between the input meanings and the meanings in the identity standard. That is, his behavior is a function not only of the degree of masculinity/femininity (meanings) he perceives about himself in the situation but also of the degree of masculinity/femininity (meanings) he holds for himself in his gender identity standard.

For example, if Tom perceives 6 units of masculinity about himself in the situation, he will act to increase that amount if his standard is set at 8 units, but he will decrease that amount if his standard is set at 4 units. Similarly, if his standard is set at 6 units of masculinity, he will act to increase the level of masculinity he displays if he perceives 4 units of masculinity about himself in the situation. He will act to decrease the level of displayed masculinity if he perceives 8 units of masculinity about himself in the situation. Thus, neither the level of masculinity perceived about himself in the situation nor the level of masculinity that exists in his gender identity standard predicts his behavior. Only the relationship between the inputs (perceptions) and the standard as determined by the comparator predicts the behavior, and that is because the behavior (output) is a direct function of the error or differences as detected by the comparator.

Identity-Verification

Because an identity is a system that controls its inputs of self-relevant meanings, as described above, the basic process of identity operation may be characterized as one of identity-verification. By making the (perceived) meanings about himself in the situation correspond to the meanings in his identity standard, Tom is verifying who he is—that he is the person his standard indicates. If he is prevented from doing this, he is very likely to become upset. As Swann (1983) points out, one sure way to get people stirred up is to tell them they are not who they think they are. These emotional by-products to the identity process motivate the behaviors involved. She is motivated to bring her self-relevant meanings in the situation into alignment with the meanings of her identity standard because she gets upset when they are not in alignment, and she wants to avoid being upset. Research by Zanna and Cooper (1976) has shown that when the input meanings are not congruent with the identity-standard meanings, a subjective feeling of distress occurs that increases with the degree of incongruence and serves as a motivator to take some action. Swann and Hill (1982) present an experiment that shows how people take steps to counter the discrepancy. We take a little time to present this research because it illustrates the basic identity process of identity-verification very well, and it shows a useful manner in which to test *what* is being controlled in any controlled system such as an identity.

The Experiment

In the Swann and Hill (1982) experiment, during a pretesting session at the beginning of the semester, participants (in this case, female undergraduate students) completed a questionnaire measuring the degree to which each saw herself as a dominant person. Each participant rated the extent to which a series of five dominance-related qualities (dominant, commanding, takes charge of things, domineering, forceful) characterized her on scales that ranged from 1 ("not at all like me") to 5 ("very much like me"). The respondents were then divided into three groups, depending upon their scores on the self-perceived dominance questionnaire. The experiment concentrated on the top and bottom groups, those designated as *self-dominants,* and those designated as *self-submissives.* It should be clear that in the experiment we are about to describe, neither the experimenter nor the confederate ever learned how the participants scored on the self-conception measure.

First, we present the experimental setup. As each participant arrived at the waiting area for the experiment, she was greeted by a confederate posing as an introductory psychology student. Soon, a female experimenter brought both the participant and confederate into the experimental room and seated them at a table. The experimenter proceeded to explain that the study was designed to examine how people solve problems alone in contrast to working with someone else. In today's session, they would work together on one task and separately on another. The first (together) task was a modified version of the popular logic game called Mastermind in which the order and color of four hidden pegs is deduced from feedback to trial guesses about the color. Guesses are made by placing four colored pegs in order on a board. The feedback received for guesses indicates only the number of errors, not the location or nature of those errors. Thus, logic and trial guesses are needed to solve the problem. The experimenter set up a practice problem with four hidden pegs, and the participant and confederate proceeded to try to deduce the correct colors over a series of ten trials or until they got the correct answer, whichever came first.

The experimenter then told them to do a practice set on their own and instructed them to take turns making guesses by placing the pegs, which served as guesses to the solution. The participant was then told (ostensibly at random) she would be the first to decide how to place the pegs in the first trial. The experimenter left the room after taking any questions that the participant or confederate had. This practice session also continued for ten trials or until the solution was achieved by correctly guessing the order and color of the hidden pegs.

After the practice, the experimenter announced over an intercom that during the next set of trials, one person would act as a leader and always decide how to place the pegs that constituted the guesses. The other would act as an assistant and keep track of the clues as well as place the pegs on the board according to the instructions of the leader. The assistant was free to make suggestions, but the leader always had the final say on the placement order. The experimenter then informed the participants that they would have a couple of minutes to decide who would be the leader and who would be the assistant.

We now come to the important experimental manipulation. As soon as the experimenter asked them to agree who would be the leader and who the assistant, the confederate delivered either a dominant or submissive feedback to the participant, selected randomly from session to session over the course of the experiment. In the dominant feedback condition, she asserted, "Well, you really seem to be kind of a forceful, dominant person. Like a little bit ago when you were making suggestions during the practice session. You're probably the type who would like to direct things and be in charge of making decisions. Don't you think?" In the submissive-feedback condition, the confederate said, "Well, you really don't seem to be the dominant type. Like a little while ago when you seemed a little hesitant making decisions during the practice session. You're probably happiest when someone else takes charge of things. Don't you think?"

We, thus, have self-proclaimed either dominant or submissive individuals (the identity standard is set at dominant or submissive) who are being given self-relevant feedback (meanings in the situation that are perceived by the participant). This feedback indicates that the participants have been acting in either a dominant or a submissive fashion during the practice session. For the self-dominant persons, being told they are dominant, and the self-submissive persons, being told they are submissive, the feedback is consistent. For others, the feedback (perceptions) is discrepant with their self-views (identity standard).

The reactions of the participants were assessed under two different additional conditions. In one condition, half of the participants were allowed to respond to the confederate following the feedback. In the other condition, the rest of the participants had no further opportunity to interact or respond to the confederate. In the condition in which the participant had a chance to reply to the confederate, the confederate was instructed to remain as neutral and nondirective as possible for the two minutes this lasted. In the no-response condition, the experimenter interrupted over the intercom, immediately after the confederate provided her feedback, to say that there was an equipment failure and that the experiment could not proceed with the current task until the equipment was fixed. In the meantime, they were to work on a second (individual) task that had been explained to them earlier. This task also lasted for two minutes. At this point, the experiment was essentially over.

When the two minutes were up, the experimenter returned to the room with a booklet of questionnaires in which two dominance scales were embedded. One was the same scale the participants had filled out at the beginning of the semester, rating their own dominance-submissiveness. The other was a scale asking the participant how the confederate would rate them on these same dimensions. The experiment concluded after the questionnaires were filled out and the participants were debriefed and thanked.

We have described this experiment in some detail in order to provide a clear understanding about the conditions under which we can observe the identity-verification process at work. In this experiment we have the ability to compare the responses of persons to feedback that is either consistent or discrepant with the meanings in their self-views. The measure of self-dominance that was obtained at the beginning of the semester tells us about the meanings in each of the participant's identity standard along a dimension of dominance/submissiveness. The feedback statement about the dominance or submissiveness of the participants that was given by the confederate tells us about the nature of the input to the identity system— again, as meanings along the same dominance/submissiveness dimension. The comparator in each of the participant's identities is thus able to compare the perceived feedback (input) with the participant's standard and assess the degree of correspondence.

The identity model says that meaningful behavior (output) on the part of the participant will be a function of that correspondence as assessed by the comparator. This behavioral output, according to the model, should act to restore the perceptions of the participant toward the meanings that are contained in her identity standard. That is, it should make the inputs more semantically congruent with the identity standard. What do we observe? We return to the experiment.

Trained observers listened to tape recordings of the interactions between the participant and the confederate (in the half of the groups that had this opportunity) and rated them on a four-point scale indicating the degree to which the participant resisted or accepted the feedback. At one end, the scale indicated that the participant "accepted it willingly," and at the other end, the scale indicated that the participant "questioned or refuted it." These observers also rated the participant in the interactions on each of the five dominance scales that the participant rated herself on at the beginning of the semester. Thus, we also have observer ratings of the dominance/submissiveness of the participants as revealed in their interactions with the confederate during the two-minute interaction following the feedback.

The results of the ratings by the trained observers showed, quite unequivocally, that there was much more resistance to the feedback in the discrepant conditions. Self-dominant persons resisted being told they seemed submissive, and self-submissive persons resisted being told they seemed dominant. The ratings of the observers of the level of dominance displayed by the participant in the two-minute interaction following the feedback also showed that there was a change in the behavior of the participants. Those who got consistent feedback did not differ in the degree of dominance displayed in their interaction during that time. However, those participants who received discrepant feedback behaved very differently. How they behaved depended upon their self-views.

Let us explain this. Those who saw themselves as dominant but were told they were submissive acted in a very dominant fashion, even more than the dominant persons who received self-consistent feedback. Those who saw themselves as submissive but were told they appeared dominant acted in a more submissive fashion than the submissive persons who received consistent feedback. Thus, in each case, those with discrepant feedback acted in a manner that *over*emphasized their self-view. Overall, then, for these participants, we see them acting to manipulate the meanings in the situation. They deny and refute the discrepant meanings provided by the confederate, and they overact to produce more meanings that are consistent with their identity standard. For this to make sense, we have to assume that the participants perceived the meanings provided by the confederate as self-relevant meanings, and we have to assume that these meanings did not match the standard and that action was taken to change the self-relevant meanings available in the situation so that they would be consistent with their identity standard. Actions are taken to restore the perceptions of self-relevant meanings to accord with the identity standard.

We mentioned above that this was an excellent prototype of an experiment for the identity model. Having discussed both the model and the experiment, we now explain why this is so. A control system, such as an identity, is not like the linear cause and effect systems that are used in many social psychology theories of behavior. As William James, who understood this process in humans very well, indicated, people are adept at arriving at a single outcome through multiple means. In this case, the participants in the experiment are acting to counteract a disturbance of their inputs. To say that something is a disturbance means that we are making a comparison between the current input and what that input would be under normal or ideal conditions, that is, equal to the identity standard. To bring the input back to the level of the identity standard, the participant has to act in a way that just counterbalances the disturbance.

For the self-proclaimed submissive persons who were told they were dominant, this means that they have to act *even more submissively,* until their inputs are restored to the normal level of self-as-submissive that agrees with their identity standard. For the self-proclaimed dominant persons who were told they were dominant, this means that they have to continue to act as they have been because they are already getting feedback that is consistent with the meanings contained in their identity standards. Their feedback had not been disturbed. Notice, then, that what the experiment does is disturb the inputs that are being controlled by the identity system and then observe the reactions to those disturbances. Telling self-dominants that they are dominant does not disturb the system, and there is no special reaction. Telling self-submissives that they are dominant produces a strong reaction that counteracts the disturbance. It is the reaction to counter the disturbance that tells us that we have, in fact, disturbed something that is being controlled by the system in question. Introducing a disturbance, as this experiment does, is one of the few ways that a control system can be systematically studied, and that is why we referred to this experiment as an excellent prototype for studying identities. It helps very clearly identify the meanings that are being controlled. This is what Powers (1973) calls "the test." Disturb a perception that is being controlled, and the identity will act to compensate or counteract the disturbance. Disturb a perception that is not being controlled, and the identity will act in disregard of the "disturbance." Only in this way can we clearly identify what perceptions are controlled by an identity.

Controlling (Perceptions of) the Situation

If we follow out the implications of the identity-verification process and come to understand that this process is ongoing continuously with respect to whatever identities are active at the time, it becomes clear that humans must spend a lot of energy on this process. The amount of energy would be the amount it takes to counteract the disturbances to the self-relevant meanings that exist in the situations in which we spend our waking moments. If there are many random disturbances, and those disturbances are rather large, we will expend a great deal of energy coping. If, however, we were able to construct situations in which the disturbances would be small or nonexistent, then we would not need as much energy to cope with the disturbances. In this case, identity-verification would be routine. We would quite consistently get the feedback that matches our identity standard.

Swann has pointed out that this is, indeed, what generally happens. He calls it "developing an *opportunity structure*" (Swann 1983, p. 36), which he likens to the biological concept of a *niche* that organisms inhabit, wherein their needs are routinely satisfied. He suggests that people not only will gravitate toward opportunity structures that offer support for their self-conceptions but also will create those opportunity structures when such do not naturally exist. He goes on to outline three main ways in which people create their own opportunity structures.

The first of these is *displaying signs and symbols* of who we are, and it corresponds to the model discussed above. This is not confined to language communication; it includes clothing and cosmetics, hairstyle, and possessions such as the car we drive, the house we live in, and the artwork on our walls. It even includes changing our own body structure through diet, exercise, weight lifting, and plastic surgery. As mentioned earlier, Stone (1962) was one of the first to recognize the importance of appearance in communicating self-meanings to others so that they come to know exactly *who* we are. As he suggests, a person's appearance provide the identities, values, moods, and attitudes of the person because it arouses in others the assignment of words and meanings of who one appears be. A greasy pair of coveralls and a business suit lead to different impressions on the part of others and therefore to different treatments by them. A pair of jeans and an evening dress similarly lead to different treatments for the wearer. We dress boys in blue and girls in pink. We dress boys in pants and shirts, while girls wear dresses. In this way, we announce to the world the manner in which our children are to be treated—as boys or as girls.

The second way to manipulate our opportunity structure (for identity-verification) is through *selective affiliation*, that is, choosing the "right people" with whom to interact and the right situation in which to interact. The right people will make it easier for us to be who we are because they treat us in a manner consistent with our identities. For example, when parents encourage their children to play with certain other children and discourage them from playing with others, they are creating environments in which certain identities are encouraged and others discouraged. Now, this does not mean that one associates only with "better" others or with those who see us in a positive light. Rather, we prefer to associate with those who see us as we see ourselves. For example, Swann, Pelham, and Krull (1989) found that people who had negative conceptions of themselves preferred to associate with others who also viewed them relatively unfavorably. They found, in a study of college roommates, that if there was incongruence between how students saw themselves and how their roommates saw them, the students were more likely to seek new roommates.

The third manner in which the opportunity structure can be changed is using what Swann calls *interpersonal prompts*, that is, the use of appropriate interaction strategies. Very simply, this is a process of getting others to treat you in a manner consistent or congruent with your own identity. As suggested above, we do this partly with our appearance, but we also behave in ways that reinforce this. We saw one example in the Swann and Hill (1982) experiment described above. Here, participants changed their behavior to engage in more dominant (submissive) patterns when others were apparently not seeing them as dominant (submissive) as they saw themselves. Another experiment, by Swann and Read (1981), demonstrated that subjects who saw themselves as likable were able to behave in a manner to elicit more favorable reactions from others than were subjects who saw themselves as less likable. Moreover, this pattern was stronger if the subject suspected that the others might not like them.

Weinstein and Deutschberger (1963) used the term "*altercasting*" to represent a very similar notion to the idea of interpersonal prompts. Altercasting refers to the creation of an identity for another person in an interactive setting. This is done by casting Alter (the other) into a particular identity or role type such that your own identity and goals are maintained. As Weinstein and Deutschberger point out, altercasting may be done in a number of ways. Some are direct and explicit. For example, someone might say, "Now, Joe, as a good friend of mine, I know you would ..." Some are direct and implied as when we "come on strong" in our own role identity, thus providing a signal to Alter about how they ought to behave toward us. Some are less direct techniques such as using gestures of approval and disapproval to the various lines of action that Alter takes, thus, in a sense, "guiding" Alter into assuming the correct role identity. In all of these cases, the use of altercasting and interpersonal prompts serves to create an opportunity structure for the realization and continued maintenance of our identities.

Research by Serpe and Stryker (1987) provides a nice illustration of the process of creating an opportunity structure in a natural setting. They studied new freshmen at a large Midwestern university and followed them for several months through the fall semester. During this period, the students began to build new friendships, group memberships, habits, and behaviors in a context that was entirely new to them. Five different role identities were studied for each student, each concerned with a different set of relationships. Three of these were of primary focus in their research: athletic/recreational roles, extracurricular roles, and personal involvements (nonorganizational friendships) of the students.

The salience of each of the five role identities was measured when students first arrived on campus by having them choose, in a series of comparisons, which of each pair of identities was more characteristic of how they thought of themselves. By comparing each identity with all of the remaining, the relative salience of each was obtained. For example, if a student always chose the athletic/recreational role over all of the others, it had high salience. If, however, extracurricular activities always lost out in the comparison, it had low salience. Each of these identities, of course, was developed at an earlier time, when the students were still in high school (or earlier). Now, as new freshmen on a residential campus, they no longer had structural support for these identities. Structural support had to be built anew by joining with others in organizations and friendships if they were to have it.

What Serpe and Stryker found was that students were more likely to join organizations and enter activities related to a particular role identity to the extent the identity was salient. The more a student thought of himself or herself in terms of athletics or extracurricular activities or personal friendships, the more likely he or she was to join with others *in these particular areas* over the course of the fall semester. In this way they came to reproduce for themselves (albeit with new persons in a new context) the sets of relationships they had given up in coming to college, thus recreating opportunity structures that support and maintain the identities that were important to them.

Failure in Identity-Verification

What happens when people are not able to continuously verify their identities by keeping perceptions of their self-relevant meanings in situations close to their identity standard? We have seen that there is a strong motive for people to control the perceptions of self-relevant meanings contained in the input to their identity processes and to keep them equal in value to the meanings in their identity standards. People who view themselves as "good" want to get feedback that they are "good." And there is evidence that people become upset and suffer symptoms of stress when they are not able to achieve this congruity between situationally based self-perceptions and their identity standards or when it becomes difficult to do so (Zanna and Cooper 1976).

Burke (1991; 1996) presented an analysis of the ways in which stress arises from this difficulty or failure to achieve congruity between perceptions and standards. This analysis was based on theoretical work on the stress process done by Mandler (1982). Mandler suggested that stress was not based so much on people being overloaded with demands, as has traditionally been the case. Rather, he argued that stress results from an interruption of normal action and thought processes, including (and perhaps, especially) those related to the process of identity-verification. Interruption is the disconfirmation of an expectancy or the noncompletion of some initiated action. Sometimes, but not always, being overloaded with demands results in the interruptions that result in distress. It is the interruptions, however, and not the overload that is important. This is the *interruption theory of stress.* The basic premise of interruption theory is the well-documented finding that *autonomic activity (subjectively felt as distress or anxiety) results whenever some organized action or thought process is interrupted.* The autonomic activity instigated by interruption (stress) serves as a signaling system that demands attention. This can result in the adaptive response of increasing attention to crucial events or, in more extreme situations, of drawing attention away from other needed areas (Baddeley 1972).

The difference between overload and interruption is illustrated in research by Kirmeyer (1988). She studied police radio dispatchers whose completion of particular tasks on the job was frequently interrupted as new calls came in. She showed that the amount of distress dispatchers experienced was directly related to the number of objective interruptions that occurred per hour. The total workload (number of tasks per hour), while correlated with distress, appears to affect distress levels entirely through the *rate of interruptions* that occur.

The logic of the argument linking identity processes with the stress process may already be apparent to perceptive readers. The key is to remember the following important points. First, when an identity is activated, identity processes operate continuously through time to maintain congruence between the identity standard and perceptions of identity-relevant meanings. Second, the identity standard is a set of expectancies in the form of meanings, and the output of the identity system (meaningful behavior) is linked to its input (perceived self-meanings) primarily through the social environment. And third, an identity process is a continuously operating, self-adjusting feedback loop: individuals continually adjust behavior to make and keep perceptions of self-relevant meanings in the situation congruent with their identity standards or references. In familiar situations, this adjustment process is nearly automatic, requiring little or no attention. Since the identity process is continuous, the amount by which one's situated self-perceptions differ from one's identity standard is kept small. The existence of a relatively large discrepancy is likely to indicate some type of interruption in the identity process that has suspended the normal condition of continuous congruence between reflected appraisals and the identity standard (Stotland and Pendleton 1989).

Swann (1983, p. 50) provides an illustration of this kind of stress when he talks about midlife crises triggered when people realize that "their now frazzled and frowzy appearances no longer evoke the admiring glances they have come to expect from others." Conway's (1978) book on men in midlife crisis is full of such examples of people's reactions to the stress induced by the failure of identity-verification. The normal self-relevant meanings we have been accustomed to getting from others begin to disappear. Our actions aimed at a particular self-presentation no longer yield the expected results. Our expectations are not met, our normal identity-verification processes are interrupted, and we must find ways of reestablishing the normal identity processes, or else find new identities.

The Four Types of Interruptions

Identities are control systems that can be interrupted in a number of ways. These have been divided into four basic types (Burke 1991; 1996). The first, or *Type I* interruption, is the *broken loop*. When activated, an identity is a highly organized, continuously operating feedback loop of adjusting outputs to maintain congruence between inputs and the identity standard; breaking this continuous loop would constitute an interruption of a highly organized process and would be a major source of distress (Mandler 1982) in the form of heightened autonomic activity. Much of the literature on the impact of life events fits this type of interruption. When a loved one dies, our identity with respect to that person (brother, wife, son, parent, and so on) is interrupted.

When we move, change jobs, become promoted or laid off, our normal identity processes involving friends or coworkers are disrupted, as well as might be our identities as parent or spouse, to the extent that being a spouse or parent involves where we live or the job we have.

The *Type II* interruption of the identity process, *interference from other identities*, is understandable when it is recognized that people have more than one role identity. Because of this, it is possible that maintaining one identity acts to undermine and interrupt the processes that maintain another identity—the classic role-conflict situation. An example might be a high school student who is in both the band and the high school chorus when rehearsal times conflict. Another example would be an athlete who discovers that a friend and teammate is taking drugs. The athlete is caught between the loyalties of a friendship identity and those of a team member identity. Carver and Scheier (1988) present an idea very similar to this type of interruption, suggesting that problems in the smooth flow of self-regulation sometimes arise, as when there is conflict between identity standards (reference values in their language), which results in anxiety. For example, we might consider Marvin, a male minister, who tries to be compassionate and supportive as a minister, but independent and assertive as a male. To the extent that these meanings are incompatible, verifying one identity puts the other in jeopardy.

The third manner of interruption (*Type III*) is related to the first two but has a different source. This is called the *over-controlled identity*. As we have seen, each identity is a control system that is driven by the size of the error signal or discrepancy between the inputs and the identity standard. In a loosely controlled system (as compared with a tightly controlled system), a larger degree of discrepancy or error is tolerated before control mechanisms work very hard to reduce that error. A tightly controlled system requires more sensitivity to error (hence a larger autonomic response to discrepancy when it occurs), and it requires more attention and resources to monitor potential discrepancies, which may draw away from resources used to maintain other identities. The maintenance processes of these other identities, without proper resources, may be disrupted and lead to distress. Thus, heightened distress occurs not only from the greater sensitivity to error of the over-controlled identity but also from other identities that cannot be sufficiently attended to. The stress associated with classic Type-A personalities, who have been characterized as hard-driving, competitive, and hostile whenever their control is threatened, would illustrate the Type III interruption process (Bryant and Yarnold 1990). Another example might be a person who is a perfectionist on the job (as well as, perhaps, elsewhere). He or she spends a lot of time and energy making sure everything is exactly right and can tolerate no margin of error, becoming quite upset at the smallest deviation from what is desired. We may compare this person with another who is laid-back and never seems to be upset by deviations from what is desired.

The fourth manner of interruption (*episodic identities, Type IV*) proposed by Burke (1991) is based on the fact that people have multiple identities, not all of which are activated at the same time. In this sense, all identities are episodic in nature, and the continuity of their processes is interrupted routinely and predictably. There is, therefore, a certain amount of distress that is built into the functioning of all identities. However, there is variability in the degree to which any identity is episodic, and this variability occurs across identities, across people, and across time. Some identities are taken on briefly and infrequently, so the practiced smoothness of the control system has little chance to develop, such as being an actor in a school play. Other identities have a strong component of frequently being "on" and "off" without predictability, as with police and fire protection roles, emergency room physicians, and so on. In each of these cases, the interruptions caused by turning the identity on and off may bring about heightened distress.[8]

At this point, we have seen the main parts of the identity control system, the inputs and outputs, the comparator and identity standard. In addition, we have seen the main workings of the identity system in the process of identity-verification, which keeps the inputs close to the standard. Further, we have examined the way in which the identity-verification process creates opportunity structures that make it easier to keep inputs close to the standard, and we have briefly looked at what happens when that process is interrupted. We now turn to briefly consider the positive consequences of identity-verification rather than the negative consequences of problems with verification.

Self-Esteem as an Outcome of the Verification Process

Self-esteem refers to an evaluation of the self that is made by the self. It is a self-attitude, that is, an attitude we hold about ourselves (Elliott 1982; Gecas 1982; Rosenberg 1979). The concept highlights the reflexive character of the self: its ability to take itself as an object and to respond to that object. In this case, that response is one of evaluation, of assessing the "goodness" or "badness" of the self as an object. Self-esteem answers the slightly altered question posed by Dorothy to the Witch of the West in *The Wizard of Oz*, "Are you a good self or a bad self?"

As an attitude about the self, a feeling of value or goodness and badness, we have to ask what the source of self-esteem is. From our discussion in chapter 1, we saw that one of the contributions of William James (1890) was his view of self-esteem as a function of both our achievements and our aspirations. Recall his formula:

$$\text{SELF-ESTEEM} = \frac{\text{SUCCESSES}}{\text{PRETENSIONS}}$$

James's formulation makes clear that the self-esteem consequences of our accomplishments (successes) are relative to our goals (pretensions). Our goals set the standard for measuring our accomplishments, and the source of our self-esteem is a consequence of the relationship between accomplishments and aspirations. Thus, even if our achievements are high, our self-esteem will be low if our aspirations are higher still. Similarly, even modest achievements can boost one's self-esteem if aspirations are even more modest.

Cast and Burke (2002) present a theory of self-esteem that develops James's answer to the question of the source of self-esteem. Their view is that self-esteem, which has many functions, arises from the simple process of identity-verification. They suggest that the many functions of self-esteem (it acts as a buffer to stress, it is sometimes a motive in the sense that people act to increase self-esteem, and it is an outcome of other social and interpersonal processes) can all be accounted for as an outcome of the identity-verification process. They suggest that if we are good at controlling our self-relevant perceptions, keeping them close to the identity standard, we have cause to rejoice and our self-esteem will be increased. If we have trouble with the verification process and the error signal remains large, we will feel distressed as indicated earlier, and our self-esteem will diminish.

Cast and Burke begin with the identity model discussed earlier. They point out that, in identity theory, identities act to match perceived meanings in the situation (inputs) with the internal meanings of the identity standard (goals). This implies an important relationship between goals and achievements. They also draw upon William James's suggestion (James 1890) that self-esteem is the ratio of "successes" to "pretensions," implying a relationship between what individuals accomplish and their goals. This pairing is similar to the pairing, within the identity model, of self-relevant perceptions of the meanings in the current situation, the "how am I currently doing" ("successes"), and the meanings in the identity standard or goal, the "how should the meanings be?" ("pretensions"). Put simply, identity theory focuses on the degree to which individuals are able to achieve a match between an identity goal or "ideal" (the identity standard) and perceptions of the meanings in the environment or the "actual" performance of the self, much like James's focus on the degree to which successes match pretensions. Therefore, self-esteem is a direct outcome of the successful verification of an identity.

This would be true for any identity. Successful verification of the identity leads to increased self-esteem, while failure of the verification process reduces self-esteem. If one takes on identities that are very difficult to verify or that contain standards that are difficult to meet, lower self-esteem is likely. On the one hand, avoiding such identities is one way of preventing the loss of self-esteem. On the other hand, verifying an identity that is difficult to maintain should lead to higher self-esteem than meeting the standards of an identity that is very easily achieved. And, in general, we see that people tend to choose identities that are neither too "easy" nor too "difficult."

The Consequences of Self-esteem

When considering self-esteem as a buffer, the literature points out that people with high self-esteem suffer less from the slings and arrows of life, although the mechanism for this has not been entirely clear. For example, some have suggested that self-esteem works to maintain positive self-views by process-ing feedback in a self-serving way (Baumeister 1998). That is, individuals with high self-esteem are more likely than those with low self-esteem to perceive feedback as consistent with their positive self-views, to work to discredit the source of the feedback, and to access other important aspects of the self to counteract negative feedback (Blaine and Crocker 1993; Spencer, Josephs, and Steele 1993; Steele 1988). Others argue that those with high self-esteem have a more stable sense of self and are more stable emotionally, both qualities that provide them an "emotional anchor" (Baumeister 1998; Campbell 1990; Campbell, Chew, and Scratchley 1991). Finally, some have argued that people with high self-esteem have more "cognitive resources" at their disposal, enabling them to deal more effectively with unsatisfactory circumstances (Baumgardner, Kaufman, and Levy 1989; Spencer, Josephs, and Steele 1993; Steele 1988). Thus, self-esteem has been found to protect the self from a number of "stressors," including: (1) experiences and infor-mation that might otherwise prove "harmful" to the self (Longmore and DeMaris 1997; Spencer, Josephs, and Steele 1993), (2) distress (Cohen 1959; Coopersmith 1967; Rosenberg 1979), and (3) depression (Burke 1991; 1996; Mirowsky and Ross 1989; Pearlin and Lieberman 1979; Pearlin, Lieberman, Menaghan, and Mullan 1981).

Cast and Burke (2002) suggest that when we consider self-esteem as an outcome of the identity-verification process, we need to ask what happens to the self-esteem that successful verification produces or that nonsuccessful verification takes away. Their answer to this question is to view self-esteem as a reservoir of "energy." A cumulative stream of successes in overcoming situational disturbances to the identity fills the reservoir. Failures in over-coming disturbances drain the reservoir. The level of the reservoir indicates the level of self-esteem. In their view, the self-esteem reservoir increases when the error signal produced by the comparator diminishes, and the self-esteem reservoir diminishes when there are problems with verification and the error signal is increasing. Because it is cumulative over some period of time, immediate identity-verification problems have little impact. Persistent problems in identity-verification, however, will have a cumulative effect of reducing the level of self-esteem. And persistent success will raise self-esteem over time.

Cast and Burke (2002) also suggest that the process of working toward identity-verification uses this energy. Having sufficient energy in the reser-voir allows one to continue working toward identity-verification even when it is difficult or takes much time. This energy is used up discovering new ways to verify an identity when verification is problematic. If enough energy is not present in the reservoir, people may give up striving to bring perceived meanings into accord with meanings in the identity standard; they may become very distressed or even depressed.

In their study of the newly married couples, Cast and Burke (2002) show exactly the above pattern over the first years of marriage with respect to the spousal identity. To the extent that persons were able to verify their spousal identity, they had higher self-esteem. Cast and Burke also showed that individuals who had persistent problems verifying their spousal identity over time (from year one to years two and three) had a bigger cumulative hit to their level of self-esteem. Thus, the newly married individuals they studied showed the increases and decreases of self-esteem as an outcome of the identity-verification process.

Cast and Burke (2002) also looked at the buffering effects of self-esteem in their study of the newly married individual. They indicate that self-esteem operates as a type of personal resource that protects individuals from the consequences of problems with identity-verification, allowing individuals to remain engaged in the situation while they find new ways of verifying their identity. However, because self-esteem is used up in the process, there are limits to this buffering effect. When individuals are persistently unable to verify their identities, the decline of self-esteem is even greater, leaving individuals more and more vulnerable to the negative effects of a lack of identity-verification (including the loss of self-esteem). Therefore, when social relationships do not contribute to identity-verification, individuals may leave such relationships and seek identity-verification, and the resulting self-esteem, elsewhere. Cast and Burke show that the likelihood of separation or divorce is higher for spouses with low levels of identity-verification and low levels of self-esteem. A desire for self-esteem motivates individuals to seek both verifying and enhancing social relationships.

What is the reservoir we call self-esteem? We don't have a full answer to this. As indicated above, following Cast and Burke, we think of it as a reservoir of energy in the sense that high self-esteem (a full reservoir) allows us to continue in situations in which we are not very successful with identity-verification. In this way, we can continue searching for ways to be successful, exploring alternatives and taking some risks. This is a very useful effect. If we avoided all "costly" situations, we would not be able to find the rewards that are only possible after passing through those situations. We would avoid the long-term gain because of the short-term cost.

Studies of Identity-Verification

A study by Burke and Reitzes (1981) was one of the first to show that the connection between identities and behavior is through the meanings they share; that identities influence behavior only to the extent that the meanings of the behavior and the meanings in the identity standard are the same. They studied the student identity using a sample of college students. Using a questionnaire, Burke and Reitzes asked the students what it means to be a college student, a high school student, a graduate student, a college graduate, and a person their age who did not go to college. We will talk in more detail in chapter 5 about how such meanings are measured; but for now, we note that based on a series of descriptive adjectives, they found four dimensions of meaning that were seen by all students as being relevant to defining oneself as a student. These were *academic responsibility, intellectualism, sociability,* and *personal assertiveness.* In addition to discovering the shared dimensions defining the meanings of being a student, Burke and Reitzes also measured each student's view of himself or herself as a student along each of the dimensions. Thus, one student might view herself as very academically oriented, not very intellectual, and very sociable, for example. Another student might view himself as not very academically oriented, not very intellectual, but very sociable. Each student had a score on each of the dimensions, representing how he or she saw himself or herself on these dimensions of meaning. These dimensions constituted their identity standards for being the type of student each saw himself or herself to be.

In addition, Burke and Reitzes measured the meanings of certain behaviors along these same four dimensions of academic responsibility, intellectualism, sociability, and personal assertiveness. The behaviors they examined were two pairs: "planning to go to graduate school" versus "planning to get a job after graduation," and "frequently engaging in social activities like going to the movies, restaurants, sports events, and parties" versus "not engaging in social activities like going to the movies, restaurants, sports events, and parties." Each of these pairs of activity differed along the four dimensions of meaning. Going to graduate school and getting a job differed most in their meanings with respect to academic responsibility and personal assertiveness, while engaging or not engaging in social activities differed most in their meanings in terms of sociability and personal assertiveness.

In the questionnaire, students were asked their educational plans after college: going on to graduate school or getting a job. They were also asked the extent to which they engaged in a number of social activities including the ones mentioned above. Burke and Reitzes reasoned that one's student identity should predict his or her behavior in college only to the extent that the identity and the behavior share common dimensions of meanings. To test this, then, they looked at the association between each of the behaviors (educational plans and participation in social activities) and the student identity meanings on each of the four dimensions.

They found that educational plans were best predicted by the respondent's self-view on academic responsibility and personal assertiveness while participation in social activities was best predicted by the respondent's self-view on sociability and personal assertiveness. Indeed, they found that the strength of the tie among each of the identity dimensions and the behaviors was in direct proportion to the extent that the behavioral choices (graduate school or work and party or not party) differed in meaning on that dimension. Dimensions of meaning on which the behaviors did not differ significantly were dimensions of the student identity that did not predict the behavior, while dimensions of meaning on which the behaviors did differ significantly were dimensions of the student identity that did predict the behavior. This study thus confirmed that the link between identity and behavior is through shared meanings. People act in ways such that the meanings of the behavior reflect the meanings they hold for themselves in their identities.

Burke and Harrod (2005) examined the consequences of identity-verification and identity-nonverification using the data from a study of newly married couples (Tallman, Burke, and Gecas 1998). The identity that Burke and Harrod examined concerned the self-views of husbands and wives along an evaluative dimension of meaning that was measured by asking respondents to rate themselves from 0 to 100 on a series of scales including intelligence, physical attractiveness, likability, friendliness, and understanding. Their analysis indicated that these five items constituted a single evaluative dimension of meanings and that by averaging each person's self-ratings on the five scales, the person's self-view along this dimension of meanings could be represented numerically. These self-ratings constitute the identity standard for each of the respondents.

In addition to rating themselves, respondents also rated their spouse. These ratings were also averaged, and each score represented how the respondents viewed their spouse along the same dimension of meaning. For each respondent, then, Burke and Harrod had a self-rating representing their identity standard, and a rating by their spouse indicating how their spouse viewed them. Burke and Harrod realized that the spouses' rating was not the same as a self-relevant perception or reflected appraisal, because it was not the perception of the respondents of how they thought their spouse viewed them. The identity model technically requires measurement of the respondents' identity standard and the respondents' own perceptions of the meanings in the situation because it is the perceptions that are controlled in the model. They reasoned, however, that the actual views of the spouse would be communicated through interaction with the respondents, and that the respondents would perceive these meanings and infer their spouse's view of them. That is, the perceptions or reflected appraisals would mirror the actual views of the spouse.

Thus, for example, if I view myself as an 85 (a "B" grade) on this scale and my spouse views me as a 75 (a "C" grade), the idea is that my spouse would treat me like a 75 and I would come to perceive that treatment and understand that my spouse views me as a 75. Given some errors of perceptions, I would have, on the average, a perception of my spouse's view as being about a 75. Since my perception of how I am coming across to my spouse (75) does not match my identity standard (85) on this same dimension of meaning, the error or difference should lead me to be somewhat distressed. This was the hypothesis that Burke and Harrod (2005) tested.

And this is what they found. Respondents were distressed to the extent that their self-view, representing their identity standard, did not match their spouse's view of them, representing their perception. Further, it did not matter if their spouse's view were more negative than their own or more positive than their own self-view. Any discrepancy, either positive or negative, resulted in increased distress as identity theory predicts. This is shown in figure 4.2 below, adapted from their study. Along the X-axis is the level and direction of discrepancy between assumed perceptions and the identity standard. Along the Y-axis is the level of distress using a standard measure (Derogatis 1977). The curved line of the graph shows that the level of distress increases as we move away from the 0 level of discrepancy on the X-axis either in the positive or the negative direction.

When the level of discrepancy is small or close to zero, the level of distress is also close to zero. Burke and Harrod (2005) also found that when the distress is large enough, people begin selectively to get out of the nonverifying situation. They found that the probability of divorce among the newly married couples increased to the extent that each person's identity was not verified. By removing themselves from the distressful situation, people are attempting to reduce that level of distress.

Burke and Stets (1999) studied the spousal identity of the same couples using similar techniques as were used by Burke and Harrod (2005) in their later study. By measuring the meanings of the spousal identity as held by the respondents for themselves (their spousal identity standard) and as viewed by their partner (representing the perceptions), Burke and Stets were able to show that to the extent that respondents' spousal identity was verified by their spouse holding identical views of them, their level of distress was reduced. Conversely, to the extent that respondents and their spouse

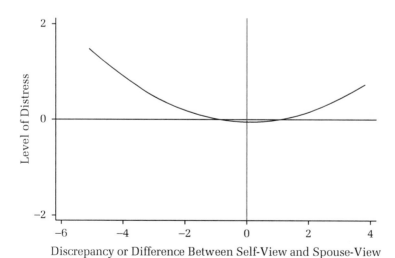

Figure 4.2. Level of Distress as a Function of the Discrepancy between Self-View and Spouse-View of Self

disagreed about the meanings involved in the respondents' spousal identity, the respondents felt augmented levels of distress. As we discuss below, however, much more was at stake than distress for the verification or nonverification of the spouse identity.

The meanings of the spousal identity standard were captured in a series of eleven interview items the respondent and the spouse answered. Each item tapped into a spousal role activity in terms of the degree to which the respondent felt that as a spouse he or she should engage in that role activity. These role activities included such examples as "being responsible for cleaning the house" and "being responsible for taking care of bills and accounts." In addition to the self-ratings on the eleven items, respondents rated their spouse on the degree to which their spouse should do those things. Again, by assuming that the spouse's feelings will become known to the respondent through interaction, those ratings can be used as a proxy for the respondent's perceptions of how he or she appears to their spouse.

Identity-verification for the respondent occurred, then, when the spouse of the respondent saw the respondent's spousal identity in the same way that the respondent saw it. That is, verification occurred when the respondent, for example, saw himself or herself as responsible for all of the cooking and cleaning and the respondent's spouse saw the respondent as responsible for all the cooking and cleaning. Similarly, if the respondent thought he should do half the cooking and cleaning and the respondent's spouse thought he should do half the cooking and cleaning, there was again verification of the respondent's spousal identity. Lack of verification occurred if the respondent felt she should do all of the cooking and cleaning and the respondent's spouse thought she should only do half or do none, for example. Burke and Stets found that when there was verification of the spousal identity, the distress level of the respondent was low but increased to the extent that his or her spousal identity was not verified.

Burke and Stets (1999) also examined other outcomes of the verification process in this study. In addition to the distress that was felt when their spousal identity was not verified or confirmed by their spouse, Burke and Stets found several positive outcomes that occurred when the spousal identity was verified. Four that we shall mention here include increased love of the spouse, trust in the spouse, commitment to the spouse, and a greater feeling of coupleness as reflected in the greater use of the term "we" as opposed to the terms "I" or "me" in couple interaction. Further, by examining these outcomes over several years, Burke and Stets showed that these positive outcomes at one point in time created greater verification in future years. That is, verification and these other outcomes tended to reinforce each other, creating what they called a "mutual verification context" in which partners verified each other and themselves and created a bond that helped maintain that relationship for continued and future mutual verification.

A final study we will mention was done by Riley and Burke (1995). They studied leadership identity in forty-eight small four-person task discussion groups. In this study, they showed that leadership meanings of an individual's behavior (high or low) generally reflect the meanings in their leadership identity standard. They also showed that these meanings are shared and understood by others in the group and that group members are dissatisfied with their role performance when their leadership identity is not verified. This is also the first study that examined four persons in a situation, each trying to verify his or her own identity in the presence of disturbances to that process created by others trying to achieve the same thing.

Each of the groups Riley and Burke studied met four times, each time discussing an issue on which the group had to achieve consensus. Two weeks before the groups met, each participant filled out a questionnaire providing background information on a number of attitudes and traits. One set of questions asked about self-views concerning the respondent's orientation to be a leader. Example questions include, "When I am on a committee, I like to take charge of things," "I try to influence strongly other people's actions," and "I try to be a dominant person when I am with people." The answers to these questions ranged from strongly agree to strongly disagree across five points. With high scores representing meanings associated with strong leadership, the answers were summed to measure each respondent's leadership identity standard. Persons with low scores did not see themselves as leaders in group situations.

Later, after each discussion, the four group participants filled out another questionnaire that concerned their perceptions of what went on in the discussion. Of interest for this study was the answers the respondents provided on items designed to measure the degree to which a person acted like a leader, that is, produced meanings that were understood in the group to reflect leadership. Included among these items were questions asking the respondents to rate each participant (including themselves) on the degree to which he or she "provided fuel for the discussion by introducing ideas and opinions for the rest of the group to discuss," "guided the discussion and kept it moving effectively," and "stood out as a leader in the group." With high scores representing meanings associated with high leadership performance, the ratings were summed to represent (1) the degree to which each actor was perceived by others as acting as a leader in the group (using other's ratings) and (2) the degree to which each actor perceived himself or herself as acting as a leader in the group.

Riley and Burke (1995) found that across all forty-eight of the groups, individuals with strong task leader identities were perceived to engage in more task leadership type behaviors by both themselves and others. This confirmed the link between identity meanings and role-performance meanings suggested in identity theory, and it also showed that these meanings are shared in the group. Not only did individuals see that, in general, the meanings of their own behavior corresponded to the meanings in their identity, but also others saw those leadership meanings. That is, if one person saw herself as not inclined toward leadership in groups (low task leader identity measured two weeks earlier), she also saw, after the discussion, that she had not performed much leadership in the discussion. Others in the group also saw that she did not engage in much leadership behavior, thus sharing her reactions to her behavior.

Further, Riley and Burke found that to the extent that there was a discrepancy between the identity-standard meanings and the perceptions of task leader behavior (meanings) for respondents, those respondents were dissatisfied with their role in the discussion. That is, persons with a high task leader identity who perceived themselves as engaging in high levels of task leadership behavior were satisfied with their role in the discussion, as were persons with a low task leader identity who perceived themselves as engaging in little task leadership behavior. People were satisfied with their role if they engaged in a great deal of leadership behavior or very little behavior as long as it matched up with the level of leadership identity that they had. The persons who were not satisfied with their role performance, according to Riley and Burke, were the persons with a high task leadership identity who, for one reason or another, did not see themselves as engaging in much task leadership behavior. Also dissatisfied were those with a low task leadership identity, who perceived themselves engaging in high levels of task leadership behavior. The inconsistency between identity meanings and behavior meanings created higher levels of dissatisfaction with their role in the group.

Summary

This series of studies illustrates empirically the relationship through shared meanings between identities and behaviors hypothesized in identity theory. The fact that the link is through meanings also implies that perception is intimately involved in the process. People control their perceptions of self-relevant meanings in the situation to make it match their identity standard. This holds for the student identities studied by Burke and Reitzes, the spousal identities studied by Burke and Stets, and Cast and Burke, the evaluative personal identities studied by Burke and Harrod, and the leadership identities studied by Riley and Burke. People choose behaviors in the situation that best match the meanings of the situation to the meanings of their identities. In addition, when they have difficulty doing that, when they have difficulty verifying their identities they become distressed and may leave the nonverifying situation to seek a situation in which they can be verified. However, as Cast and Burke found with the newly married couples, when identities are verified, individuals' self-esteem is built up, which, in turn, buffers those individuals from further problems. Furthermore, as Burke and Stets also found with the newly married couples, when they find situations in which their identities are verified, they tend to form strong ties and commitments with the others in that situation in an attempt to keep a good thing going. Thus, verification brings good things for both individuals and groups.

5

Meaning, Resources, and Interaction

In the last chapter we said that identity standards hold meanings that define who we are. For example, what does it mean to Rachael that she is a district manager? What does it mean to Joseph that he is the manager of a store? These meanings, as we have seen, guide the actions of individuals when they act in terms of these identities, for example, as a district manager or a store manager. And we have seen that when people verify their identities, they act to control perceived meanings in the situation to make them congruent with the meanings contained in their identity standards. That is, the verification process seeks to alter the perceived situational meanings (indicating how the person is coming across in the situation) to match the meanings in the identity standard. Clearly, the idea of meaning is central, but we have not yet made clear exactly what we mean by "meaning." In this chapter, we take some time now to spell out more clearly the nature and facets of meaning as understood in identity theory.

Meaning

Signs and Symbols

Identity theory has expanded the sense of meaning from the usual symbolic form as generally considered in symbolic interaction theory by returning to Mead (1934), who distinguished the concept of signs from symbols. We touched on this in chapter 2. Mead divided the general concept of signs into the two categories: natural signs and conventional signs. A natural sign or simply "sign" is a stimulus that is perceived regularly to be connected with

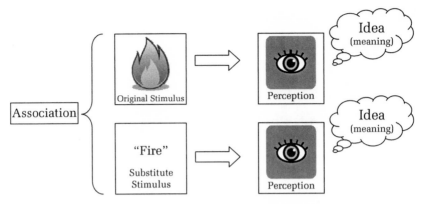

Figure 5.1. Substitute Stimulus Gives Rise to Same Idea (Meaning) as Original Stimulus

something else. The natural sign and what it indicates occur together in the same situation, that is, both are parts of the same concrete situation, and the two become associated. This is shown in figure 5.1.

The term "sign," as we indicated, is a more general concept than symbol. Symbols are a special class of signs, which have shared meaning. A symbol has the same meaning for all persons who share a particular culture. The meaning conveyed by symbols is conventional (arrived at by social convention) and is therefore somewhat arbitrary, being guided by what is shared in a culture. In English, we use the symbol "fire" to represent a particular phenomenon. This term is arbitrary. Other languages use other representations, for example, "le feu" in French, "feuer" in German, and "fuego" in Spanish. The actual representation is arbitrary and doesn't matter so much as the fact that it is a shared agreement with other individuals with whom we communicate. All the words in this book are symbols that give rise to meanings in the readers that are the same as those for the authors. Symbols allow communication because of this shared meaning.

Signs, however, are not necessarily shared. Signs give rise to meaning in the person who responds to them by direct experience. Signs allow persons to experience meaning directly. Clouds may be a sign that it will rain; turning leaves may be a sign of the coming of winter. The position of a needle on a dial may be a sign of the flow of oil in a pipeline; the clicking of a Geiger counter may be a sign of radioactivity in the environment. Signs are not arbitrary; their meaning is not determined by social convention or consensus but is acquired through direct experience.

By returning to the ideas of Mead and expanding our idea of meaning beyond the usual symbolic character that is discussed in symbolic interaction theory, we are able to expand our understanding of what is involved when identities control meaning in a situation. We can move out of the realm of verbal (symbolic) communication into the realm of action. This is important because much of what people do is take action with respect to a variety of objects and processes. We do more than talk; we act on the environment, and we control resources.

Measuring Meaning

As we indicated in chapter 1, meaning is a response to signs and symbols as they represent things and relationships outside of us. As we outlined in that chapter, the idea of meaning as a response was developed much further by theoretical and empirical work done by Charles Osgood and his collaborators as outlined in their book *The Measurement of Meaning* (Osgood, Suci, and Tannenbaum 1957). In this book, they indicate that meaning is not a characteristic of any object or stimulus in a situation. Rather, meaning is a response to a stimulus or sign. It is a particular kind of response to a particular kind of stimulus. The particular stimulus is called a substitute stimulus. Recall from chapter 1 that this draws on the work of Pavlov, who found that dogs will salivate to the bell, which is a substitute for the food powder with which the bell has been associated in the past. Again, this is represented above in figure 5.1.

The particular response to a substitute stimulus Osgood has called a representational mediation response. This is an internal response (an idea or feeling) to some stimulus or sign that mediates between the initial perception of the substitute stimulus and the final external response. This internal response is a representative portion of the original response to the original stimulus or object. For example, when we respond to the word "fire" (the substitute stimulus for an actual fire), we have an internal response that is not the full response that we would have to the original stimulus of a fire. Rather, it contains only some of that response, a representative portion. This smaller portion is enough for us to distinguish the word "fire" from similar words such as "light" or "heat" or "burn," but no more than is necessary to make that distinction. The substitute stimulus can even represent things with which we have no direct experience. The word "zebra" is understood through pictures and other association by most children, though most have never encountered one.

The representational mediation response is both a response to the substitute stimulus and is a stimulus in its own right; it mediates between the initial stimulus and our subsequent responses to it. This is shown graphically in figure 5.2. Osgood, Suci, and Tannenbaum recognize that the two sets of responses—that is, to the original stimulus and to the substitute stimulus—do not have to be identical to have the same meaning. The reduced set of responses has enough of the original set of responses so that it can function in place of the original set of responses in appropriate contexts. Thus, in Pavlov's experiments, the bell came to have the same meaning as the food powder in its ability to produce salivation.

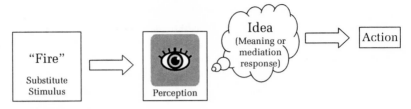

Figure 5.2. The Idea (Meaning) Mediates between the Substitute Stimulus and Further Action

This internal mediation response (meaning) is bipolar in nature and occurs along a number of dimensions labeled in terms of their two ends or poles. Osgood developed a measurement technique, called the semantic differential, to measure these responses. He did this by asking persons to respond to word stimuli using a pencil mark on a series of scales defined by adjectives that were polar opposites (bipolar scales). For example, the meaning of (response to) the word "father" might be ascertained by having people respond to a long series of bipolar adjective scales as follows:

FATHER

happy	____:____:__X__:____:____:____:____ sad
hard	____:__X__:____:____:____:____:____ soft
slow	____:____:____:____:__X__:____:____ fast

In this case, the respondent rated the substitute stimulus "father" as somewhat happy, fairly hard, somewhat fast, and so on. The meaning of "father" to this respondent is thus contained in the set of ratings/responses across all of the bipolar adjective scales. The underlying dimensions along which people respond in terms of their ratings are of interest. It is those that define the relevant dimensions of meaning along which mediation responses are made.

Osgood and his colleagues have investigated these underlying dimensions through a statistical procedure called *factor analysis* and have found that there are three primary dimensions of response that occur to a wide variety of stimuli and account for about fifty percent of the variability in people's responses. These three dimensions are evaluation, potency, and activity, often referred to as EPA dimensions. Evaluation is our feeling of the goodness or badness of the stimulus object. The potency dimension is our feeling of how strong or weak is the stimulus object. And the activity dimension is our feeling of how active and lively or passive and quiet is the stimulus object. These three dimensions have been documented across many cultures and may be part of human nature (Osgood, May, and Miron 1975). While the EPA dimensions are primary, it is clear that there is another fifty percent of the variability of person's responses that are not contained in these three dimensions, and the number of dimensions that is needed to capture this more complete set of meanings is probably fairly large.

For our purposes, however, we see that meaning is a set of responses that people make to a stimulus or sign. To the extent that people share these responses to signs, then the signs become symbols and form the basis of symbolic communication. We see that symbolic and sign meanings can be measured using the semantic differential technique.

Building on this idea, we can measure the meanings people hold for themselves by using the self as a stimulus. This is precisely the technique suggested by Burke and Tully (1977) when they devised a procedure to measure the self in terms of one's gender identity using children in the sixth, seventh, and eighth grades. The idea was to capture what it means to children to be a boy or a girl. By using the semantic differential, meaningful responses to the self as an object could be captured, taking advantage of the fact that the self is reflexive and has the ability to respond to itself. Thus, the gender aspect of the self to be responded to using the semantic differential procedure was: "as a boy I am..." or "as a girl, I am..."

Before this could be done, however, a number of issues needed to be solved. The first was the selection of relevant bipolar adjectives to capture potential dimensions along which meanings (responses) might be made. Burke and Tully (1977) did not feel that the EPA dimensions in themselves would capture the important meanings the schoolchildren held about what it means to be a boy or a girl. By talking with boys and girls in the relevant grades, they ascertained the terms that were felt to be important and relevant for the respondents themselves. For this study, they ended up with thirty-four different bipolar adjective scales that were deemed as potentially important in defining the meaning of being a boy or a girl. Examples of these include timid/bold, strong/weak, wild/gentle, and clumsy/graceful.

The second issue was to understand meaning not in an absolute sense but in a relative sense. There are a number of ways in which boys are like girls; they are both children, they like to play games, and so on. Of interest, however, was what it meant to be a girl as opposed to being a boy. Part of the symbolic interaction understanding of what it means to be someone is an understanding of what that someone is not—what is me and what is not me (McCall 2003). Part of what it means to be a girl is not to be boyish; part of being a boy is not to be girlish. Thus, Burke and Tully wanted to capture the dimensions that distinguished being a boy from being a girl.

To do this they obtained responses to the concept "boys usually are..." and to the concept "girls usually are..." by all the children across all thirty-four bipolar adjectives using the semantic differential procedure. Then a statistical procedure called *discriminant function analysis* was used to find those bipolar adjective scales, which best distinguished between the meaning of being a boy and the meaning of being a girl (Burke and Tully 1977). It turned out that five bipolar adjective scales were sufficient for these schoolchildren to distinguish between ratings of girls and ratings of boys with ninety percent accuracy across all subjects: boys and girls, as well as sixth graders, seventh graders, and eighth graders.[1] It was thus the consensus of these schoolchildren that the particular five polar adjectives captured the important dimensions of meaning distinguishing boys and girls. This procedure thus yielded information about which of the thirty-four bipolar adjective scales best discriminated between the meanings of being a boy from the meanings of being a girl for these schoolchildren. The five dimensions that worked best for everyone were soft/hard, weak/strong, girlish/boyish, not emotional/emotional, and rough/smooth. Two other dimensions that came close to being included but were not quite as good were clumsy/graceful and brave/cowardly.

With that, it is now possible to examine the responses of boys and girls to the concepts "as a boy I am..." or "as a girl I am..." on these particular five bipolar adjectives to quantitatively characterize their own location along the dimension distinguishing what it means to be a boy or a girl. Such a procedure results in being able to assign a numerical score to each child along this dimension that ranged from about −3 through 0 (the midpoint) to about +3. At one end (−3) were the very boyish meanings; at the other end (+3) were the very girlish meanings. Each child was assigned a score based on how he or she saw himself or herself along this scale. The scale itself, as we saw, was derived from the responses of all children in the sample defining the contrasting meanings of being a boy and being a girl. This score, then, represents the identity, in gender terms, of the person to whom it is assigned.

As an example, suppose Billy rates himself as follows on the items measuring gender meaning:

AS A BOY I AM...

hard	____ :	X :	____ :	____ :	____ soft
strong	____ :	X :	____ :	____ :	____ weak
girlish	____ :	____ :	____ :	X :	____ boyish
emotional	____ :	____ :	____ :	X :	____ not emotional
smooth	____ :	____ :	____ :	____ :	X rough

These items would be coded 2 on hard/soft, 2 on strong/weak, 4 on girlish/boyish, 4 on emotional/not emotional, and 5 on smooth/rough. The formula for calculating the gender identity score starts with a score of .9 and then adds (for the first two items) or subtracts (for the last three items) Billy's score multiplied by .3. The values of .9 and .3 in the formula result in a person's score ranging from −3 (strong masculine) to +3 (strong feminine). For Billy, and the way he answered the bipolar items, this would result in a score of −1.8 (that is, $.9 + .3*2 + .3*2 − .3*4 − .3*4 − .3*5$). The score of −1.8 for Billy puts him on the masculine side of the scale but not as extreme as he might be, that is, not at −3.

The distribution of all of the identity scores of boys and girls along this dimension indicated that boys and girls were arrayed across the dimension, that boys were generally toward the boyish end (−3) and girls were generally toward the girlish end (+3). The distribution also indicated that there was considerable overlap in the self-meanings of boys and girls along this

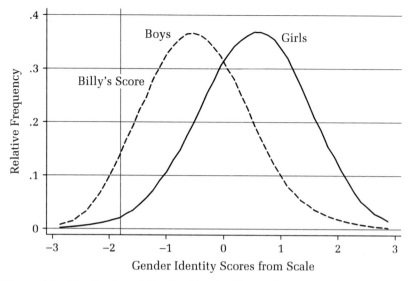

Figure 5.3. Distribution of Gender Identity Scores for Boys and Girls

dimension. Figure 5.3 shows the distributions of gender identity scores for the sample of boys and girls studied by Burke and Tully (1977) and includes the position of Billy's example score.

We see in the figure the bell-shaped curve for the distribution of scores for boys, which is centered just above the score of −1. We also see the bell-shaped curve for this distribution of scores for girls, which is centered just below the score of 1. Most of scores for girls are above the 0 point on the scale, and most of scores for boys are below the 0 point on the scale.

This procedure has subsequently been used to quantitatively measure the meanings contained in the standards of a number of identities including the gender identities of adults along the dimension of masculine/feminine (Burke and Cast 1997; Stets and Burke 1996); the student identities of college students along the four dimensions of "academic responsibility," "intellectualism," "sociability," and "assertiveness" (Burke and Reitzes 1981); the age identities of older persons along dimensions of "feeling useless" and "Personalism" (Mutran and Burke 1979a; 1979b); the body image identities of adolescents (Stager and Burke 1982); the spousal identities of newly married couples along a dimension that distinguishes husbands and wives (Burke and Stets 1999); the environmental identity along the dimension of "anthropomorphism" and "ecocentrism" (Stets and Biga 2003); and the moral identity along the dimensions of "justice" and "care" (Stets and Carter 2006). With this measurement procedure, we can now be very specific when we talk about meanings, whether it is the self-meanings held in any identity standard or the perceived meanings of signs and symbols in the situation that are relevant to the self. When we say that a person changes the situation so self-relevant perceived meanings are altered, we mean that, for example, if Billy seems to be coming across in a situation as if his gender identity score were −.8 (rather than the −1.8 that was measured for his gender identity standard), he will act in the situation to change the way he is coming across. He will change his behavior to be more masculine (more toward the −3 end of the scale) until he perceives that he is coming across with a meaning value of −1.8, thus matching his standard.

What is not clear from the measurement procedure as presented above is that meaning as a response to a sign is not just a cognitive response concerned only with understandings and knowledge. Rather, the meaning response includes emotions and feelings as well as cognition and knowledge. It includes all of the psychological, physical, and chemical reactions that we have to the stimulus. It includes the denotative aspects of the sign as well as the connotative aspects. The word "moonlight" refers not only to the light of the sun reflected on the surface of the moon to which we can point. It also refers to the romantic feelings that might also be generated by the word or to the fears that might be generated in another context (as in a werewolf movie). Meaning as a response must be understood to include the full array of internal events that result from the stimulus. Ideally, our measurement procedure would capture as many of these aspects as possible in the responses used in measuring meaning.

Social Structure: Further Considerations

Hopefully, at this point we have provided some understanding of meaning as a mediational response to signs and symbols and we have provided an understanding of the way in which those meaning responses can be measured to provide numerical scores that represent the meanings along relevant dimensions, such as masculine/feminine. As we have discussed meaning and its measurement, however, we have focused primarily on the responses to symbols. We have viewed identities as agents for controlling the symbolic meanings that reflect how we define ourselves symbolically in particular roles. What does it mean to be a boy, a teacher or a student, or a president or a secretary?

We now expand this view of identities by returning to the point made in chapter 1 that identities control sign meanings as well symbolic meanings.[2] It is through the control of sign meanings that the resources that sustain us are themselves controlled: the food we eat, the clothes we wear, the cars we drive, and so on. Although we do live in a symbolic world of language and communication, we also live in a physical world of energy and resources. We will return later to the relationship between these two, but before we do, we want to enlarge our view of social structure from that presented in chapter 1.

To begin an understanding of social structure from this point of view, imagine the flow of oil in a pipeline, perhaps from the northern part of

Alaska down toward Fairbanks and Anchorage. Imagine it flowing into huge storage tanks at the end of the pipeline and then onto tanker ships, and it being carried and put into more storage tanks in another port and from there being moved into a processing center and transformed into gasoline. Imagine the flow of this gasoline from the processing center into still other storage tanks, and from there to tanker trucks, to gasoline stations, and into the automobiles and trucks that we drive.

Or imagine the digging of iron ore from the ground and the hauling of that ore by train to steel mills. Imagine that ore being transformed into iron and then into steel, and the steel being transformed into automobile parts, truck parts, train parts, oil rig parts, pipeline parts, and storage tank parts. Imagine all of these parts then being transformed into the automobiles we drive to the gasoline stations, the tanker trucks and ships that haul gasoline and oil, the oil rigs that bring up the oil, and the pipelines and storage tanks that move and hold it.

Imagine the movement not only of these objects and things but also of energy, information, and data around the world. Imagine the transformation of these objects, things, energy, information, and data from one form to another. Imagine data being transformed into research findings, and research findings being transformed into manufacturing processes, which, in turn, may transform other resources from one form to another, for example, oil to gasoline or ore to iron to steel to automobiles. What we are imagining is a vast and interconnected network of flows and transformations of a multitude of resources across and around our country, indeed around the world (Freese 1988).

We can broaden this even further, expanding our view of the resources that go into this vast network. Imagine now the flow of love, esteem, power, support, and authority from person to person in a group or organization. Respect, admiration, friendship, as well as hostility, fear, and hate serve as resources to support individuals and groups of individuals, as much as do heat, light, buildings, and rooms. This network of resource flows and transformations is vast indeed, but it is structured and highly organized.

In chapter 1 we spoke of social structure in terms of people and the relationships among them as evidenced by the patterns of their behaviors as they interact with one another. Positions in the social structure were characterized as consistent patterns in the behavior of persons who occupy those positions (for example, insurance investigator, truck driver, or teacher), and at an abstract level we talked about the flows of persons into and out of such positions. Now, we want to combine with this view of social structure as patterns of behavior the idea of this vast network of flows and transformations of resources that we have been previously imagining. The question we shall pursue is how these two views of structure are linked and, indeed, form a unitary whole.

The answer we propose lies in the actions of identities organized into *systems of interaction* that operate across time and situations (Freese 1988;

Freese and Burke 1994), which we explain below. Identities organized into systems of interaction provide the structure and organization to the network of resource flows and transformations in terms of their agency and accomplishment. For example, a municipal police department may be a system of interaction. It controls the flow of persons into police positions and accused criminals into jails. It controls the flow of vehicles that the police can use in their work. It controls jails, guards, paper, pencils, desks, issuing citations, and many other resources that allow the organization to do its job. The police department as a system of interaction, however, is not located in one place. The personnel are probably never all together in one place. The business of the department is carried out across situations and across time.

However, looking at the network of resource flows, we see that the structure and organization of the system of interaction is built to maintain such flows and transformations of resources. These flows and transformations of resources are the ends to be maintained by the system of interaction of the police department.

Let us briefly look at this idea of a system of interaction more closely, though we will return to it later in the chapter for more extensive treatment. We should warn, first of all, that not only is this concept very abstract but also it runs counter to the usual ways we think about society and social structure. It concerns not the linking together of interacting people but the linking together of resource flows and transformations, about which more will be said below. Clearly people are involved in this linking, as we can point to the individuals who turn valves, press keys, and monitor gauges as crude oil is transformed into gasoline. The important point in this analysis, however, is not to think of the persons but rather to think of the functions to be accomplished. The person in the link is not important; the function is. The person is only an agent used by an identity to accomplish the function. The coordination and sequencing involved in the valve-turning, the key-pressing and the gauge-monitoring is made possible, in part, by the orders and instructions of other persons, also acting as agents for identities, the information supplied by other agents, and the valves, computers, and gauges supplied by still other agent-persons. Keeping in mind the functions, then, we build a picture of how these many and diverse functions are interconnected to keep the resources flowing and the transformations occurring. It is this large, interconnected set of functions carried out through the behavior of persons that constitutes the system of interaction. The person, however, is simply a vehicle for the function. A person is, of course, much more than this function. But when considering systems of interaction, it is important to highlight the function of the person, as this makes the concept of a system of interaction clearer.

Before going on to discuss resources in more detail, we need to introduce one additional concept: that of a situation of interaction, in contrast to the concept of a system of interaction just mentioned (Freese and Burke 1994). A situation of interaction is the place in which interaction happens. For example, let us focus on a particular location. Imagine a steel mill. Imagine the flow of iron ore into the mill, the dumping of the ore from the railcars, its movement on conveyer belts. Imagine the flow of coal and coke to the mill, the flow of electricity, and the flow of water. Imagine the flow of heat, slag, and contaminated water out of the mill and the flow of steel out of the mill.

Imagine the flow of people into the mill on a workday and home again in the evening. Imagine the flow of skills, information, actions, and behavior through the mill and the flow of equipment, supplies, order forms, computers, pencils, trucks, cranes, and so on through the mill. Imagine the flow of money, credit, and debit through the mill and between the mill and other parts of the economy. Imagine the flow of esteem and respect and of fear or anger to various managers and workers within the mill.

The steel mill in this example is a location (actually, a set of locations) for the coming together and intertwining of these resource transfers and transformations. It provides one illustration of a situation of interaction in the sense of a place where the functions defining a system of interaction are carried out, where signs and resources are manipulated, controlled, and transformed by particular people—a place of action and agency with respect to resources. Action is thus always situated, but the situation alone is not enough to understand that action. The action first and foremost must be understood in terms of the systems of interaction and the role that action plays in sustaining the resource flows and transformations.

In the next section, we present a more detailed picture of the nature of resources as they are conceptualized here. Following that, we will return to the discussion of situations and systems of interaction to pursue the connection between the two views of social structure as systems of resource flows and as systems of relationships among identities.

Resources

Following Freese (1988), we define resources as anything that supports individuals and the interaction of individuals. This is different from the usual notion of resources in two ways. First, it is a definition of resources as processes rather than as entities. Second, it does not presume that resources are zero sum in that what one person gets another looses, nor does it assume that resources are scarce (light is generally not scarce), valued (air usually has no price tag), or necessarily even desirable (children may not want their medicine).

Resources As Process

Defining resources as that which sustains individuals and the interaction of individuals tells us what resources do, not what they are, and is therefore a process definition. Thus, anything that supports individuals and their interaction is a resource. Food is a resource, not an entity, and is a process that includes ingesting, digesting, circulating, and chemically using and transforming food. This is a process that must occur at a certain rate and is controlled by the individual. Milk is a food, but only if it can be digested and utilized. For some people, milk is, therefore, not a food, because it cannot be digested. Some people may not be able to ingest milk that is too old or too warm. Such milk is not food for them. This, of course, is common sense, but it warns us to be careful in what we label as a resource. It is easy shorthand to think of the entity as the resource, but, although we may often be able to get away with such shorthand, we can get into trouble by doing so. A container with only air in it would be considered empty by most people, but the "contents" of that empty container can serve to sustain the life of a scuba diver under water.[3]

Thus, to say that a resource can be anything is thus not to say that everything is a resource. Whether something is in fact a resource means that it is functioning to sustain individuals or interaction.

Resources and the Support of Individuals

When we consider the things (processes) that sustain persons, we need to consider the physical as well as the social and psychological (i.e., cognitive, emotional, and relational) aspects of the individual. Although science has only the most limited knowledge of what things sustain a person cognitively, emotionally or relationally, there is still much to be learned even about the requirements of the physical beings of individuals—the nutrients, vitamins, minerals, warmth, light, touch, and so on, that keep us alive. Of course, such knowledge of the biological and psychological requirements of the individual may belong more properly in the province of the biologist or psychologist than in the province of the social psychologist or sociologist. Still, it is individual and collective behavior and the social organization of that collective behavior that assures that individuals, in fact, are sustained (or not sustained). Thus, we would do well as sociologists and social psychologists to understand the social organization of behavior as it is tied directly to the lives and livelihoods of individuals, for those lives and livelihoods would appear to underlie all social organization (Freese 1988).

Consider, for the moment, how much of our activity is given over to self-sustaining processes. We need to eat, and we spend a good deal of time and effort not only in the process of consuming food and water but also in associated activities such as the preparation of food and drink for consumption at home or the searching out of places (restaurants, etc.) for the consumption of food and drink away from home, including time spent reading menus, ordering, and waiting for what we have ordered. We spend time dressing ourselves to keep us warm, to protect ourselves from embarrassment, and, perhaps, to gain respect and admiration. We spend time with personal grooming, bathing, and going to the bathroom. And, of course, in our culture, all of these self-supporting activities require the use of additional resources, which must be obtained and maintained. We may need dishes and flatware, napkins and candles, tables and chairs, music and atmosphere for a dinner, not to mention stoves, refrigerators, pots and pans, sinks and garbage disposals, water and sewer services, gas and electrical services, and so on. The list goes on and on and each layer of resources requires other layers.

Consider, too, how much of our activity is given over to our social needs above and beyond our biological needs such as food, clothing, sleep, exercise, and shelter. We spend time and effort seeking and maintaining friendships and support networks, engaging in recreational activities, acquiring skills and knowledge from others who have them, for example, by attending school or taking lessons. Support, love, attention, admiration, and respect all come from our association with others, but they do not come automatically. Although there may be individual variation in the degree to which each of these is necessary to sustain us as individuals, we all spend time and engage in a variety of behaviors and interactions with others to assure that we have enough of each of these social resources, as we might call them. To have a friend, we must be a friend; to earn respect, we must act in a manner that deserves respect; to enjoy intimacy we must act in a way that earns the trust and love of others. Our lives are filled with these actions and behaviors so that we may sustain ourselves by drawing upon and using resources.

Resources and the Support of Interaction

The definition of resource given above indicated that resources support not only individuals but also the interaction between individuals. We are, perhaps, moving to a higher level of abstraction when we consider resources that support the interaction of individuals, as opposed to individuals directly. However, it makes sense to consider such resources separately because they apply to a different entity than the individual. They apply to the couple or to the group or to the organization or company. We are talking here about those things or processes that sustain and support interactions that take place between and among individuals. Just as at the individual level, some resources, such as nutrients, sustain the cells and organs that make up the individual, other resources, such as love, help sustain the entire individual and not the cells or organs that help make up the individual.

At the group level, parliamentary rules as embodied, for example, in Robert's Rules of Order support the orderly interaction that occurs in business meetings. A clock may support interaction by coordinating the times people meet, the time classes start, or the time for a luncheon engagement. At an organizational level, having a building may help organize a company by providing a place for interaction and the tools for the accomplishment of tasks. Robert's Rules of Order, a clock, and a building do not support individuals but are resources that support interaction and groups.

We now want to distinguish between resources in use and resource potential. Resources in use are actively supporting persons or interaction. As examples of resources that support interaction, consider a workgroup meeting in a room at Acme Enterprises. The members of the workgroup are meeting in a room with light and various furnishings. The light is a resource in use that allows the members to see one another. A table around which they interact is another resource in use, as are the chairs upon which the members sit while interacting with one another. A whiteboard and markers are also resources in use as they are utilized by the workgroup members to present and clarify ideas. Each of these resources is supporting not individuals as such but the interaction among the individual group members. They are resources in use by the members of the workgroup.

In addition to these resources in use, which we may term "actual resources," there is another class of resources, which is also important. This other class might be called potential resources and contains objects and processes that, in the right form and at the right time and place, have the potential to be used to support persons or interaction. Returning to our example of the workgroup meeting at Acme Enterprises, the telephone in the corner of the meeting room is a potential resource, as is the money in the group leader's pocket, both of which will be used to order sandwiches for everyone. The sandwiches are food that will help sustain the individuals, but having the sandwiches here in the room will help sustain the interaction of the members of the workgroup. The information that is being presented on the whiteboard in the meeting is a potential resource that may be used at a later point to redistribute advertising dollars and increase sales, which in turn helps sustain the organization and the workgroup. Much of the control of resources is control over resource potentials—getting resources in place at the right time and in the right form to be used to sustain persons or interaction or to sustain other resource flows and transformations, thus acting indirectly to sustain persons and interaction.

The distinction between actual and potential resources is not always clear, for it depends upon what is to be supported. Consider a bakery, for example. The flour that goes into making bread is a potential resource that can sustain an individual as food. That same flour, as it is being used in the bakery to make bread, is an actual resource that sustains the actions and interactions of persons in the bakery. This can easily be seen if we consider what would happen if the flow of flour to the bakery were to be interrupted. In that case the bakery would have to close temporarily or at least curtail many of its activities. The continued flow of flour is necessary for those activities to be sustained. In our example, therefore, flour is both an actual as well as a potential resource, so the distinction between actual and potential resources is an analytical distinction, not a concrete distinction. Being an actual or potential resource is not a property of the object itself. Rather, it is a relationship between the resource in question and the persons or interactions it may support. If the resource in question is involved in the current support of persons or interaction, it is an actual resource or a resource in use. Otherwise it is a potential resource for those persons or for that interaction. In either case, it may also be a potential resource for other persons or for other interactions.

Resources and Meaning

The distinction between actual and potential resources is an important one, for it allows us to see that much human activity is involved with the manipulation of potential resources so that they may become actual resources at the time and place they are needed. For example, Tom may consult with friends or colleagues about their recommendations on a doctor or dentist if he has moved and needs to change whom he sees. In purchasing a new camera or audio system, Mary may consult friends and reviews in publications. She may visit different stores looking for the best buy; she may talk with sales persons about the advantages and disadvantages of various models. In the realm of politics, Rachael talks with friends about various politicians; she reads the newspapers and magazines to understand the issues and see where various politicians stand with respect to these issues. All of these activities may be thought of as a prelude to the using of the resource: the doctor when Tom is sick, the audio system for Mary's peace and harmony, the politician (through voting) for sustaining Rachael's style of living. All of this also involves symbolic activity, for the resources themselves may not even be present. Thus it is not the resource itself these people are dealing with, but the idea, the knowledge, the concept, or the meaning of the resource. Symbols make it possible to deal with potential resources.

Indeed, Freese and Burke (1994) have argued that the function of symbols as they have evolved from signs is precisely to deal with potential resources. They suggest that to every configuration of symbols there corresponds a set of potential resource transfers. Symbols are thus the means by which people transcend the experience of immediate signs and the resource transfers that they signal—the means by which they store information about signs learned, make plans about signs, and coordinate and regulate their plans and information. In short, this is the process of developing and transmitting a culture.

We can now return to the distinction between signs and symbols presented earlier. A sign was defined as a stimulus that calls up a response that is the same as or similar to the response previously evoked by some other stimulus. A sign is thus a substitute stimulus, the meaning of which is our response to it. If our response to the sign is the "same" as our response to the original stimulus, then the meaning of the sign is the same as the meaning of the original stimulus. A symbol is a special type of sign. Here, the substitute stimulus is one that is socially agreed upon. For example, the word "sun" is a socially agreed upon symbol that refers to the source of light and heat that seems to hang in the heavens. The word "sun" is a symbol for that source of heat, light, and life. The feeling of sunshine on your face, however, is a sign that the sun is shining; no social conventions are necessary in this case.

Recall other examples of signs from chapter 1, such as the readings on a thermometer as a sign of the temperature and the needle on a car's gas gauge as a sign of the amount of fuel in the gas tank. These illustrate that signs are tied to objects and resources in our immediate environment or situation of interaction. When we respond to signs, we are responding generally to the immediate levels and flows of resources. Behavior oriented to signs is behavior that has consequences in the situation of interaction, and when that behavior is coordinated with the behavior of others also concerned with signs, we might then refer to resource interactions (Freese and Burke 1994). Resource interactions are based on signs and deal with the transfer and transformation of resources in the immediate situation of interaction.

In this way, we distinguish, at least analytically, resource interactions (based on the signs of immediate experience) from symbolic interactions (based upon the symbols reflective of meaning outside the realm of immediate experience). Symbols reflect the potential resources that may come to be realized under the right conditions, and symbolic interaction manipulates those symbols and meanings that govern potential resources. Symbolic interaction coordinates plans, analyzes possibilities, and controls representations. It reviews and records and provides collective memory from which we can learn.

Of course, any concrete interactions among persons include both symbolic as well as resource interactions. For example, while Tom is talking to Manuel from the local heating company about converting his home to solar energy (a symbolic discussion about potential resources), Tom is also taking notes on a piece of paper with a pencil; and both Tom and Manuel are seated in chairs and using the tabletop as a platform on which to write. Tom passes the notes across to Manuel, the heating company representative, who adds some comments and suggestions using his own pen. This all involves sign behavior that manipulates, transfers, and transforms resources in the situation (pens, ink, paper, table, chairs), which, in turn, facilitates their interaction (though the content of the writing is symbolic).

We thus arrive at a picture of resource interactions organized around signs that deal with the flow and transformation of resources in the immediate situation of interaction and of symbolic interactions organized around symbols that deal with the potential of resources, which may or may not be present in the immediate situation. Together, these organized and patterned resource and symbolic interactions and the resources and symbols that are being manipulated by these interactions constitute social structure in the context of identity theory.

Bringing Identities Back In

Now the question may be raised as to what maintains the patterned and coordinated flows and transformations of resources that we are calling social structure. "People's actions accomplish this" is one's most likely initial response, but this answer is not really correct, as we have already suggested. Rather, it is the functions that individuals provide through their behavior and the organization of that behavior. To understand these functions and their organization for a more adequate answer to this question of what maintains the patterned and coordinated flows and transformations of resources, we move to the other level of our analysis and talk about identities. That is, if we view the patterns, flows, and transformations of resources as they occur between individuals and situations as one level of analysis, while we view the nature and agency of identities within individuals as a second level of analysis, it is to this latter level we return.

We have noted earlier that the basic operation of identities is a control system seeking to match perceptions (inputs) with standards. And we have noted that both perceptions and standards are coded in terms of meanings, both sign meanings and symbol meanings. The fundamental action of identities is, therefore, to alter situations in such a way that the meanings of the signs and symbols that are perceived in the situation match the meanings held in the identity standard. This fundamental action of identities, thus, brings us right back to the ideas of resource and symbolic interaction (dealing respectively with signs and symbols) as discussed above. Resource interactions and symbolic interactions are accomplished by the operation of identities doing their job of matching perceptions to standards. Recall that the output of identities is an error signal resulting from the difference between perceptions and standard. We talked about the output being behavior on the part of the person holding the identity. This behavior has meaning (is interpretable to the self and others), and it alters both sign and symbol meanings in the situation. The behavior itself is the action of the person acting as an agent for the identity that has been activated. Each person acts as the agent for many identities, as many as the person holds. This view turns much sociological thought on its head. Rather than signs and symbols being the mechanisms that provide a link between persons, this view says that persons are agents that link signs and symbols to identities (Freese and Burke 1994). We will see, however, that this inverted view helps provide a rather parsimonious view of social life.

We had asked earlier what maintains the patterned and coordinated flows and transformations of potential and actual resources. The answer is now clear: identities using persons as their agents maintain the patterned and coordinated flows of resources. Identities (not persons) are responsible for the vast network of resource transfers and transformations. Furthermore, because symbols refer to potential resources, when the meanings of symbols perceived in a situation do not match the meanings encoded in an identity standard, potential resources are not the way they are "supposed" to be (according to the identity standard). When the sign meanings perceived in a situation do not match the meanings encoded in the identity standard, actual resources are not the way they are "supposed" to be. Thus, to modify the signs and symbols in a situation is to modify the actual and potential resources in the situation. When the perceived actual and potential resources in a situation are modified to match the encodings in the identity standard, when they are transferred or transformed in particular ways, the signs and symbols are then brought into accord with the identity standard. It is the normal operation of identities as they verify themselves by bringing the perceived meanings of signs and symbols into accord with the meanings of their standards. This, in turn, alters and thus controls the flow and transformation of resources in the situation.

Of course, all of the identities activated in the situation are doing this, and it is not likely that the standards of all of the activated identities are identical. Consequently, the effects of the agency of one identity are likely to introduce disturbances that must be compensated and countered by another identity in an ongoing and continuous process of resource and symbolic interaction. There is no state of rest. Perturbation and disturbances in the identities of sets of persons are the foundation for continual order-defining and sense-making activities, for negotiations and renegotiations, for positioning, explaining, accounting, and manipulating, and for rearranging status and role relationships. These are all carried out to bring the perceived flow and transformation of actual and potential resources into agreement with identity standards through the mechanism of matching the meanings of signs and symbols with the meanings coded into the standards.

Systems and Situations of Interaction

It is one thing to suggest that it is the normal operation of identities, acting through persons as their agents, that provides the functions that coordinate the vast network of resource transfers and transformations about which we have been speaking. It is another thing entirely to show how such operation results in the patterns and organization that network demonstrates. To help move us in this direction, we want to elaborate further on two concepts that we introduced earlier in the chapter: systems of interaction and situations of interaction. A situation of interaction is a place or location where actual and potential resources, signs and symbols, are manipulated, transferred, and transformed by identities using persons as their agents. The location might be an office, a meeting room, the shop floor, a street corner, or a bar. The people present are engaged in a variety of symbolic interactions (in the bar, for example, ordering a beer, talking about problems at home) and behaviors (picking up a mug, placing it under the tap and drawing the beer, listening sympathetically, and providing support). This is the place where money is transferred, where beer is transferred, where support and sympathy are provided; it is a situation of interaction.

A system of interaction, as suggested above, is a more abstract concept and involves the linking of flows and transformations of resources across time and situation into some synthetic whole as a social system whose boundaries may not always be clear. The bar, considered as a system of interaction, involves the identities of the owner, the manager, three bar-keeps, several servers, kitchen staff, janitors, a bookkeeper, many patrons, beer, liqueur, wine and food suppliers, licensing authorities, union officials, building inspectors, health inspectors, waste service suppliers, water and electric suppliers, heating and air conditioning suppliers, and so on, all of whose person-agents act and interact in many places and time periods to keep the bar functioning. All of these actions and interactions involve the transfer and transformation of actual and potential resources as necessary to counteract disturbances and keep the sign and symbol meanings perceived in a multitude of situations congruent with the meanings in the identity standards of all the identities involved.

Now, the bar as a situation of interaction contains more interactions than just those relevant to the bar as a social system. Jennifer and Raphael, two lawyers discussing cases over lunch at the bar, are engaged in interactions relevant to another social system in the form of a legal firm. Jennifer and her husband, Ron, meeting after work to share a drink, may engage in interactions relevant to their family social system. At the same time, Jennifer, Ron, and Raphael are also engaged in interactions relevant to the social system of the bar by acting as patrons and ordering food and drink. A situation of interaction materializes with a gathering of assorted persons, each bringing assorted interpersonal inputs (signs and symbols). It results in a variety of behavior that is both symbolically meaningful and situationally resourceful, having impact upon the symbol and resource flows in the situation.

Note that Jennifer in the above example is an agent who acts respectively for the identities of attorney, wife, and patron (among others), depending upon which identity is activated at the moment. Each identity has inputs of sign and symbol meanings that are relevant for itself alone. These inputs are perceptions made by Jennifer acting as an agent for the activated identity. As a person, Jennifer may have input perceptions that are relevant to more than the identity that has been activated at that point in time. Such input may serve to activate other identities that can monitor that input. For example, Jennifer as a patron overhears the waiters talking about a new restaurant that has just opened and is supposed to be excellent. That symbolic information (dealing with potential resources) may be relevant to Jennifer as a wife, who wants to go to a nice restaurant with her husband, Ron, to celebrate their wedding anniversary. As each identity is activated, the relevant sign and symbol meanings are perceived and compared with the identity standard. The results of that comparison give rise to actions that seek to bring the perception into congruence with the identity standard.

Identity Standards As Goals

As we have indicated, the identity standards contain sign and symbolic meanings that are used as a reference for the perceived sign and symbolic meanings in the situation. People act, as agents for identities, to modify the sign and symbolic meanings in the situation so that they correspond to or match those meanings in the standard. This is the process of identity-verification. We have also indicated that the identity standards contain information about the way the sign and symbolic meanings in the situation are "supposed to be." This latter phrasing is from the point of view of the person holding the identity. There is a sense of the way the levels of actual and potential resources in the situation are supposed to be that is taken from the identity standard. People become upset or distressed in varying degrees when the situational meanings are not the way they are "supposed to be," as we indicated in chapter 4. And they act to change the situation so that perceptions match the identity standard.

This way of looking at the process allows us to see that the identity standards are therefore goals to be achieved or realized in the situation as it is perceived. Since there are disturbances in the situation—that is, others acting to change actual and potential resources from their own point of view, as well as normal processes of wear and tear on equipment, or resources being used up or degraded—people must continue to act not only to achieve the goal but also to maintain the goal in spite of these disturbances. Joseph, the store manager, doesn't just do what store managers do like he is following a script, but he accomplishes the goals that need to be accomplished and maintained in spite of changing circumstances, in spite of changing personnel, and in spite of changes in the competition. Joseph, as the store manager, is an active agent, seeking out ways to accomplish what needs to be accomplished so that he can say that right now things are the way they are "supposed to be." Sarah, in driving her car on the highway, has the goal of keeping her car in the middle of the lane. She cannot predict the exact movements of the steering wheel she will need to make to do that. Instead, Sarah responds to the disturbance of wind, turns in the road, and so on, as they occur to achieve and maintain her goal.

This is true for all identities. Identities use the agency of persons to achieve and maintain the levels, flows, and transformations of actual and potential resources—that is, signs and symbols—in the situation to achieve the goals set in the identity standards. The actual behavior that will achieve these goals may not be known in advance, because the disturbances, their sources, and magnitudes may not be known in advance. For each role, the identity tells how resources are supposed to be and the agency of the person makes it happen.

Resources in Support of Identity-Verification

As the person, acting as an agent for an identity, adjusts actual and potential resources in the situation to bring them into accord with the dictates of the identity standard, the person uses resources to accomplish that. It takes resources to verify identities. Sarah uses the steering wheel to accomplish keeping the car in the middle of the lane. Joseph, the store manager, uses the telephone, the computer, stationary, billing sheets, and so on, to achieve the level of sales that might be one of the goals of the identity standard of store manager identity. In short, there are two different sets of resources, the perceptions of which are controlled by an identity. The first set is the resources whose levels, flows, and transformations are indicated in the identity standard, and the second set of resources are used to accomplish the control of the first set. The first set contains the resources that define the social structure as we have reconceptualized it, that is, the resources controlled by interrelated systems of interaction. Hector is a truck driver who delivers gasoline to stations in a certain district. Controlling the gasoline delivery by Hector is an example of the first set. The truck that Hector uses to deliver the gasoline and the roads that he uses to deliver the gasoline are examples of the second set. Earnings (resources from the second set) that Hector gains by accomplishing the delivery of gasoline (verifying Hector's identity as a truck driver) are used (in part) to buy the truck that allows Hector to deliver the gasoline.

Because some resources (the second set) are used to control the resources that bring about identity-verification (the first set), persons or agents that have control of more of this second set ought to be in a better position to verify the identities that the agent has. If Hector earns very little money delivering gasoline, he may not be able to keep up payments on the truck that allows him to verify his identity as a truck driver. If Hector has more money, not only can he keep up payments on the truck, but also he can afford to keep good tires on the truck, pay a mechanic to keep it running well, and have a music player in the cab to make the driving more comfortable. All of these extras will help Hector better confirm his identity as a truck driver.

A number of research studies have examined the link between identity-verification and resources. A study by Cast, Stets, and Burke (1999) showed that husbands and wives were able to maintain their spousal identity standard against unwanted change over the interval of a year if they had more education and a better job. If their level of education or job status were less than their partner, their spousal identity tended to change over the year in the direction defined by their partner. The identity standard was not able to be maintained according to the respondents' own preferences.

Stets and Harrod (2004) looked at the verification of three different identities that respondents had as measured in a survey. The first had to do with the respondents' job, which they labeled a worker identity. The second had to do with the respondents' achieved level of education, which they called an academic identity. And the third had to do with the identity of friend. Verification of these identities was measured in terms of the difference between how they saw themselves on these identities (their identity standards) and how they reported others saw them in terms of these identities (reflected appraisals). A larger difference between the standards and the reflected appraisals indicated a discrepancy or inability to verify the identity, while a smaller difference or no difference indicated a better ability to verify the identity. For both the worker identity and the academic identity, those persons with more education (representing a higher level of resources available) had a higher level of verification of their identities. The resource of more education did not seem to influence respondents' ability to verify their friend identity. We can only speculate that other resources may have been helpful for verifying the friend identity.

Every position in the social structure is expected (through identity-verification) to control relevant resources for the maintenance of the social structure (by controlling sign and symbolic meanings). For that reason, legitimate access to those resources is built into every position. The nature of the access and the nature of the resources vary by position, as does the amount of resources made available to the position. For example, the role identity of CEO of Microsoft has more resources available for control than does a programmer hired to code a section of a new product. Control of resources is not the same as status, but status is accorded to persons in part by the amount of resources that are controlled by the person. The CEO of Microsoft has more social status than the programmer.

Using status as a surrogate for resources, in another study of the spousal identity, Burke (2008) showed that both husbands and wives were better able to verify their spousal identities if they had higher status. Two different indicators of status were used in this study: race, with whites having higher status than nonwhites in our society, and a combined index of education and occupational status, with those having better jobs and more education having higher status. In both cases, those with higher status (and therefore more access to resources) were better able to verify their spousal identities.

Stets and Cast (2007) examined the issue of the relationship between identity-verification and access to resources in more elaborate detail than the other studies. In addition to the spousal identity that was examined before, they also looked at a more personal identity for each individual: how they saw themselves in terms of the characteristics of being friendly, understanding, and likable. They also looked at three types of resources, which they labeled personal, interpersonal, and structural. Personal resources included a combination of self-worth and self-efficacy, which might be viewed as indicating general self-esteem. Interpersonal resources reflected the ability of individuals to access resources through interpersonal relationship. For this, Stets and Cast combined indicators of the individuals' ability at role-taking and how they were perceived by their spouse in terms of being liked and trusted. Structural resources were represented by combining indicators of the level of education, occupational status, and personal income. When Stets and Cast analyzed all of these data, they found that each of these different types of resources was in fact helpful for verifying the respondents' role and personal identities. Thus, from all of these different studies, we see that resources of a variety of types are helpful if not necessary for persons acting as agents to verify identities that they have.

Summary

In this chapter, we examined in more detail the nature of meaning as a response to signs and symbols in the situation, and we reviewed a procedure to measure the meanings of the self in terms of the identities contained there. This procedure was based on Osgood and his colleagues' (1957) semantic differential to capture the internal, connotative, and emotional responses to symbols. We then extended our understanding of meaning by looking at the connection between signs, symbols, and resources. Controlling perceived meaning in the situation is thus equivalent to controlling actual resources, based on sign meanings, and potential resources, based on symbolic meanings. In this way we saw that identities, through the process of verification, do the work of creating and maintaining social structure either in terms of a set of related positions or, in our new view, as a connected set of resource flows, transfers, and transformations. Identity standards act as goals for agent-persons to control the perceived sign and symbol meanings to accomplish this. Finally, we noted that the control of signs and symbols through the verification process uses resources, and we reviewed research that supports the idea that persons who control more resources are better able to carry out the task of verification through the control of actual and potential resources.

6

Bases of Identities: Role, Group, and Person

Since the development of identity theory, identity researchers have focused on the categorization of the self as an occupant of different *roles* in the social structure such as being a student, worker, or spouse (Thoits and Virshup 1997). As we saw in the previous chapter, researchers have studied the *meanings* people attribute to themselves while in various roles (one's *role identity*), and these meanings are distinct from the behaviors people enact while in these roles (Burke and Reitzes 1981; McCall and Simmons 1978; Stryker 1980 [2002]; Thoits 1983). In this chapter, we discuss the idea that there are more bases for identities than roles. Individuals can also have *social identities* and *person identities*. To make the distinction clear, while role identities are based on the different social structural *positions* individuals hold, such as spouse, worker, and parent, social identities are based on individuals' memberships in certain groups as in persons being Democrat, Latino, or Catholic. Person identities are based on a view of the person as a unique entity, distinct from other individuals. Here, the focus is on the qualities or characteristics individuals internalize as their own, such as being more (or less) controlling or more (or less) ethical.

At the outset, we point out that role, social, and person identities all operate in the same way. Identities from each basis have identity standards that serve as the reference and guide behavior in situations. Whether it is a role, social, or person identity, individuals act to control perceptions of who they are in a situation to match the feedback they receive in the situation. A discrepancy between self-in-situation meanings and identity-standard meanings is identity-nonverification. Individuals will experience negative arousal, and they will act to reduce the negative feelings by changing their behaviors, perceptions, and, at a slower pace, their identity standard.

Alternatively, a correspondence between identity-standard meanings and feedback (perceptions) results in identity-verification and positive feelings, with behavior and perceptions continuing in an uninterrupted manner. Therefore, although we are making an analytical distinction between the different ways individuals are tied to identities at the role, group, or person levels, their underlying operations are the same.

Historically, the emphasis on role identities emerged out of structural symbolic interactionism, the orientation that forms the basis of this book. Sociological social psychologists in this orientation have taken seriously the idea that people's location in the social structure—the roles they assume—importantly shape how they see themselves and how they behave. Alternatively, psychological social psychologists have been instrumental in informing us as to how individuals see themselves as group members. From this has developed social identity theory (Abrams and Hogg 1990), which we will discuss at some length in this chapter, particularly with respect to how it is similar to and different from role identity in identity theory (Stets and Burke 2000). In recent years, identity theorists have begun to recognize person identities, and understand the person as a third basis of identities (Stets 1995; Stets and Burke 1994; Stets and Carter 2006). Social identity theorists and identity theorists have discussed person identities, but they have generally remained peripheral to both theories. As a third basis for identities, we give more attention to person identities in this chapter, particularly as they relate to role and social identities.

In chapter 3, we discussed role identities as they emerged in the thought of McCall and Simmons, Stryker, and Burke. In this chapter, we will give a more general view of role identities that all identity theorists share. We will then discuss social identities, making it clear that they are different from role identities but also are important in understanding the types of identities that serve as the basis for one's identity standard in interaction. Given that person identities are the "new kid on the block," we will discuss these identities in the latter part of the chapter. Person identities are underdeveloped in identity theory, so there is still much to investigate about person identities both theoretically and empirically.

Role Identities

For the early identity theorists, identities based on roles were *the* identities of central importance (Burke 1980; McCall and Simmons 1978; Stryker 1980 [2002]). The emphasis on role identities was likely due to identity theorists' symbolic interactionist roots, especially the focus on individuals playing out roles in interaction (Thoits and Virshup 1997). Roles provide structure, organization, and meaning to selves and to situations. To understand role identities, we first need to briefly review *social positions* and *roles*, which are tied to social positions.

A social position is a category in society or an organization that an individual occupies. Some social positions are considered normative given one's life trajectory such as student, worker (for example, teacher, carpenter, or artist), spouse, and parent; but they may also include those that are counternormative, such as criminal, alcoholic, or homeless person. Other social positions are categorizations based on one's interests, activities, or habits (for example, "activist," "hockey player," "dreamer," or "maverick"). These social positions are known as "social types" or "the kinds of people it is possible to be in a given society" (Stryker and Statham 1985, p. 323).

A role is the set of *expectations* tied to a social position that guide people's attitudes and behavior. For example, tied to the social position of "student" are the roles of learning new knowledge and skills, establishing an area of study, passing courses, acquiring a degree, and so forth. Associated with "teacher" are the (role) expectations of being knowledgeable and instructive. The position of "friend" may include the expectations of being supportive and trustworthy. We learn the expectations tied to different social positions from others such as our parents, peers, educators, and the media.

There may be more than one expectation tied to a social position. Further, expectations can be specific or general in the behavior to which they refer. They can require specific performances, or they can simply provide an outline within which much flexibility is possible. For instance, a general expectation of a "mother" is that she be nurturing. Some women may fulfill this expectation by being physically affectionate, while others may fulfill it through encouraging their child and engaging in supportive talk. Expectations can also be held for the goals or outcomes that one should achieve in a role, without explicit indications as to how those should be achieved. For example, a delivery person is expected to make all of the deliveries without specific instructions about how to deal with traffic, road closures, or the exact order of deliveries. Expectations can also refer to a minimal part or a large part of one's range of interactions. For example, the role of "male" carries with it many expectations such as being dominant and assertive and taking the lead. These expectations will be applicable to a wide range of interactions such as at home, at school, at work, and with friends. In contrast, the role of "fraternity member" carries with it expectations that typically are relevant with friends or at school; thus, they are applicable to a smaller range of interactions.

A *role identity* is the internalized meanings of a role that individuals apply to themselves. For example, the role identity of "teacher" may include the meanings of "mentor" and "friend" that a person applies to himself or herself while playing out the role of teacher. As we mentioned in chapter 3, the meanings in role identities are derived partly from culture and partly from individuals' distinctive interpretation of the role. The first part is the conventional dimension or *role* part of a role identity (McCall and Simmons 1978). Individuals are socialized into what it means to be a student, friend, or worker. Importantly, they learn the meanings of a role identity in interaction with others in which others act toward the self *as if* the person had the identity appropriate to their role behavior (Burke 1980). In this way, role identities acquire meaning through the reactions of others. The second part is the idiosyncratic dimension or *identity* part of a role identity (McCall and Simmons 1978). Here, it is individuals' own understandings as to what the identity means to them. It is the part of role meanings that uniquely is defined by the role-holder and is not necessarily shared by others.

Role identities generally contain a large set of meanings. Thus, individuals may turn to more than one characteristic to describe what the role means to them. Further, different individuals may have different meanings for the same role identity. For example, for one person, the student identity may mean being academic and taking one's schoolwork seriously, while for another student, identity may mean being sociable and having fun with one's peers at school. When role identity meanings are not shared, individuals must negotiate the meanings with others who may have a different understanding of that identity (McCall and Simmons 1978). Individuals may find that they have to settle on a compromise as to the role identity meaning one can claim and the behaviors that correspond to that meaning.

Irrespective of the content of the role identity meanings, identity meanings relate to the meanings implied by one's behavior. There is correspondence between the meanings individuals apply to an identity while in a role and their behavior (Burke and Reitzes 1981). For example, if the role identity of "student" involves the meaning of being academically responsible, the performance of student should match this meaning by attending class, taking lecture notes, doing homework assignments, and passing exams (Burke and Reitzes 1980). Alternatively, if the student identity entails the meaning of being sociable, a person's behavior should correspond to this meaning as spending time with one's friends and going to parties.

When two people interact, we see these two persons as relating to each other not as whole persons but as persons relating to each other only in terms of specific roles. Interaction is guided by the principle of role reciprocity. For every role that is played out in a situation, there is a counterrole to which it is related. As Turner (1962, p. 24) earlier argued, "A role cannot exist without one or more relevant other-roles toward which it is oriented. The role of 'father' makes no sense without the role of child; it can be defined as a pattern of behavior only in relation to the pattern of behavior of a child. The role of the compromiser can exist only to the extent that others in a group are playing the role of antagonists."

If roles are related to counterroles, then by extension, identities are related to counteridentities (Burke 1980). For example, the student identity has a corresponding counteridentity of professor. Because each person is assuming a different identity in the situation, correspondingly there will be different perceptions and actions between individuals. For instance, a person in the student identity will have particular goals, use specific resources, and engage in certain behaviors that may be different but interrelated to the goals, resources, and behaviors of the professor identity. A student may desire to master a subject area; use resources such as printed texts, videos, the computer, discussions with friends on the subject matter, and so forth; and engage in behaviors such as attending lectures, doing homework assignments, writing papers, and taking exams. Correspondingly, the professor may seek to have a student understand a subject area; provide resources to transmit the subject matter such as books, movies, newspapers, speakers, web-based computer material, and so forth; and employ behaviors such as lecturing and stimulating class discussions. Notice that rather than the student and professor acting alike in their identities, they are acting differently, but as unique, individual agents; each person's perception and action is interconnected and complementary in the situation.

In order for the interrelatedness of identities and counteridentities to work in situations, individuals must negotiate the different meanings and corresponding behaviors tied to each identity (McCall and Simmons 1978). Individuals have their own interests, resources, and goals to fulfill, and these may compete with the interests, resources, and goals of others in the situation. Thus, actors need to make compromises for effective role performance of everyone in the setting. Each needs to give up some of their own meanings and expectations tied to a particular identity in favor of another's meanings and expectations of that identity. Through this interaction and negotiation, meanings come to be shared.

Ultimately, all actors in a situation want to verify their identities. As we have already mentioned, "identity-verification" means that perceptions of the person in the situation are consistent with the person's identity-standard meanings. However, a lack of identity-verification occurs when the perceptions about the person in the situation disconfirm the person's identity-standard meanings. Practically, individuals attempt to achieve identity-verification by enacting role performances that will keep perceived meanings of who they are in a situation consistent with the meanings held in their identity standard. If all goes well, all actors in the situation will mutually accomplish their respective identity-verifications. However, this may not happen automatically in a situation. Mutual identity-verification in a situation often requires cooperative and mutually agreed-on arrangements of role performances. Since each actor's role performance is not the same as the other in the interaction given the role identities and counter-role identities that each is taking on, actors' performances must reflect this complementarily in a coordinated manner. This coordinated effort might involve individuals modifying their role performance somewhat or altering their identity standard a little in order to accomplish identity-verification and facilitate the verification of the other's identity.

To illustrate how noncooperative role performances can generate problems in identity-verification, let us take a student-professor interaction. If Jane, the student, claims the meaning of "academic" as part of her student identity standard, then we expect her to attend the professor's course and complete the assignments. Correspondingly, if the professor, Dr. Jackson, claims the meaning of "educator" in the professor identity, we expect him to provide the tools for learning such as lectures and books, and we expect him to create assessments such as assignments and exams to test the student's mastery of course material. If Jane does not attend class or attends class but surfs the Internet on her laptop or text messages her friends on her cell phone, she is not verifying her student identity, and she is not providing the feedback necessary to the professor to verify Dr. Jackson's identity as instructor. Alternatively, if Dr. Jackson does not test Jane's knowledge of course material, then he is failing to verify his professor identity as well as the identity of his counterpart—the student.

If individuals do not obtain verification for the identities they claim, they will become less satisfied with their roles, and they may withdraw from an interaction. For example, as discussed earlier, research on the leadership role identity reveals that when individuals cannot negotiate leadership performances in a group that match their leadership identities, they become less satisfied with their roles and are less inclined to remain in the group (Riley and Burke 1995). Alternatively, when they can negotiate leadership performances consistent with their identities, they are more satisfied and more likely to stay in the group. Other research shows that when different but interrelated and complementary spousal role behaviors in a marriage are successfully negotiated by spouses, what develops is a strong emotional attachment to the spouse, commitment to the marriage, and a movement away from a self-focus (an "I") to a global unit (a "We") (Burke and Stets 1999). Thus, role identity-verification is a result not just of one's own action but also of one's action in relation to others' actions.

In chapter 4, we noted that self-esteem is an outcome of the identity-verification process, and, although we talked about self-esteem as a single entity, it has become increasingly clear that there are three major bases for self-esteem or the general positive evaluation we have of ourselves. These are *self-efficacy* or a sense of competency, *self-worth*, or a general sense of being found worthy and valuable, and *self-authenticity*, or the feeling that one is being one's true self. As we will see, these different bases of self-esteem arise from the verification of identities that are tied to the three bases of identity.

When considering role-based identities, we note that they activate a sense of efficacy when they are verified (Stets and Burke 2000). Individuals want to feel competent and effective in their environment (Gecas 1989). By verifying role identities, that is, behaving in ways consistent with the meanings and expectations associated with role identities, individuals come to have a heightened sense of self-efficacy. As a result of this high-level belief in one's own abilities, persons with higher self-efficacy are more likely to engage in difficult behaviors that they have not tried before because they have the general expectancy of ability to accomplish outcomes. Persons who have low levels of self-efficacy are more likely to shy away from problematic situations, feeling that they will likely make a mess of it.

Because self-efficacy arises from the successful verification of role identities, there is some degree of a self-fulfilling prophesy about self-efficacy. People with high self-efficacy try more things and thus have the opportunity to learn they are successful, while people with low self-efficacy tend not to make the effort and thus may not have the opportunity to learn about the things they are good at.

Therefore, what one *does* given one's role identity is important. We remind the reader, however, that performing one's role properly not only facilitates confirming one's one role identity but also, in coordinating it with the performance played by the other in the counterrole, confirms the other's identity and at the same time creates and confirms the social structures within which the identities are embedded.

Social Identities

The second basis for identities is the social group. A *social identity* is based on a person's identification with a social group (Hogg and Abrams 1988). A social group is a set of individuals who share the view that they are members of the same social category. Through a social comparison and categorization process, persons who are similar to the self are categorized with the self and are labeled the ingroup. Correspondingly, persons who differ from the self are categorized as the outgroup. Having a particular social identity means being like others in the group and seeing things from the group's perspective. It is assumed that individuals as group members think alike and act alike. Thus, there is uniformity in thought and action in being a group member. Individuals do not have to interact with other group members in order to think and act like the group. Simply identifying with the group is enough to activate similarity in perceptions and behavior among group members.

Examples of membership into particular social groups include parents who become active in their local Parent-Teacher Association; children who join their school choir; college students who enter a fraternity or sorority, enlist in the military, or enter the peace corps; workers who become active in a union; or physicians who join the American Medical Association or local country club. All of these memberships imply an ingroup and an outgroup, and, correspondingly, a sense of "us" versus "them."

The set of features that distinguishes ingroup members from outgroup members also allows some differentiation among ingroup members. The idea of a group *prototype* contains these features and is therefore central in understanding this internal differentiation. Prototypicality represents the degree to which a group member exemplifies or is representative of the stereotypical attributes of the group as a whole by being most like ingroup members and simultaneously most different from outgroup members. The prototype is the interrelated set of perceptions, attitudes, feelings, and behavior that captures similarities among ingroup members and differences between ingroup members and outgroup members (Hogg 2006). For example, a prototypical member of the environmental activist group Greenpeace would be a person who embodies the belief that we need to defend our oceans, forests, and air from further degradation and to reverse the process. Anger and disgust likely emerge when this person witnesses environmental exploitation such as logging or the dumping of waste in our oceans. Behavior may include social movement participation in rallies, sit-ins, boycotts, and so forth.

Prototypes follow the *metacontrast principle* in that their "profile" maximizes the similarities among members within a group as well as the differences between these group members and members in other groups (Hogg 2006). For this reason, prototypes do not describe the typical or average ingroup member; instead, "they are polarized away from outgroup features and describe ideal, often hypothetical, ingroup members" (Hogg 2006, p. 118).

When individuals view themselves as the embodiment of an ingroup prototype, *depersonalization* has occurred. Rather than seeing themselves as *unique* individuals, they see themselves in terms of the prototypical attributes of ingroup members. For example, when individuals categorize themselves as Greenpeace members, rather than seeing themselves as having specific individual characteristics such as being kind, smart, short in stature, or shy, they see themselves in terms of being environmentally aware and protective of the earth's scarce resources. Depersonalization does not mean that individuals "loose" their sense of who they are, rather, they simply identify with a particular group and take on the group's identity.

When individuals take on a group-based identity, there is *uniformity* of perception among group members (Oakes, Haslam, and Turner 1994). Group members see things in the same way. They act in concert, identifying and evaluating themselves and others in the group positively and identifying and negatively evaluating others not in the group (Hogg 2006). From this develops a sense of "we" or "us" (toward the ingroup) and "them" (toward the outgroup). Interestingly, research reveals that for individuals to take on a social identity, they need not even interact with other ingroup members.

The "minimal group" experiments in social identity theory have revealed that simply categorizing a person as a member of a group rather than having the person interact with other group members is sufficient for the person to identify with that group (Turner, Hogg, Oakes, Reicher, and Wetherell 1987). For example, naming a person as a member of a group labeled "A" while others belong to a group labeled "B" is enough for the person named as part of group "A" to identify with group "A" and *dis*-identify with group "B." Correspondingly, members of group "A" quickly evaluate their group more positively than group "B"; likewise, members of group "B" evaluate their group positively and evaluate group "A" negatively. According to social identity theory, the positive evaluation associated with an arbitrary group is rooted in individuals' desire for a positive social identity (Tajfel and Turner 1979). As we will see with the self-enhancement motive discussed below, people have a desire to learn positive information about themselves because it makes them feel good. Positively evaluating an arbitrary group of which one is a member is in keeping with the self-enhancement motive.

A social identity becomes relevant or active in a situation through two processes: *accessibility* and *fit* (Oakes 1987). Accessibility has to do with readily available social categories such as gender, race, age, or other categories that are important to individuals and that are chronically accessible in memory or are easily accessible in situations. People use these accessible categories to make sense of immediate situations. For example, they may ask themselves how well these accessible categories account for similarities and differences among individuals in the situation (comparative fit) or how well these accessible categories help account for people's behavior in the situation (normative fit). If the fit is not good—for example, gender, race, or age do not account for the similarities and differences among individuals in the situation—or if they do not help account for people's behavior in the situation, then people will turn to other social categories until they find one that best fits the situation. Perhaps religion or political affiliation is a better fit with the situation because it best distinguishes among individuals in the situation and best explains people's behavior. The category that best fits the situation becomes the activated category.

To illustrate the above, you may be at a party and find two people (Bill and Linda) are arguing with two other people (Sue and Bob). Bill and Linda are arguing on the merits of a wife not working outside of the home, while Sue and Bob are defending a wife's decision to have a career. You might determine that for Bill and Linda, the identity of conservative is active in the situation and members of the outgroup (Sue and Bob) are liberal. It would account for the similarities and differences among them (comparative fit), and it is the expected position you would predict for those having a conservative compared to liberal identity (normative fit). In this way, the social identities help organize the situation and make sense of people's behavior.

Two important reasons for joining groups include self-enhancement and uncertainty reduction. Self-enhancement is the desire to seek positive information about the self. Membership in groups generates positive distinctiveness or the view that one's own group is better than an alternative group (Hogg 2006). Essentially, what is occurring is a social comparison of ingroup members with outgroup members along particular dimensions that lead ingroup members to judge their group positively and the outgroup negatively, thereby raising their evaluation of themselves as ingroup members. For example, if the ingroup consists of members of the military, the value of "serving one's country" would benefit the members of the ingroup and degrade the value of outgroup members who do not share this value. Knowing that members of the ingroup share this value makes the ingroup more attractive to ingroup members and makes one glad to be a member.

The social identity process also satisfies uncertainty reduction (Hogg 2006; Hogg and Mullin 1999). Individuals want their environment to be predictable. By joining groups, prototypes help guide one's own behavior as well as others' behavior and thus facilitate predictability over one's environment (Hogg 2006). Categorizing self and others in particular ways and expecting particular thoughts, feelings, and behaviors to follow from these categorizations enables individuals to have some control. In this way, belonging to groups also enables individuals to be effective agents in their environment.

Finally, having one's social identity as a group member verified activates a sense of belongingness and raises one's self-worth (Stets and Burke 2000). Worth-based self-esteem, or self-worth, is the second base for self-esteem that Gecas (1982) discussed after self-efficacy. Self-esteem based on worthiness is often rooted in the reflected appraisals process in which people feel that others accept and value them. With high levels of self-worth, people have a degree of existential security that provides value and meaning to their lives. When one is a member of a group and is similar to others in thought and action, one will receive recognition, approval, and acceptance from other group members, thus verifying their social identity as a group member; and in turn, they will experience positive feelings. Thus, feelings of self-worth rise when individuals join groups and feel accepted and are judged valuable on the basis of *who they are* and not *what they do* (Cast and Burke 2002).

Integrating Role and Social Identities

Some have argued that role identities and social identities reference the self in terms of *me* and *we,* respectively (Thoits and Virshup 1997). To have a role identity is to refer to the self as an individual "me" and to identify oneself in a role such as "*I* am a student" or "*I* am a friend." In this way, role identities are individual-level identities. Individual-level *me*'s are derived through taking the role of others in a situation and responding to their expectations and feedback as to how one is coming across (Thoits and Virshup 1997). Individual-level role identities function to provide positive self-conceptions, and through their role identity enactment, they help maintain the broader social order in which roles are embedded.

Alternatively, Thoits and Virshup maintain that social identities involve identification with others who belong to the same category or social group, for example, "*We* are women," "*We* are Jewish," or "*We* are Democrats." Collective-level *we*'s are derived from such cognitive processes as group categorization (one sees himself as the embodiment of the ingroup prototype) and group evaluation (one positively evaluates the ingroup and negatively evaluates the outgroup). Collective-level identities function to foster conformity (to the ingroup). Should intergroup conflict emerge between the ingroup and the outgroup, the resolution could lead to potential social change in society. Interestingly, Thoits and Virshup argue that sociologists and psychologists need to think of roles *and* categories as being individual *and* collective identities. How is this possible? Let us first address role identities.

For sociologists, because role and counterrole relationships help shape and determine interaction, specific role and counterrole identities emerge out of specific contexts. For example, the role identity of husband and counterrole identity of wife emerge out of a marital interaction. The role identity of employer and counterrole identity of employee emerge out of the work situation. The teacher-student identities surface in the education setting. Thoits and Virshup point out that in these contexts, individuals can identify themselves not only as a role-holder but also as a member of the social group, for example, the organization in which the employer and employee exist or the school in which the student and teacher exist.

Husband and wife roles are embedded in the family group. Employer and worker roles are part of an organization or company. Teacher and student roles are part of a particular school. Clearly, roles are embedded in groups. Having a role identity thus provides a social identity in terms of the group or organization in which the role is created. Activating the student identity in the context of a particular teacher in a class does not necessarily activate the school social identity. However, at a basketball game with another school the social identity may become activated, and being a teacher or a student would be less relevant than being a member of the ingroup school and winning against the outgroup school.

The distinction between role identity and social identity, therefore, is primarily analytic. In any empirical case, role-based identities and social-based identities are often fused. Further complication can occur when a role-based identity becomes a social identity as when workers (as a collective) are pitted against managers (also as a collective). Mother is a role identity, but in the slogan "mothers of the world, unite!" mother becomes a social identity.

Thoits and Virshup have this confusion in mind when they point out that when one identifies with a group, the identification may not only be on the basis of a social category but also be on the basis of being a particular role-holder. Thoits and Virshup suggest that we should not draw a distinction between social identities and role identities, because both can be individual or collective identities. Instead, they suggest we draw a distinction between the psychological state that is activated (a *me* or *we*) and the social functions it provides (an ego function that satisfies needs of the self or inter/intra-group function that satisfies needs of the group). Their point about potential confusion is a valid one. We need to be careful about understanding when a person is acting in a role on the basis of a role identity or is part of a collective or group and acting on the basis of the social identity. The common feature defining the social group is less relevant. It may be geography (I am a Californian), an organization membership (I am a graduate of Harvard), or political grouping (I am a member of the machinists' union).

As we have mentioned elsewhere (Stets and Burke 2000), role-based identities and group-based identities correspond to the theoretical distinction in sociology between organic and mechanical forms of social integration (Durkheim 1893 [1984]). Mechanical integration, common in primitive societies such as hunting and gathering societies, involved individuals tied to one another based on similarities and shared experiences. Differences among individuals were minimized, and role specialization was relatively absent. Organic integration,· more likely in modern, industrial societies, involved a complex division of labor, with individuals dependent upon one another to perform certain roles and tasks that they themselves could not perform. We see that people are tied mechanically to their groups through social identities, and they are tied organically through their role identities within groups. A complete understanding of society must incorporate both the mechanical/group and organic/role forms since each is but an aspect of society that links to individual identities in separate but related ways.

To illustrate this idea, let us take the identities of manager and worker. On the one hand, manager and worker are roles that are defined within the group/organization of a corporation. There are meanings and expectations tied to each of these roles regarding performance and the relationships between these roles. On the other hand, manager and worker are social categories or groupings that constitute an ingroup and an outgroup. For a manager, other managers would constitute the ingroup and workers would constitute the outgroup. Here, the focus is more on membership than on performance, and the membership that distinguishes managers from workers is their occupation. However, not all roles are intimately tied to groups. For example, the roles of husband and wife within the family have meanings and expectations tied to them, but the social categories of husband and wife only occasionally constitute an ingroup and an outgroup pairing. Only rarely would we expect husbands to see their wives as the outgroup and thus negatively evaluate them. The persistence of such ingroup and outgroup pairing could lead to divorce.

Whether one is a manager or husband, he is at once in a role *and* in a social group. In focusing on the role, we consider the group (for example, the organization to which the manager belongs) and the relationship among the different roles within that group. These are intragroup relations. In focusing on the categorical aspect or the social group, we look at the fact that the manager and all other roles in the group (for example, CEO, workers, secretaries, and so forth) comprise the organizational group, and sometimes these individuals act as a member of the organization as when they attend a company picnic or party or when they play on the organization's baseball team against another organization. These are intergroup relations.

To push the point a little further regarding individuals taking on both role and social identities, we turn to additional examples. Dr Jackson may play out the professor role identity in the classroom, but he is also a member of a department, so he may cast a vote for a particular new faculty hire. He is also a member of the university, so he may volunteer to participate on a university committee; and finally he is a member of his profession, so he may run for a particular professional office. Similarly, Jane may enact the student role identity in the classroom; but as a student, she may also be a member of a sorority on campus, play for the school's basketball or soccer team, and be involved in a club of her major such as the business club or psychology club. What we see in these examples is that one is always and simultaneously in a role and in a group, so that role identities and social identities are frequently and at the same time relevant and influential in individuals' perceptions and actions. Thus, we cannot easily separate role from group empirically (Deaux 1992; Thoits and Virshup 1997). They are analytic distinctions that help organize the ways in which different identities operate within and across situations.

If we cannot easily disentangle social identities from role identities in an empirical instance, we also cannot easily separate group and role identities from the person identity. Both social identity theorists and identity theorists have discussed the person identity, but they have largely neglected an examination as to how the person identity might be incorporated into their theories. We turn next to the person identity.

Person Identities

In social identity theory, the *personal* identity involves seeing oneself as a unique and distinct individual, different from others. It is the "idiosyncratic personality attributes that are not shared with other people" (Hogg 2006, p. 115). What guides behavior is one's own goals rather than the goals or expectations of the group or role. When a social identity becomes activated in a situation, depersonalization has occurred. One has shifted attention away from the self as a unique individual toward a view of the self as a member of a group (Hogg, Terry, and White 1995). Essentially, the *me* becomes *we* (Thoits and Virshup 1997). Depersonalization does not mean that one loses his or her personal identity; rather, there is simply a change in focus from the individual to the group. In social identity theory, because the personal identity and the social identity are mutually exclusive bases of self-definitions, both are unlikely to be operating at the same time.

In identity theory, the term "person identity" rather than "personal identity" is used (and we will continue with this usage throughout), but the term is conceptualized in a manner similar to how it is understood in social identity theory. The *person identity* is the set of meanings that define the person as a unique individual rather than as a role-holder or group member (Stets 1995; Stets and Burke 1994). Early on, McCall and Simmons (1978) maintained that although a social identity defined an individual in terms of broad social categories, such as one's military rank, a personal identity was a set of categories that defined an individual in a unique way, such as John Doe of Portland, Maine, or Jane Doe, daughter of John Doe of Portland, Maine.[1]

In identity theory, person identity meanings are based on culturally recognized characteristics that individuals internalize as their own and that serve to define and characterize them as unique individuals. These meanings serve as identity standards, guiding the identity-verification process (Burke 2004a). They may include such characteristics as how masterful, dominant, and controlling the person is (Burke 2004a; Stets 1995; Stets and Burke 1994; 1996), how moral the person is (Stets and Carter 2006; Stets, Carter, Harrod, Cerven, and Abrutyn 2008), or what the person values (Gecas 2000; Hitlin 2003). Because the person identity meanings of being controlling or moral and so forth are culturally shared, others will draw upon these same meanings to identify the individual and thus facilitate the verification process.

In the same way that individuals regulate the meanings of their role and social identities, they also regulate the meanings of their person identities. Thus, person identities are *not* predispositions to act in a particular way. Rather, like role and social identities, they are maintained by the perceptual control process that is the basis of identity-verification. Further, because person identities consist of meanings that constitute a person as an individual, verification of person identities leads to increased feelings of authenticity, that is, one who is able to be who one really is (Burke 2004a).

Authenticity is the third and newest base of self-esteem to receive attention in social psychology. It is the feeling that one is being one's true self. Most often in sociological literature this is discussed with respect to feelings generated in the workplace where people may feel that they cannot be themselves. A frequent example is the airline flight attendant who must smile and be nice to airline passengers, even those who are being disruptive, inconsiderate, and generally making a nuisance of themselves (Hochschild 1983). Smiling and acting friendly is not consistent with the flight attendant's emotions, so some feelings of inauthenticity are generated in that situation. Not feeling authentic is a negative state. Authenticity or self-authenticity is not the same as feeling competent or feeling worthy. Rather, it has to do with what might be called the core self: who one is as a person across situations, across time, across relationships. Thus, as verification of role identities fosters self-competence and the verification of group identities fosters self-worth, the verification of person identities fosters self-authenticity.

Unlike role identities but like social identities, the person identity is conceptualized as operating across various roles and situations. Person identities are more likely to be activated across situations than role identities because they refer to important aspects of the individual. Persons don't "put on" and "take off" these characteristics as they might "take on" and then "exit" particular roles. The meanings form an essential ingredient as to whom they are. For example, an individual may be a very controlling person, and this control will show its face in the different roles the person takes on and even in the different groups he or she joins.

Consistent with the above, early research on person identities attempted to link person identities to role identities by arguing that they may be related through a common system of meaning, that is, the meanings of person identities may overlap with the meanings of role identities (Stets 1995). For example, Stets found that the masculine gender *role* identity is linked to the mastery *person* identity through the shared meaning of "control." Meanings of masculinity such as dominance and competitiveness are consistent with meanings of mastery that involve control over one's environment. When Stets examined the predictors of control over one's partner, she found that those with a more masculine gender identity were more likely to control their partners than those with a feminine gender identity. However, those with a feminine gender identity were more likely to control their partners when they had low mastery. Stets argued that more feminine people will react when the meanings in their person identity of mastery gets too low by being more controlling to raise their mastery level. This is because the motive to have mastery is important to individuals; they need to have a certain level of control over their environment. What we see here is that when the meanings of a role identity (here, femininity) conflict with the meanings of a person identity (mastery) in terms of controlling another, people may act without regard to their role identities in order to maintain their person identities.

Person identities likely figure more prominently into interaction than identity theorists are aware. This is because they are constantly activated and thus are generally very high in salience (Burke 2004a). Related to this is the idea that given the constant activation of the person identity and its high salience in the hierarchy of identities, it operates like a master identity (Burke 2004a). Conceptually, what this means is that if we arrange role, social, and person identities in the hierarchy of perceptual control (and we will discuss the hierarchy of perceptual control in the next chapter), person identities would be ranked higher than role or social identities. As a result, the meanings in the person identity would influence the meanings held in one's role and social identities more so than the other way around. For example, if one sees himself as high on the moral dimension, as in being ethical, principled, caring, and honest, he may be more likely to choose roles that reflect these characteristics. He may become a social worker, minister, or police officer and may belong to groups that are consistent with these moral qualities such as church group or volunteer organization. The influence of person identities to role identity and group identity choices assumes that individuals are in a society in which roles and group memberships are voluntary; in less open societies in which people have little choice as to their roles and groups, the person identity likely will be shaped more by the roles and groups that individuals assume rather than the other way around (Burke 2004a). However, we need to keep in mind that even in open societies, choice is not always available, as when we are born into a particular family, must attend a particular school or church, and so forth. Here, person identities will again be influenced by the nature of our roles and groups.

Integrating Role, Social, and Person Identities

In chapter 5, we indicated how the process of verification of identities is accomplished through the control of active and potential resources through the manipulation of meaning using signs and symbols in the situation. This is true whether we are discussing role-based, group-based, or person-based identities. These three different bases for identities all operate in much the same way, with the same perceptual control processes and the same verification processes. They are distinguished from each other by the way in which each of the identities is tied into the social structure and consequently by the way in which the verification process works.

Recall from chapter 5 that we defined resources as anything that supports individuals and the interaction of individuals. Viewing resources in this manner provides insight because many of the expectations and goals that are part of identity standards involve controlling both the active and the potential resources that sustain us. People act to verify their identities; in doing so, in the face of distractions and disruptions, they enact the processes that define the social system. We are now in a position to better understand the different bases of identity in terms of the resources controlled by each.

A social identity based on membership in a group or category gives one self-meanings that are shared with others in the group (Stets and Burke 2000). One is tied to many similar others; in verifying the self as a group member, one receives recognition, approval, and acceptance from those others. One's ties to the others are like their ties among themselves. One is verified as a member by being like the other members. Being verified in terms of a social identity reinforces group-nongroup distinctions, thus maintaining boundaries and supporting the continued differentiations and cleavages in the social structure.

In contrast, a role identity is tied to other members of the role set; verification comes by what one does, not who one is (Stets and Burke 2000). Verification is tied up in mutual, complementary, and reciprocal processes. The output of each role is the input to its counterrole. The verification of each identity depends upon the mutual verification of the counteridentity in a reciprocal process. One is verified not by being like the other but by performing in a way that confirms and verifies the other's role identity and is matched by the other's performance in a fashion that verifies one's own role identity. In contrast to the social identity, in which one is linked to many similar others, with the role identity, one is linked to a few different others. Being verified in a role identity reinforces the importance of a role within a set of role relationships. Each role becomes necessary to sustain its counterroles and thereby sustains itself.

Finally, verification of a person identity sustains the individual as a biosocial being. By acting, controlling, and verifying the meanings of who one is as a person, the person distinguishes himself or herself as a unique, identifiable individual with qualities that other individuals can count on and use to verify their own person identities (or group or role identities). Individual names may set each of us apart and identify us in relatively unique fashion, but our meaningful traits and characteristics make us who we are: levels of dominance or submissiveness, levels of energy, being tense or easygoing, being emotional or stoic, and so on.

Although the types of resources and the consequences of their manipulations through the verification of role, social, and person identities vary across these bases, we need to think of social, role, and person identities as simultaneously operating in situations. Within groups, there are roles, and persons play out these roles in different ways. For example, the role identity of student is within the larger category of a school (the ingroup) compared to an alternative school (the outgroup). When enacting the role of student, some students are hardworking while others are lazy. Some are kind and helpful while others are unkind and hard-hearted.

Which identity we focus on will highlight some issues and not others in the situation. For example, in focusing on the categorical aspect of membership in the school compared to another school, we attend to shared perceptions and uniformity in action among students, such as school chants, the wearing of school colors, and other symbolic displays of school pride, and how membership in the school facilitates belongingness. In addressing the role identity of student, we examine how it relates to the counterrole of teacher, and we address how the successful performance of a role leads to a feeling of self-efficacy. Finally, in emphasizing the personal aspect of being a student, we focus on the individual as a unique entity, distinct from others in how he or she performs the role of student.

By integrating role, social, and person identities into theory and empirical work, we have the opportunity to examine how identities operate at the organizational level and within interpersonal interactions. At the organizational level, for example, we might study intergroup and intragroup relations. Specifically, the different roles that one assumes in a group may enhance or reduce identification with the group depending upon, for example, one's power and status. For instance, higher-status persons have been shown to be more oriented to the group as a whole than lower-status members. Additionally, occupants of roles that are defined as more important to the group may hold greater hostility toward outgroup members than occupants of roles defined as less important to the group. At the interpersonal level, an analysis of the group, role, and person may help us better understand such motivational processes as self-worth, self-efficacy, and authenticity. As we have already discussed, it is possible that people primarily feel *good* about themselves when they associate with particular groups; typically, they feel *confident* about themselves when playing out particular roles and generally feel that they are "real" or *authentic* when their person identities are being verified. Research will want to test whether the different bases of identities produces these different outcomes.

More generally, although identity theory has historically examined primarily role identities, as it develops, it is broadening to include these other bases of identities. We need to examine the conditions under which these different bases mutually support one another in situations as well as the conditions under which they conflict with one another. In thinking about the integration of these different bases, there are a number of issues that can be raised for future research. We discuss these avenues of future research in chapter 10.

Summary

Table 6.1.   Defining Features of Person, Role, and Social Identities

Features	Person Identity	Role Identity	Social Identity
Bases	Individual Self-Concept	Expectations Tied to Social Positions	Social Group
Definition	Meanings that Define Person as a Unique Individual	Meanings Tied to a Role	Meanings Tied to a Social Group
Cognitive Representation of Identity	Identity standard	Identity Standard	Prototype
Activation of Identity	Salience	Salience	Accessibility and Fit
Behavior	Independent of Others	Complementary to Others	Similar to Others
Self-Reference	Me	Me as Role	We
Verification Outcome	Authenticity	Self-Efficacy	Self-Worth

Table 6.1 outlines the defining features of person, role, and social identities. This should give the reader a clearer sense as to how the different identities are both similar and different. Given that identity theorists have devoted much of their attention to role identities, they should redirect some of their focus on social and person identities. As we mentioned at the outset of this chapter, we conceptualize person, role, and social identities as operating in the same way, that is, according to the principles of the perceptual control process. For this reason, the theoretical insights that we have obtained from studying role identities can be applied to person and social identities, including how identity-verification gets accomplished and how things get resolved when identity-nonverification occurs.

7

Multiple Identities

Much of our discussion about identities up to this point has been on what identities are and how they work. Moreover, although we have mentioned that people have multiple identities and that there are many identities from many people in operation in any situation of interaction, we have not considered the implications of this. Identities do not always operate in isolation, but they interact with other identities in particular situations. Thus, we must consider the importance of this observation for understanding more clearly some of its social implications. For this, we break the problem into two parts and first consider the situation in which different identities are held by the same person. Second, we consider the situation in which different identities are held by different persons interacting together in a social setting.

An example of the first is a situation in which an adolescent, who is both a friend and a daughter, is interacting in a situation that activates both of these identities at the same time, for example, when the daughter has a friend visit and her parents are present. In this situation, what it means to be a friend (perhaps by acting "sophisticated" with the friend) may be at odds with what it means to be a daughter (not acting "sophisticated"). An example of the different identities being held by different persons would be two persons, a professor and a student, interacting in a situation. One of the persons has a professor identity and the other person has a student identity. These identities may be at odds if what the student expects of the professor (give me a passing grade so that I can stay in school) differs with the identity of the professor (give grades according to merit and fairness with other students). In each of these cases, it may or may not be possible to verify all the identities involved at the same time. The consequences of these possibilities are numerous. We consider first the case of many identities within a person.

Multiple Identities within a Person

As we mentioned earlier in the book, William James (1890) was among the first to note that we have as many "selves" as we have others with whom we interact. The idea of multiple selves has changed somewhat since James wrote, and we now talk about identities rather than selves, but the basic components of the concept have remained. We take on many identities over the course of a lifetime, and at any point in time we have many identities that could be activated. A person could be a student in one context, a friend in another, a mother, a daughter, a teacher, a blood donor, a homeowner, and so on. Each of these identities acts to control meanings/resources in a situation, such that relevant identities are verified.

When considering these multiple identities within a person, it helps to distinguish two approaches that might be taken. We can look at these identities from an internal framework or from an external framework. The internal focus attends to issues of how an individual's multiple identities function together within the self and within the overall identity-verification process. How does the identity-verification process work for the multiple identities? The external focus addresses how the multiple identities that an individual has are tied into the complexities of the social structure in which the individual is embedded. Here we need to consider one's commitment to the multiple identities and the way each identity ties one to a particular location in the social structure. We turn to each below.

The Internal Framework: Multiple Identities within the Perceptual Control System

When considering the relationship among identities within the hierarchical perceptual control system in which all identities reside, questions arise as to how the multiple identities relate to one another, how they are switched on or off, and, when they are on, how the person manages to verify each. Included in this last part is the question of what happens when one or more of the identities cannot be verified.

Prior work on the relationship among multiple identities within a person has focused on the way in which the multiple identities do or do not share meanings. For example, Linville's (1985; 1987) self-complexity theory dealt with the idea that individuals with more complex selves were better buffered from situational stresses. The complexity of the self was defined as the number of "distinct" self-aspects one has. By distinct aspects we mean the number of roles, relationships, traits, or activities that do not share attributes or meanings. The suggestion was that if one self-aspect or identity has problems, such problems will not spill over to other aspects, because they do not share meanings. Identities that share meanings, then, from their viewpoint, are potentially problematic because problems can spread from one identity to another along lines of common meaning.

Where do such complex selves come from? Stryker (1980 [2002]) suggests that the complexity of the self is a reflection of the complexity of society. As society becomes more differentiated in terms of groups, organizations, and roles available to persons, persons who take on more of these as identities become more complex themselves. The premodern self was generally simpler (with fewer affiliations and, therefore, identities) than the postmodern self. Further, because the networks of the premodern era were more embedded within one another, there was more sharing of cultural meaning and expectations (Pescosolido and Rubin 2000).

Consequently, the different identities in the postmodern era have less common or shared meanings compared with those in the premodern era. Thus, not only are there more identities available, but also they have less in common with one another. This means that the verification of these multiple and disparate identities calls for the manipulation of more and disparate meanings across more and disparate settings. Common meanings shared across identities would facilitate identity-verification, as there would be fewer different meanings to control. It would make sense, then, that people would select to occupy positions in the social structure that, as much as possible, shared meanings, thereby taking on identities that shared meanings.

Stets (1995) looked at the relationship between gender role identity and mastery, a person identity, and suggested that the two are related through a common dimension of meaning concerning the degree to which the person controls aspects of his or her environment. Because of this common meaning, she suggests, enactment of one identity has implications for the other, since each is controlling the same shared meaning. Deaux (1992; 1993) also proposed this idea of common characteristics shared among social and personal identities. She used the concept of common "traits," though one could substitute the idea of common meanings with the same effect.

Shared among all of these researchers is the idea that identities that have common meanings are likely to be activated together whenever those meanings are present in the situation and that multiple identities might work together in the identity-verification process to control those meanings in the situation or might suffer together when there are problems dealing with the shared meanings. Additionally, Deaux suggests that identities that share many meanings are more prominent or important because of that sharing, and such identities may work together to control the meanings of identities lower in the prominence hierarchy. Identity theory further develops the idea of shared meaning and the extent to which one identity may control another, but it does so within the context of the hierarchical control system, and we turn to that now.

Salience, Prominence, and Commitment

The salience of an identity is the likelihood that it will be activated. Identities that are more salient are more likely to be activated in any situation. By being activated, you recall, we mean that an identity is attempting to verify itself. This means that perceptions of relevant meanings are being made, the comparator is assessing the degree to which the perceived meanings match those in the identity standard, and the comparator is sending an appropriate signal to the output system. Depending upon whether or not the identity was being verified, this output would continue behavior unchanged (no error) or modify the social behavior. Behavior would be modified to counteract any disturbances and alter the situational meanings in order to reduce the error or difference between their perceptions and the identity standard. Although a person may have multiple identities, if only one of them is activated at any point in time, then, for that period, they may as well have only the one identity.

If more than one identity is activated in a situation, we expect that the identity with the higher level of prominence, or the identity with the higher level of commitment, will guide behavior more than an identity with a lower level of prominence or commitment. As McCall and Simmons (1978) suggest, performances strongly suggested by more prominent (important) identities are more likely to be carried out than are those suggested by less prominent identities. If one identity is more important than another is, then verification of that identity is more important than verification of another. In a similar fashion, an identity that has more commitment than another (that is, more other people depend upon that identity than the other), that identity is more likely to be verified, thus fulfilling our commitments to the many rather than to the few. Thus, prominence and commitment not only influence the level of salience of an identity but also help sort out the question of what to do next when multiple identities are activated. If one identity or another has to wait for verification because we cannot work on all of them at once, those that are less prominent and those that have lower commitment are the ones to wait. In this way, identities can be distinguished and compared in terms of their prominence and level of commitment. However, identities are also related more directly in terms of the hierarchy of control in which they are embedded.

The Hierarchical Control System

To understand this idea of the hierarchy of control of meanings that is central to identity control theory, we need to understand the hierarchical nature of the overall perceptual control system in which identities are located. The overall perceptual control system, as we noted, is composed of an interlocking set of individual control systems at multiple levels (Tsushima and Burke, 1999) such as that depicted in figure 7.1. To facilitate the presentation, we

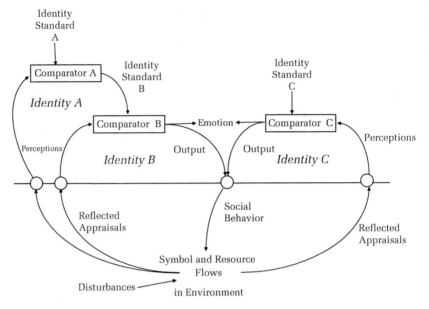

Figure 7.1. Model for Three Identities within a Person

will first discuss the relationships among identities located at the same level in the overall control system, such as those labeled B and C in the figure. We will then discuss the relationship among identities at different levels in the system such as those labeled A and B in the figure.

At the lowest level of the hierarchy, we consider the two identities labeled B and C in the figure. Each of the identities has its own standard and its own perceptions of meanings, and each modifies its own output (behaviors in the situation) to verify itself by keeping the perceived situational meanings in agreement with the meanings in its standard in the manner we discussed in chapter 4. Although we consider only two identities for the person, the ideas can be generalized to a larger number of identities that might be labeled D and E and so on. Because all of these identities exist within one person, we note that the output of all of these identities must combine to control the social behavior of that individual. The individual's behavior controls situational meanings to make them congruent with the meanings held in all of the identity standards. That is, each identity is controlling meaning by adjusting the behavior of the same individual. Thus, although there are possibly many identities, there is only one behavioral output stream because there is only one person to act. This implies that the behavior of an individual must "satisfy" several individual identities simultaneously by altering the situation in ways that change all of the self-relevant meanings perceived by all of the different identities. If a person has the identities of professor and spouse and both are activated, the person must adjust perceived meanings to confirm or verify both the professor identity and the spousal identity.

This process occurs for all activated identities in a situation, so that perceptions of all of the self-relevant meanings of all of the activated identities are simultaneously controlled. For this to happen, all of the meanings must be either unrelated or aligned. They cannot remain in opposition. Were, for example, two self-relevant meanings perceived in the situation to be in opposition with each other, as one was brought into alignment, the other would be moved out of alignment. One cannot both be good and bad, for example, or both strong and weak. When different identity standards require oppositional meanings, as in our above example of the daughter/friend trying to be "sophisticated" to her friend, but not so sophisticated to her parents, the system is put into an impossible situation in which one or both identity standards cannot be verified. To the extent this happens, the identity standards themselves must shift as people's identities change to remove the conflict. People re-identify themselves, changing the self-meanings held in their identity standards. To understand this idea of identity change and how it works, as we will in chapter 9, however, we must understand the hierarchical structuring of identities. We will discuss that in the next section.

When the meanings held in different identity standards are unrelated to one another, an action that changes meanings in the situation to verify one identity will leave the other unaffected. For example, getting an ovation for an excellent scientific talk may verify one's scientist identity but may be irrelevant for one's spousal identity.

When two identities share common meanings, the situation is much simpler. Control of the situation to change self-relevant perceptions on the shared dimension of meaning helps both identities. Verifying one of the identities will help verify the other and the two identities can coordinate their outputs to verify both. For example, consider a married person with children. If the spousal identity includes standards for providing material support for one's spouse, and if the parent identity includes standards for providing material support for one's children, then getting a well-paying job will help verify both identities.

Levels of Control

We move now to identities that are above those at the lowest level in the hierarchy. In doing so, there are additional ways in which identities relate to one another. At levels other than the "lowest," the outputs of each individual control system provide the standards for identities that are at lower levels in the control system. Figure 7.1 shows two identities within a person that are hierarchically arranged. Note that the output of "higher" identity (A) is the standard of the "lower" identity (B). Although the lower identity follows the model we have been discussing, with its perceptions, standard, comparator, and output of social behavior that matches the meanings of perceptions and standard, the higher identity differs in that it does not control social behavior directly. It has its perceptions, comparator, and standard, but its action is to control the standard or goals of the "lower" identity. The lower identity acts to match the meanings in the situation to those meanings held in its standard (its goals), but those meanings are set by the higher identity. Thus, what the lower identity actually does depends upon the goals set by the higher identity. Since the higher identity in some sense controls the lower identity, they cannot be in conflict—the lower identity is the servant of the higher identity. The higher identity does not tell the lower identity how to verify itself; it only tells the lower identity what meanings need to be verified.

Consider, for example, the identity professor as the lower identity. In addition, consider one's gender identity as the higher identity. How one verifies the professor identity would depend upon the setting of one's gender identity. Being male provides a set of meanings for the professor identity that are different from the meanings for the professor identity that are provided if one is female. The professor identity standard, or what it means to be a professor, varies by the kind of gender identity one has.

There are many possible arrangements for the identity at the higher level. The output of one higher-level identity may serve as the standard for several lower-level identities. In this way, all the lower-level identities can be seen as in the "service" of the higher-level identity, and the lower-level identities are thus coordinated in their endeavors. For example, the way in which I am a professor and the way I am a parent are both influenced by a higher-level gender identity. Indeed, as Burke (2001) has shown, the coordination needed by different identities, each seeking their own verification, can only be provided by having a common higher-level identity.

It is also possible that several higher-level identities contribute their outputs to a single standard for a lower-level identity. This was the model Burke (1997) used in creating an identity model for network exchange. Several higher-level identities, each controlling a different set of meanings in the situation, had their outputs combined into a single standard for a lower-level identity that controlled negotiation behavior. Finally, it is possible that these arrangements can be combined in various ways with multiple higher identities controlling multiple lower identities in the overall control system.

Levels of Perception

We discussed the hierarchy of control in which higher-level identities control lower-level identities by slowly adjusting the standards of the lower-level identities. This is what one might call the output side of the system. On the input side, perceptions are also hierarchical, and, since it is the perceptions that are controlled, perhaps we should have discussed this side of the control hierarchy first. What makes some control systems "higher" than others? Is it possible that the higher and lower control systems in the hierarchy could switch places? How do the levels differ? The answer to these questions lies in the nature of the perceptions that are controlled. Perceptions that are higher in the control hierarchy are more complex in that they consist of patterns of perceptions at lower levels. For example, perceptions of lines and angles are at a lower level, while perceptions of squares and triangles are at a higher level, consisting of patterns of angles and lines. Controlling perceptions of squares and triangles necessarily involves controlling perceptions of their lower-level components, angles, and lines. It is this relationship between the "parts" and the "whole" that distinguishes levels in the control system. Control of perceptions of "wholes" occurs at a higher level than control of perceptions of "parts." Control of perceptions of wholes is achieved by controlling the lower-level perceptions of parts. The levels cannot be reversed.

Following this logic, identities at a higher level are more general than identities at a lower level. Tsushima and Burke (1999) examined parent identity standards that exist at two different levels, which they called a principle level (higher) and a program level (lower). They indicated that both the perceptions and the standards that exist higher in the hierarchy are more abstract and more general. These higher perceptions and standards organize perceptions and standards that are lower in the hierarchy and that are more concrete and situated. Principle-level standards are conceptualizations of abstract goal states such as values, beliefs, and ideals. Program-level standards of the parent identity are more concrete goals accomplished in situated activity, such as going to the store or making sure the children get off to school. In their study, Tsushima and Burke (1999) interviewed fifteen married and fifteen single mothers with children in elementary school. Questions for the interview were organized in three areas concerning standards for education, for discipline, and for the parent identity in general. Coders were trained to examine the interviews and classify the responses discussing each standard in terms of whether the standard was at a principle or program level. Tsushima and Burke discovered that parents were primarily oriented either toward program- or toward principle-level standards for parenting, and that it was possible to classify parents as to being mainly oriented toward principle-level or program-level goals.

Tsushima and Burke provide examples of goals or standards at each of the two levels to help illustrate this rather abstract discussion. With respect to education, some parents spoke of begging, forcing, or harping on their children to do homework. Begging, forcing, and harping are programs of activity that these parents used with the goal of getting the children to do their homework. With respect to discipline, programs including confrontation, setting timers, and grounding the children were mentioned, each with respect to some situational disturbance created by the child. Each of the different programs of activity with respect to education and discipline were used to accomplish the lower-level goals of getting the children to act in particular ways within particular situations. They were immediate, short-term ways of dealing with immediate problems.

In contrast, other parents had parent identity standards that provided higher-level meanings/goals for education and discipline. These higher-level standards were higher in that they helped organize and relate various lower-level programs. For example, one parent spoke of her educational goals being to challenge her children, to be a good teacher. With respect to discipline, another parent said that it was important to listen to her children, to give them love, and to be consistent. These higher-level standards do not prescribe particular activities or programs of activity, but they do provide ways to evaluate programs of activity in terms of their ability to achieve the higher-level goals. These are longer-range goals that are achieved over time by selecting more immediate situational programs of activity that are consistent with the long-range goals.

These examples illustrate different levels at which identities and identity standards exist in the control hierarchy. Perceptions at the higher levels are composed of patterns of perceptions at the lower levels. Control of perceptions at the higher levels involves controlling the patterns of perceptions at the lower levels. The accomplishment of programs of activity by the parents involves controlling perceptions of activities and meanings such that the programs are carried out. For some parents who had not developed parental identity standards at higher levels, this was all they could attempt. Managing perceptions at the higher level of general principles and values involves seeing patterns at the program level and controlling those patterns. The higher-level standards are met when perceptions indicate that the lower-level programs are functioning in such a way to match the patterns indicated at the higher level.

Although this discussion has been in terms of lower- and higher-level standards for the parent identity, the same principles hold for identities in general. For some parents, the parent identity consisted of particular programs of activity; but for other parents, the parent identity consisted of general principles that guided all of the programs in which they might engage. In a similar fashion, one's moral identity, which is a higher-level identity, would have standards that are met when perceptions of patterns in the programs of activity in any of the many role or social identities match those high-level standards (Stets, Carter, Harrod, Cerven, and Abrutyn 2008). Perceptions of the meanings of actions as a spouse, as a worker, as a parent, or as Rotary club member all contribute to one's perceptions of oneself as a moral person. On the output side, being a moral person is realized by one's actions in all of these roles. On the input side, the pattern of perceptions of accomplished meanings in all these roles contributes to the perceptions of oneself as a moral person.

The hierarchical organization of identities in these various ways within the perceptual control system helps to maintain self-relevant perceptions close to their identity standards at all levels simultaneously. This general principle holds for all identities at whatever level. All of the comparators shown in figure 7.1 act to measure the difference between perceived meanings and those meanings held in the identity standards. The outputs of these comparators (each a function of the difference between perceptions and standards) work either to change behaviors in the situation for the lowest-level identities, or, for higher levels, change the identity standards for identities at lower levels. This is the identity-verification process, which is a dynamic, ongoing, continuous process of counteracting disturbances that occur in the situation. Such disturbances may be the result of others' behaviors in the situation, one's own behavior in the situation, or ongoing physical processes in the situation.

Through the identity-verification process, actions (output behaviors acting on the meanings and resources flows in the environment) are taken that alter the situation and hence the self-relevant meanings in that situation to bring them into congruence with the standards held in the identity. To the extent that identity-verification succeeds or fails, and perceived self-relevant meanings are or are not brought into congruence with their standards, three concurrent outcomes result. Emotional reactions that are positive occur when the discrepancy is decreasing or nonexistent, and negative emotional reactions occur when the discrepancy exists or increases. We talk more about this in the next chapter. At the same time of this ongoing emotional response, the output of lower-level identities brings about behavior that changes the meanings in the situation. This moves one's perception toward the standard, and higher-level identities change their outputs (changing meanings held in the identity standards) to move the standard of the lower-level identity toward the meanings perceived at that level (though at a much slower rate). In the longer run, the identity system moves toward congruence between perceptions and the identity standards at all levels through the operation of both mechanisms.[1]

The External Framework: Multiple Identities within the Social Structure

This last idea of the nexus of identities within a person leads naturally to our other perspective of looking at the multiple identities as multiple ties to the social structure. Sociology has long conceptualized persons as occupying multiple positions or roles within the organized matrix of social relations we call the social structure (Linton 1936; Merton 1957; Parsons 1949; Turner 1978). That these multiple positions may come into conflict with one another within the individual was a logical next step that has been explored in a number of ways using the ideas of role conflict (Gross, Ward, and McEachern 1958), role strain (Secord and Backman 1974), and status inconsistency (Jackson 1962; Jackson and Burke 1965; Lenski 1954).[2]

Although this work was conceptualized in terms of the multiple positions that people hold and the multiple sets of expectations held for them rather than the multiple identities of those individuals, a translation to the latter perspective is straightforward. Indeed many of the effects of role conflict or status inconsistency (for example, to create distress of one sort or another) only make sense when the individual cares about the conflicting expectations. They would care if they have internalized them as standards for themselves. This idea is very close to our current understanding of the concept of identity and the conflicts that can arise between them when the different identities attempt to control the same meanings to different contrasting set points held by the different identity standards as discussed above.

The viewpoint that identities are tied to social structural positions (i.e., that individuals' memberships and roles in the groups, organizations, and networks to which they belong form the basis of many of their identities) grows out of the ideas of structural symbolic interaction theory (Stryker 1980 [2002]). This perspective suggests a number of ways in which the identities may relate to one another in terms of the way in which the positions are connected within the social structure. From this perspective, we note three different conditions: (1) persons may have multiple role identities within a single group, (2) persons may have the same role identities but in different groups, and (3) persons may have different role identities within intersecting groups.

For each of these three conditions, we are talking about multiple identities that are simultaneously activated. If an identity is not activated, it has no effect, since no identity-verification is taking place and no behavior is being used to control perceptions relevant to that identity. For this reason, the abstract concept of multiple identities makes sense when there may be multiple identities for people to call up (activate) on different occasions. The overall number of identities held by a person may influence the likelihood that activated identities may conflict with one another. It is likely that, aside from sleep or otherwise being inattentive, one or more identities is always activated, providing guidance for our perceptions and behaviors. The question then is what are the conditions for multiple identity activation?

Multiple Identities within a Single Group

There are two forms of this condition. One may have several roles within a group (e.g., husband, father, son, and brother within an extended family reunion, or task leader and social emotional leader in the same task group). In this case, these different identities will often be concurrently activated, and this will have both internal and external consequences. Internally, we hypothesize that the concurrent activation of these identities will lead, over time, to the identities developing similar levels of salience and commitment for the individual, as well as developing shared meanings. We suggest that the similar levels of salience will develop because the identities are often activated together, and with similar levels of activation, they should develop similar levels of salience or the probability of activation. Those that are activated together frequently will become more salient; those that are activated together less frequently will become less salient.

There are also external consequences. For example, with respect to commitment or the number and depth of ties to others in terms of the identity, when identities are activated together, they are activated in the presence of a common set of others present in the situation. Thus, these others will come to know the person in terms of those identities and develop ties with the person in terms of those identities. The more (or fewer) persons that one knows in terms of these commonly activated identities, the greater (or lesser) is the level of common commitment to the identities.

With the identities being concurrently activated, we also expect that they will develop common, shared, or overlapping meanings. Others in the group in which the multiple identities are commonly activated are likely over time to develop expectations about the way one engages in behavior relevant to each of the identities, such that the meanings defining the identities are consistent, shared, and mutually reinforcing. In this way, each of the identities becomes tied to the overall structure and functioning of the group in ways that make the verification process for all of the identities much more coordinated and shared. For example, if one person has the role of secretary and the role of treasurer in a group, and these two identities though initially separate are activated frequently together, the two will come to share meanings and perhaps merge into a single role. However, if there are times when the two roles cannot be activated together, or if there are restrictions on their being performed concurrently, such a merger is less likely and the sharing of meaning will be less.

Indeed, this was found by Burke (2003) in a study of task leadership identities and social emotional leadership (maintaining interpersonal relations) identities in small groups. Each group member was conceived to have some level of both of these identities. Some persons saw themselves as generally high on task leadership; others saw themselves as generally low or somewhere in the middle on task leadership. Similarly for self-views (identities) on social emotional leadership, some saw themselves as being high, and others saw themselves as low. These two identities were independent across persons, so that knowing how persons viewed themselves in task leadership terms did not predict how they saw themselves on social emotional leadership terms. Burke found that these identity meanings were predictive of the kind of social behavior group members engaged in along the same dimensions of meaning. Those who generally saw themselves as low on task leadership did not perform much task leadership activity, while those who saw themselves as high on task leadership did so. Similarly, those who generally saw themselves as high on social emotional leadership did perform more social emotional leadership activity, while those who saw themselves as low did not do so. Further, there was evidence that when identity and performance did not match, performance was adjusted upward or downward over time to bring about a closer match. For example, those who saw themselves as high on task leadership, if initially performing at low levels of task leadership (a mismatch), over time increased their level of task leadership performance (bringing about a closer match between identity meanings and performance meanings).

Because the two identities were independent across group members, one would expect that the activities would be independent across persons. And that is what Burke (2003) found for persons who were not legitimated by external authority as coordinators for their groups. However, for persons who were designated as coordinators for their groups, the two types of activity were positively correlated. Persons who were high on task leadership activity were also high on social emotional leadership activity. Being in the coordinator role apparently changed performance expectations compared to expectations for persons not in the coordinator role. It was expected that the coordinator would engage in both types of leadership somewhat independent of the level of their self-view on each of the dimensions, while such expectations were apparently not held for persons who were not in the coordinator role. Coordinators therefore tended to do both types of leadership or neither type.

In the short run, this change in leadership performances for coordinators may have had little effect. However, if such coordinated task and social emotional leadership performance persisted over longer periods, we would expect that the self-views of the coordinators would change to become more consistent with their performances as constrained by expectations of the group members. They would come to see themselves as high on both dimensions or low on both dimensions or somewhere in the middle. There would come to be a blurring of the separation of the two types of leadership for coordinators as their identities changed.

A second form of multiple identities within a single group exists when a person has an activated identity in one group and something in the situation activates an identity that the person has in another group. For example, I am in a board meeting as the director of a company division and something calls up my golfer identity or my spouse identity. This is the perspective that Stryker (2000) seems to suggest in his analysis of competing identities within the context of social movements. He raises the question of why all members of a social movement are not equally committed and active within the movement—a question that is not often raised by persons studying social movements—but a question that is certainly relevant to an activist within the movement. By taking an identity perspective, Stryker points out that persons have multiple identities, which need to be verified, and people have different levels of commitment and salience for each of the identities, with the result that people spend more or less time in each identity. People may have, for example, spousal identities or worker identities that preclude the full participation in a social movement. With two or more identities activated, the person engages in behavior that attempts to verify, to whatever extent possible, all of the activated identities, with the result that each is influenced by the requirements of the other.[3]

As another example, consider Harriett, who is a professor, at a faculty meeting, and her faculty identity is activated. At that meeting, someone mentions having seen and enjoyed a movie playing in town. This information is relevant to Harriett's spousal identity, as she and her husband had been contemplating seeing the movie. As a result, Harriet's spousal identity becomes activated, and she stores away the information about the movie to convey to her spouse later. However, while her spousal identity is activated, she is engaging in identity-verification processes with respect to that identity as well as the faculty member identity, with the result that she may attempt to speed up the faculty meeting in an attempt to accompany her husband to the movie that evening. In this way, each of the activated identities may influence the salience and commitment of the other, with the likelihood that the more salient identity will have greater influence on the less salient identity.

Multiple Identities Based on a Common Role within Multiple Groups

Here we consider the case in which the multiple identities are multiple in a sequential sense and not necessarily activated at the same time. For example, a person may have the identity "friend" in separate nonoverlapping groups or "treasurer" in several nonoverlapping voluntary associations. Each of these role identities resides in the same individual, and many of the meanings of these identities are shared, having arisen in a common culture. That is, what it means to be a friend of A is similar to what it means to be a friend of B. As a result, we would expect that any differences in the different friend identities a person has would diminish over time. Parsimony would argue that where the friend identities did not have to be different, they would become alike, reducing the information load for carrying around different expectations and meanings. Additionally, we would expect that such identities would become highly salient because of the extended network of connections to others through the identities (commitment). That is, as a number of studies have shown, increased commitment to an identity leads to the increased salience of the identity (e.g., Stryker and Serpe 1982).

Multiple Identities in Intersecting Groups

Here we consider the case in which the different identities that a person has in different groups become simultaneously activated if and when the different groups come into contact or overlap in some way. As in our earlier example, a person may have the identity "friend" to a peer and "daughter" to her parents. The two groups may intersect when the peer visits in the person's home while her parents are present. Within this situationally aggregated set of persons, both identities will be activated, and sets of meanings and expectations from both identities will be relevant. This is often the situation when role conflict is present. The meanings and expectations for each identity come into conflict when both identities are activated. Under such conditions, we would expect the identity standards involved to shift meanings, with the more salient or more committed identity shifting the least. However, to the extent that the identities share meanings, these meanings and expectations should reinforce each other rather than be in conflict. The increased number of ties in the larger network of others (parents and peers) will increase the level of commitment to the shared meanings and hence the identities that share those meanings.

The Person As a Container for Multiple Identities

Finally, it should be noted that having multiple identities also creates a nexus of those identities that are affected by the fact that a single individual holds them. Events and conditions that affect the individual have the capacity to affect all the identities held by that individual. For example, the individual may become overwhelmed by events with respect to one identity and suffer performance degradations with respect to otherwise unrelated identities, as when work suffers while an individual is going through a divorce or an individual who is sick may have trouble verifying any of their identities.

There is another way in which the common nexus of identities within a person becomes important. These identities may relate to one another through the transfer of information or other resources from one identity to which they are available to another identity held by the person. A simple example is that as a professor, I receive a salary. Some of this salary may be used by the professor identity to maintain that identity, but more of it is used by other identities, such as spouse or parent or homeowner to verify them. Because these identities are housed in one person, they can easily communicate with one another to make available these resources. This transfer of resources is sanctioned by society. However, other resources I gain as a professor (for example a laptop computer or a video camera) are not to be made available to other identities I have. Society has developed elaborate rules that indicate appropriate and inappropriate transfer of resources among identities held by one person. And the development of these rules is brought about because the multiple identities held by individuals do transfer resources between themselves. Misappropriation of funds, embezzlement, insider trading, and making personal long-distance calls at work are other examples in which the multiple identities held by persons inappropriately transfer resources among themselves.

Not all interidentity transfers are inappropriate. As we mentioned, using a salary in one identity that has been earned in another identity is appropriate. Using information one learns from a friend to plan an outing with one's spouse and children is also appropriate. Using the skills one learns as a student while on a job is not only appropriate but also expected. The person is the common nexus of multiple identities, and through the person, those identities have opportunities to communicate, plan, share resources, and otherwise facilitate their mutual verification.

Because people are the carriers of identities, identities meet and interact when people meet and interact. One can meet others because of a shared group membership (for example, belonging to the same union) or role relations (for example, doctors meet patients, nurses, and drug salesmen). Because individuals hold many identities, when one individual with a certain identity meets another because of the context of that identity, the identities of the two persons other than the ones that brought them together may become relevant and activated in unexpected ways.[4]

Consider, for example, a person who has a daughter in kindergarten. She may meet the mother of her daughter's kindergarten friend while picking up her daughter at school. At first, the two adults may know each other as the mother of her daughter's friend. Over time, however, other identities may become activated and known to each other. One may know, through her work identity, of a job opportunity that the other, with her work identity, could fulfill. Through this mechanism, identities become interconnected in somewhat random ways, both within and between people. This random character results from the structural arrangements of society, the connection of individuals to those structures, as well as the multiple identities that are housed within any given individual. Highly salient identities become activated and known to others who may then find additional ways to relate to the person through activating other identities of their own. Thus, the network of relations expands as identities find new ways of verifying themselves by activating relevant identities in other individuals. Lovers may meet at church, skiers at work, friends in voluntary association meetings, and coworkers at fraternal gatherings.

An Ecology of Identities

Smith-Lovin (2003) points out that people live in an ecology of identities that are made available by the culture we live in. In preliterate or premodern societies, there may be only a few identities that are available for individuals; for example, wife, mother, sister, and gatherer may encompass most of the identities available to a woman in such a society. In societies that are more complex, there are thousands of different identities available as roles, groups, categories, and divisions proliferate. The likelihood of having multiple identities activated would certainly depend upon the number of identities one has, and that depends, in part, on how many are available to us. So, clearly, having multiple activated identities is more likely in modern or postmodern societies than in premodern societies. However, Smith-Lovin (2003) also points out that the ecology of identities is not spread equally throughout complex societies. Children, for example, have fewer identities available to them than adults have, and adults who are higher up in the status structure have more identities available to them than adults lower in the status structure have. Persons who have more resources available may use those resources to access more identities. We know, for example, that persons with higher education (both a resource and a source of status) are more likely to join one or more voluntary associations, thus adding to the number of identities they have.

Identities Provide Meaning

One of the early views of identity that grew out of the symbolic interaction framework, with its emphasis on symbols and meaning, is that identities provide "meaning" for individuals' lives. Though it was never clear what "meaning" was in this context, it was good to have meaning and not good not to have meaning. A life without meaning is a life that is full of anomie; it has no purpose, no structure, and no framework. Without meaning, people have low self-esteem. Thoits (1983; 1986) and a number of other researchers suggested that identities provide a sense of purpose and meaning in life, integrating us with the actions and expectations of others. Identities do this because they define who we are as well as how and why we are to behave in normatively specified ways. Identities thus increase self-esteem and reduce depression and anxiety (Thoits 1983). From this view that identities provide positive "meaning," it was a natural step to suggest that if one has more identities, one would have greater meaning, with the consequence of increased self-esteem and reduced depression and anxiety. More identities are, from this point of view, better.

Yet, as Thoits (2003) points out, this view runs counter to much earlier work on role conflict that more roles (identities) lead to greater chance of conflict between and among the roles (Bailey and Yost 2000; Goode 1960; Merton 1957). The competing demands of multiple roles, they argued, increased the distress of individuals. This idea was the core of what was known as stress theory. And, indeed, not all the research was fully supportive of the idea persons with more identities had higher self-esteem or lower distress. Often persons with more role identities had higher distress. At the same time, identity accumulation, or taking on more identities, did seem to benefit persons when considering some identities but not others.

To better understand this set of conflicting findings, Thoits (2003) suggested that it is important to distinguish between two different types of roles or identities: voluntary and obligatory. Voluntary identities, she argues, are those that are freely chosen by individuals and are easily exited. Obligatory identities are more compelling and, when taken on, are difficult to exit. Membership in a voluntary organization would be an example of a voluntary identity, while spouse, parent, and worker are examples of obligatory identities. By making this distinction, Thoits was trying to separate identities that could lead to distress from those that may be more beneficial. The idea, in part, was one of agency or motivation. By freely choosing some identities (voluntary), presumably a person would take on only those for which there was some personal benefit. And, for these identities, if problems began to ensue, the person could exit the identity and not suffer the consequences of increased distress. The net result, of course, is increased benefit for those voluntary identities we maintain.

Another aspect of voluntary identities is suggested by Thoits (2003). People who are able to choose their identities are persons who have control over their lives compared to others who are induced by life's circumstances into particular identities. Being in control of one's life is, of course, a form of efficacy and is one basis for having high self-esteem. Thus, the cards are stacked for people to have high self-esteem by having identities that they choose, and among these identities, perhaps more is better.

This is what Thoits (2003) found, considering voluntary identities in contrast to obligatory identities: persons with more voluntary identities did seem to have greater self-esteem, greater mastery, and lower distress. Further, examining the data over time suggested that persons who gained voluntary identities had their self-esteem increase. Correspondingly, those who lost voluntary identities had their self-esteem decrease.

Identity theory has an alternative interpretation for both these results as well as for the issue of the effects of identity accumulation on self-esteem and depression. As Cast and Burke (2002) point out in their theory of self-esteem as we discussed in chapter 5, from the point of view of identity theory, it is the verification of identities that makes people feel good in general and feel good about themselves especially. Conversely, if identities are not verified, people feel bad, distressed, and angry (Burke 1991; 2004b; Burke and Harrod 2005). It does not matter whether the identity is a voluntary identity or an obligatory identity, whether it is a role identity, a person identity, or a social identity. The general principle is that identity-verification leads to good feelings and problems with verification leads to bad feelings. This general principle has been confirmed many times. Further, it makes sense that the more identities that are confirmed, the better one feels. Thus, accumulating multiple identities should have benefits, but only if the accumulated identities are all verified. If the accumulated identities are not verified, then there should be increasing distress, depression, and lower self-esteem.

We suggest that the voluntary identities a person holds are more likely to be verified, but not necessarily because of any intrinsic merit of them as opposed to obligatory identities. Rather, if an identity is being verified, and that makes us feel good about ourselves, we will want to continue in that identity. Whether it is more or less difficult to exit is not relevant, because we want to stay in it. We are successful at it. However, if we are not able to verify an identity, or if we are having a great deal of trouble verifying an identity, we will want to leave.

Cast and Burke (2002) showed, for example, that when couples verify their spousal identities, their feelings of self-esteem and self-efficacy are increased and their distress and depression decreased. Further, they found that people who have verification difficulties that persist over time are more likely to become separated or divorced. This, of course, results in giving up the spousal identity. Thus, one way to deal with identities that are not verified is to leave them. However, if the identity is difficult to exit (like marriage), then fewer will leave the identity when there are verification problems. The result will be more problem (unverified) identities in the obligatory identity group than in the voluntary identity group and as a result more people with lower self-esteem in the obligatory identity group than in the voluntary identity group, which is consistent with what Thoits finds, but not for the same reason. The accumulation of multiple identities would appear, then, to have benefits only if they are verified. However, accumulation of verified identities would be good whether they were obligatory or voluntary identities.

Indeed, the accumulation of verified obligatory identities may be better than the accumulation of verified voluntary identities. The reason is that obligatory identities have another characteristic in society. These identities are difficult to leave because society makes it so. Moreover, society makes it so because it is important to society that there be continuity with respect to these identities. One has to think twice before taking on one of these identities because it is difficult to leave. This adds a level of importance to these identities in culture, and for individuals there is a built-in bias that such identities are taken as important, that is, have high prominence. We suggest that the verification (and nonverification) of prominent identities has more impact on emotions and feeling-states than the verification (or nonverification) of less prominent identities. Verifying an important identity should result in stronger feelings of self-worth or efficacy than the verification of a less important identity. Similarly, the failure to verify a prominent identity should have stronger negative consequences. This would lead us to expect that verification of obligatory identities should produce higher self-esteem than the verification of voluntary identities.

Multiple Identities Across Persons

We turn now to an examination of multiple identities within a situation rather than within a person. For now, we will assume that each person has only one identity; but with several persons interacting in a situation, each trying to verify his or her identity, we must be concerned with their effects on one another. In chapter 4, we saw how one identity functions to verify itself in the face of disturbances. Our concern now is that those disturbances are often other identities in the situation. Examples would include friends playing bridge, husbands and wives interacting, and members of a task group accomplishing their goal. Each of the persons has an activated identity and is engaging in behavior that both portrays the meanings of the identity and defends against discrepant meanings that are indicated or implied by others in the situation.

To facilitate this discussion, in figure 7.2 we adapt the figure of the identity model (figure 4.1) to a situation in which there are two persons, each with an active identity, like a professor and a student. Again, each of the identities has all the components that we have talked about, including the identity standard, perceptions, a comparator, and output of meaningful behavior to the situation. Since the multiple identities are in multiple persons, each has its own output of meaningful behavior in the situation, unlike the case of multiple identities within one person. Each identity is trying to control its own perceptions of situational meanings to match the meanings held in the identity standard of that particular person/identity. The situation that one identity is controlling is the same situation that the other identity is controlling. So although there are two sets of meaningful behaviors, there is only one set of meanings in the situation, and that set is being produced by both persons and is being perceived by both persons.

Three possible scenarios can arise. Each identity may be trying to control the same meanings in the situation to be the same level that the other identity is trying to control. In this case, the identity standards of the two identities agree with each other as to what the meanings in the situation should be. As a result, the two identities can be seen to support each other; what one does to the situation is exactly what the other wants. In effect, they are on the same team. Perhaps, for example, two persons want the situation to be romantic in a similar way, so they cooperate to make it so.

The second scenario is that the two identities are trying to control the same meanings in the situation to be different levels. For example, one identity wants the situation to be romantic, while the other wants the situation to be businesslike and definitely not romantic. This is a case of true conflict because as one person moves the meanings in the situation to be in accord with their identity standard, the meanings in the situation are moving further

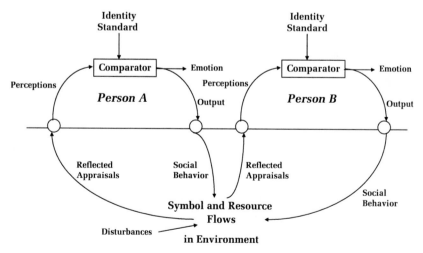

Figure 7.2. Identity Models for Two Interacting Persons

out of accord with the meanings in the identity standard of the other person. With those identities and identity standards, the situation cannot verify both. Indeed, no situation could. As the situation moves toward a more business-like atmosphere, the romantic identity is not verified; as the situation moves toward a more romantic atmosphere, the business identity is not verified. In this situation, each identity is a disturbance to the other identity.

There is a third (perhaps less interesting) scenario. In this, the meanings that one identity is trying to control are not relevant to the meanings that the other identity is trying to control. Two children are playing on the same beach, one building a sandcastle, the other digging a hole that is deep enough to be below the water line and fill up with water. Now, as long as the castle does not go over the hole, or the hole does not go under the sandcastle, what each is doing neither helps nor hinders what the other is doing. Each is controlling perceptions of meanings in the situation that are irrelevant to the other.

Each of these scenarios is, of course, a pure type. In most situations, the interaction is more complex in the sense that some meanings may be controlled in conflict, others in agreement, and others still that are irrelevant to one or the other of the identities involved—a mixture of types. Married couples provide a good example. Each spouse seeks to verify his or her own spousal identity in interaction with the partner. But, as any spouse knows, there are times when it works, and there are times when it does not work, or does not work as well. It works very well when what each does verifies not only the self but the other as well. It does not work well when what one does to verify the self "drives the other crazy" (that is, does not verify the identity of the other).

In our study of newly married couples (Burke and Stets 1999), we found exactly this result. Using procedures we discussed earlier, we measured the spousal role identity of about three hundred first married couples with no children who were interviewed right after they got married and then again a year later and a third time two years later. We measured the spousal identity of each partner. We also measured what each partner thought the spousal identity of the other ought to be. The spousal identity—that is, what it means to be a spouse for each person—was based on eleven items indicating various tasks or activities that are understood to be part of the spousal role. Each person was asked to what extent he or she felt he or she should do each of the activities, such as "work around the yard" or "shopping for the family." The extent to which each thought he or she should engage in these activities defines, in part, for each individual, what it means to be a spouse. This, of course, would vary from individual to individual.

On the one hand, if the partner's view of one's spousal identity is consistent with the self-view, then the partner is likely to engage in activities toward the self that are consistent with the spousal self-meanings, thus verifying the self's spousal identity. On the other hand, if the partner's view of one's spousal identity is inconsistent with the self-view, then the partner's behavior is not likely to verify the self's spousal identity. We thus have a situation in which each partner is behaving in a common context, the household, trying to verify his or her own spousal identity, and this requires some coordination with their partner.

An analogy would be each person trying to keep the temperature of the home at a comfortable level. If one likes the temperature at 68 and the other likes the temperature at 72, then as one adjusts the thermostat to make the temperature comfortable, that setting makes the temperature uncomfortable for the other. In order not to argue about the temperature setting, the two will have to come to some agreement about the appropriate level for the temperature. This is also true about the spousal identities. If one person feels he or she should do all of the cooking and the partner would like to do half of the cooking, the behavior of one trying to confirm his or her spousal identity will result in the other partner not being able to confirm her or her identity. However, if one partner feels that his or her spousal role calls for him or her to cook most of the time, and the other partner feels his or her spousal role calls for him or her to cook some of the time, the two identities will support and reinforce each other.

We found there was quite a bit of variability across households in the degree to which the two spousal identities worked together in a complementary fashion. Although only about three and a half percent of the couples had perfect agreement across all eleven different activities, almost all couples agreed with each other within a point across each of the eleven activities. Of course, being newlyweds, these are people who are in love with each other, have known and dated each other for some time, and found themselves compatible enough to get married. We would therefore expect some compatibility in their self-views. Nevertheless, an average disagreement of one point on spousal activities has consequences, as we found (Burke and Stets 1999).

We examined a number of consequences that occurred as the degree of discrepancy increased from the zero of the few couples in complete agreement at one end of the spectrum to a maximum that averaged a little over one point across the eleven items. Two of the consequences that were examined were the degree to which each partner felt positive and negative self-feelings when the identity was or was not supported. We found that as the amount of discrepancy between the self-views of being a spouse and the views expressed by the partner for them increased, they felt an increasing amount of distress and depression. At the same time, as the discrepancy was lower, they felt an increasing amount of self-esteem and self-efficacy (Burke and Stets 1999). Being with a partner who confirms your self-view as a spouse makes you feel better about yourself. It also makes you feel competent and able; being with a partner who acts in ways that create situational meanings that do not support your self-view (because he or she has a different view of the way you should be in your spousal role) makes you feel depressed and distressed. Many identities interacting in the same situation, each trying to verify itself, works when they are controlling meanings in the same way and producing good feelings for the individuals involved.

When there are discrepancies or differences, the situation deteriorates for the individuals.

In addition to the self-feelings, we also examined the degree to which the partners trusted each other. It turned out that to the extent that persons' spousal identities were confirmed by their partner in the household situation, they also developed a deeper trust for their partner. Their partner, after all, has behaved in ways that help them maintain their own spousal identities and feel good about themselves. As this happened for each of the partners, each became more trusting of the other—a situation of mutual trust developed. Along with this increasing mutual trust, the husband and wife developed an increased feeling of "we-ness" or couple orientation, and each was much more likely to speak of "we" rather than "I" in conversations with the other. The increased trust among these mutually verifying couples had its own consequences. The increased trust led to increased levels of mutual commitment and emotional attachment or love, which in turn helped keep the couples interacting even when times were more difficult.

These results led us to conceptualize something we called a "mutual verification context," that is, a situation in which all the parties involved (the two spouses in our study) work together to create a context in which they can verify each other's identities and have their own identity verified by the other's identity. Such a mutual verification context is something that people desire and will maintain when they have it. A group of friends who all get along with one another might be an example. A family in which each member finds it possible to be himself or herself and each member likes and appreciates the others in the family might be another example. We further hypothesized that when such contexts cannot be developed or maintained, people would prefer to leave the situation in favor of a situation in which such a context is possible. Over time, this would result in an increase in the number of such mutual verification contexts, as ones that developed were maintained and ones that did not dissolved. Of course, this assumes that people are free to enter and leave such sets of relationships, and that is not always the case.

More Than Two Persons

A study by Riley and Burke (1995) examined a context in which there were multiple persons each trying to verify an identity in the same situation. This situation was a little more complex than with the couples because there were four persons in the situation trying to maintain an identity, each with respect to three others. Counting each pair of persons, a total of six relationships needs to be maintained. The identity that Riley and Burke investigated was a leader identity in the context of a small group. They measured the extent to which each member of a four-person group generally thought of himself or herself as a group leader. This was not a question of yes or no, but of degree. Some people thought of themselves as very much dominating and leading groups; some saw themselves as persons who avoided that role, doing it very little, while others saw themselves at various points along the whole range in between.

Because people try to act in ways that verify their identities—that is, produce self-relevant meanings in the situation that match the meanings held in their identity standard—we expect that the meanings of the behaviors will ordinarily match those in the standard. Thus, people with strong leadership identities will act more like leaders, and those with weak or low leadership identities will not act like leaders or will do so much less. In the group, however, each person is not free to do what each wants to do. Each is constrained by what others are doing. For example, if two persons want to act as strong leaders in the group, they may end up competing with each other, neither being happy with his or her performance, because it does not match his or her strong leadership identity. Each may feel some distress because his or her leadership identity was not verified.

An additional feature of interaction in groups is that the members must share their interpretations of behaviors (i.e., share meanings) in order for them to coordinate their activities and accomplish the task. Thus, the behavior in which person A engages to display the meanings of his or her leadership identity must be similarly interpreted by person B. If what A does to show leadership is not what B takes to be leadership (because they don't share meanings), then B will not respond in ways that verify A's leadership identity. For the system to work, B must perceive A's behavior in the same way that A perceives A's behavior—taking the role of the other.

The groups Riley and Burke studied were laboratory groups composed of four randomly chosen student volunteers who were put together to solve a series of four human relations problems. Each problem was discussed in a separate discussion, and measures of perceived performance of each of the members were taken after each of the four discussions. They measured the leadership identity meanings of each of the participants prior to any of the discussions, they measured each person's perceived meanings of their own leadership behavior after each discussion, and they measured the meanings of each person's leadership behavior as perceived by others in the group after each discussion. From this they showed that each person's leadership identity did predict his or her leadership behavior as perceived by himself or herself and by others across all the discussions (though the predictions for own perceptions were better than for other's perceptions, as would be expected if people controlled their behavior to match their own perceptions of it). Riley and Burke also found that the perceptions of self and other were very highly correlated across the four discussions, thus indicating that self and others interpreted the meanings of the self's behavior in very similar ways; they shared meanings.

Finally, Riley and Burke showed that the degree to which a person's leadership behavior was not predicted by his or her leadership identity influenced members' satisfaction with his or her role performance in the group (but not their overall satisfaction with the discussion). Group members who performed more or less leadership activity than was consistent with their leadership identity were less happy than persons who performed at the expected level. And the degree of discrepancy or difference between actual and expected performance predicted the degree of dissatisfaction with their role in the group, confirming one of identity theory's major points that people are distressed and upset by a failure to verify their identities.

In a further extension of this research, Burke (2006b) showed that when a group member performs more (or less) leadership in the group than would be expected on the basis of his or her leadership identity during one of the four discussions, that person changed his or her behavior in the next discussion to engage in less (or more) leadership activity. This was done, apparently, in an effort to counteract the disturbances in the system that caused him or her to perform too much (or too little). Thus, not only did the members feel bad when they could not perform at the level of their identity, they also attempted to do something about it when they had a chance. Persons with a strong leadership identity who were pushed out of that role in one discussion worked harder in the next discussion to (re)gain the role that was consistent with their identity. Similarly, persons who found themselves, for one reason or another, performing more leadership than was consistent with their identity backed off in the next discussion in an attempt to verify their identity. With more people in the situation, each trying to verify an identity, others in the situation may find it difficult to verify their own identity unless and until all the persons in the situation can establish a mutual verification context so that all identities can be verified simultaneously.

Summary

In this chapter, we examined the complexities that can arise when we consider more than one identity at a time operating in a situation to verify itself. Because each identity is a control system that operates to maintain consistency between perceived meanings and meanings in the identity standard, there are problems when two or more identities cannot agree on what those meanings should be. Whether the different meanings are held by different identities within a single person (being a student and a friend and a family member, for example), or the different meanings are held by different persons with different identities in a situation (a professor interacting with a student, for example), the meanings must be consistent or at least independent. They cannot be in disagreement without serious problems resulting either in identities changing or in people leaving the situation. In either case, the emotional reactions of the persons involved are quite negative. If the identities change so that they mutually verify one another in the sense that when one is verified other identities are also verified, people will feel good and will work to keep that situation as it is—what we called a mutual verification context. Such contexts are inherently stable and provide stability to the social structure of which they are a part.

8

Emotion

In this chapter, we focus on the role emotions play in identity theory. We discuss not only how emotion fits into the theory but also the extent to which the empirical work thus far supports the role emotion plays in the theory. The majority of the chapter will be devoted to discussing emotion using the perceptual control emphasis in identity theory because this is where the relationship between emotion and identity processes has been advanced. In the last part of the chapter, we discuss how we might develop the role of emotion further in the theory. Clearly, we have only touched the surface as to how emotion informs us about the meanings of one's identities.

To begin, emotions generally refer to the feelings individuals experience in situations. Although there is a host of feelings people can experience within and across situations, their emotions generally are categorized into primary and secondary emotions (Turner and Stets 2005). Primary emotions form the core from which all other emotions are derived. Persons around the globe can identify these emotions; thus, they are universal, and they appear to be evolutionarily and biologically based in that they are present in other primates and have a distinctive physiological response (Ekman 1992). The primary emotions include happiness, fear, anger, and sadness. Notice that three of these four primary emotions are negatively valenced. Secondary emotions stem from primary emotions and generally are conceptualized as a mixture of primary emotions (Kemper 1987; Plutchik 1980; Turner 2000). For example, fear and anger lead to the secondary emotions of hate, jealousy, and envy, while fear and happiness generate wonder, awe, and hope (Kemper 1987).

Generally, when identity theorists discuss emotions, it is not with respect to specific emotions such as those listed above. Instead, it is with respect to whether individuals are experiencing negative or positive feelings in situations (Turner and Stets 2005). Indeed, if we conceptualize emotions as on a continuum from negative to positive, individuals can move along this continuum in any one situation, such that at one point they may respond negatively and at a later point they may respond positively. Identity theorists do not examine this possible shift in emotional tone in a situation. Rather, they are interested in identifying the eliciting condition(s) that produce the negative or positive feelings. Further, in their early work they were not interested in identifying *which* emotions individuals might feel in a situation. Rather, they were interested only in whether the emotions were positively or negatively valenced. Given that the list of possible emotions could be very long, predicting the specific emotion individuals will likely experience has not been a goal in the theory. Instead, identity theorists are interested in the valence of these feelings, that is, whether individuals feel good or feel bad since these outcomes influence other cognitive and behavioral responses that they are interested in explaining. For example, if individuals feel bad, how will they resolve these feelings behaviorally and cognitively? Before we examine emotions in greater detail in identity theory, we return to the roots of identity theory to see how its key thinkers have theorized about emotion.

Early Theorists

George Herbert Mead

Although all symbolic interactionists draw inspiration from the work of George Herbert Mead (1934), surprisingly, Mead had little to say about emotion. He focused on the self as a cognitive entity rather than an emotional entity. His emphasis on such processes as actors' ability to take themselves as an object and think about themselves as others would think about them, or actors' ability to take-the-role of the other in a situation and consider the other's view when acting, directed our attention to the cognitive aspects of the self and not the affective aspects of the self. Indeed, he claimed that the primary structure of the self was a cognitive rather than emotional phenomenon (Mead 1934).

However, Mead did not ignore emotion altogether. He was interested in the display of emotion and how it served as a signal to others to respond in a particular way as prescribed by culture (Ward and Throop 1992). For example, the intent of shaking one's fist to express anger is to evoke a response in another to apologize, flee, or psychologically withdraw. The intent is not to induce the other to shake his fist and express anger as well, although this could happen and lead to escalatory behavior rather than de-escalatory behavior. Similarly, when one feels sorrow over the loss of a loved one, the intent behind shedding tears is to evoke responses of empathy or sympathy in another. The intent is not to call forth tears in another as well, although it could have this unintended consequence.

As Turner and Stets (2005) point out, a place where Mead could have given more attention to the self as a feeling entity was in his theory of the four stages of the act: the impulse, perception, manipulation, and consummation stages (Mead 1938). According to Mead, the moment an individual experiences an interruption in ongoing activity, it sets in motion the first phase of the act, the *impulse* stage. Impulses heighten perceptions in a situation and initiate response options to return the self to its ongoing activity. For example, it is evening, you are reading a novel, and the reading light goes out. The light going out disrupts your ability to continue reading, and the disruption calls forth a response within you to resolve the problem so you can get back to reading. According to Mead, following the impulse stage is the *perception* stage in which one evaluates what may be going on in the situation. You might ask yourself, "Does the bulb need to be tightened into the lamp socket?" "Has the lamp cord come loose from the outlet?" "Did the bulb's filament blow?" Each of these questions leads to a unique way to respond in the situation. In the *manipulation* phase, one carries out actions consistent with his thoughts. Therefore, you might tighten the bulb into the lamp socket, press the lamp cord firmly into the outlet, or examine the bulb's filament to see if the bulb needs to be replaced. In the *consummation* stage, one assesses whether he or she has resolved the problem. If the evaluation is that the problem is unresolved, one returns to the manipulation phase to try out other responses, or, alternatively, one returns to the perception stage to entertain new ideas. Thus, if you tighten the bulb in the lamp socket and the light does not turn on, you may press the lamp cord into the outlet. If this still does not turn the light on, you may replace the bulb. If the light still does not turn on, you may entertain new ideas, for example, the filament in the current replacement bulb also has blown, and you need a second bulb for replacement. Once the light comes back on, you can return to reading your novel.

Now, throughout the phases of the act as discussed above, we see an actor who is a "thinking" entity but not a "feeling" entity. Nowhere does Mead mention the actor's emotional reaction to an interruption in ongoing activity or to an unconsummated act. An interruption in what one is doing or an unresolved state of affairs can generate negative feelings such as fear, disgust, sadness, frustration, and even anger. One's goal is blocked. These negative feelings can be directed inward. For example, feelings of shame may emerge if one cannot find the source of the problem, and one may say to himself, "I'm so stupid." They may also be directed outward, for instance, blaming others for causing the interruption as when you might say to your partner, "You know you broke this socket when you dropped the lamp on the carpet because the bulb won't fit." Further, if one has to continually work on the problem to resolve it, negative feelings could intensify. These intense negative feelings could block implementing appropriate action (e.g., you could break a light bulb in an attempt to replace it), or they could block clear thinking (e.g., you cannot think of further reasons for the light going out). An alternative is that negative feelings become repressed, which may activate defense mechanisms such as displacement (e.g., you yell at your neighbor for the loud music he is currently playing outside the window where you were reading) that may also get in the way of a clear resolution to the problem (Turner 2006).

As the above reveals, we can easily incorporate emotions into Mead's theory of the act, and this is where identity theory has an affinity with Mead's theory. One can conceptualize an interruption in ongoing activity (Mead's impulse phase) as analogous to a person's identity not being verified in a situation (see chapter 4). According to identity theory, when identity-nonverification occurs, it produces negative emotions for the self. In response to the negative emotions, a person will think about and then act in the situation (Mead's perception and manipulation phases) to return the self to a verifying state. If identity-verification occurs (Mead's consummation phase), the negative feelings are eliminated and a person feels positive emotions. If identity-verification does not occur, the self will continue to feel negative emotions and act upon the environment until verification is achieved. In general, therefore, identity theory makes explicit what Mead left implicit as to the role of emotions for the self.

Charles Horton Cooley

Charles Horton Cooley (1902), a one-time colleague of Mead, was far more attentive to the emotional aspect of the self than Mead. Cooley saw sentiments or emotions to be at the core of the self. For Cooley, emotions are social because they are based on images the self experiences in response to how others see them. The alternative would be that a person just ignores the views of others. The idea that we consider others' views of us is best revealed in Cooley's *looking-glass self*. Recall from chapter 2, the idea behind the looking-glass self is that as persons get feedback from others across situations, this feedback becomes a mirror or "looking glass" as to how persons come to see themselves. Their reflection conjures up three things. First, they *imagine* how they appear to others. Second, they imagine how others would *evaluate* that appearance. Finally, they experience a *feeling* given the evaluation of their appearance. For example, Tom may imagine that others see him as intelligent. He may then infer that others see him in a good light because intelligence is valued in American society. What likely follows from this inference—that others evaluate him positively—is a feeling of pride in Tom. Alternatively, Tom may imagine that others think he is lazy. He may then surmise that they see him in a bad light because laziness is not valued in American society. Following this negative evaluation, Tom likely will feel shame. Cooley highlighted the feelings of pride and shame. Pride emerges when persons evaluate their appearance (in the eyes of others) in positive terms, and shame emerges when persons evaluated their appearance in negative terms. These were "self-feelings" because they were feelings individuals directed toward themselves in response to the imagination and evaluation of others.

Cooley was ahead of his time, not only in bringing emotions into the self, but also in bringing "specific" emotions such as pride and shame into the self. Symbolic interactionists such as Scheff (1988; 1990; 2000) have built on Cooley's idea of pride and shame. For the most part, identity theorists have been more likely to study emotions in more general terms—as positive or negative feelings—rather than as a specific emotion that actors may feel. As we will see, it is only very recently that identity theorists have attempted to bring specific emotions into the theory (Stets and Burke 2005b).

Contemporary Identity Theorists

Recall that in chapter 3 we identified three theoretical emphases in identity theory: the interactional, the social structural, and the perceptual control focus. Theorists in these three areas have discussed the role of emotions in identity theory, but the most development on emotions in the theory has come out of the perceptual control area. Before discussing the perceptual control view of emotions, it is important to review the contributions of McCall and Simmons and Stryker on emotions.

The Interactional Emphasis

For McCall and Simmons (1978), a person's feelings emerge in a situation when an identity that is prominent or important is challenged. Essentially, others in the situation do not agree that the individual's behavior is consistent with the identity the person is claiming. For example, a friend of yours may claim to be a "computer wizard" but then is unable to solve a computer problem you have. The lack of support from others for one's behavior produces negative feelings for the individual, and the person may employ any number of strategies to get rid of these negative feelings.[1] As we mentioned in chapter 3, McCall and Simmons label these "mechanisms of legitimation," and they include such strategies as selective perception, rationalizing one's behavior, deprecating or rejecting others who are nonsupportive, or withdrawing from the interaction. We point out that McCall and Simmons do not identify the type of negative emotions individuals experience in response to the lack of support, for example, anger, sadness, or shame. Further, it is possible that a particular negative emotion will influence adopting one strategy compared to another to get rid of the bad feelings. For example, feeling shame may influence one to attend selectively to feedback in the situation that confirms her identity while disattending to feedback that disconfirms her identity. This helps her cope with her shame by counterbalancing negative feelings with positive feelings. Anger may lead an individual to deprecate or reject those who do not support one's behavior. Future research will need to investigate whether there is a connection between the specific negative emotion individuals experience in a situation and the way they try to get rid of the negative feeling.

In general, the strategies that McCall and Simmons discussed enable persons to escape the painful feelings associated with a lack of support for identities they claim in situations. What is interesting about McCall and Simmons's strategies is that they come close to the notion of "defense mechanisms" that other symbolic interactionists studying emotions indicate are important in understanding how individuals manage negative emotions or more generally any threat to the self (Turner 2002). Defense mechanisms are those tactics people use to protect themselves from the pain associated with negative feelings. They may include *repression*, in which individuals push the painful emotion below the level of consciousness thereby making them oblivious to the pain. It might also include *projection*, in which people assign their negative feelings to others rather than attributing them to themselves. For example, Mary may remark to John that he seems depressed when it is Mary who is really feeling depressed. In addition, it might include *displacement*, in which people's negative feelings are directed at others. For example, Mary may feel angry rather than depressed, and she may direct that anger at John by insulting him.

As we will see in the perceptual control emphasis of identity theory, theorists discuss how individuals cope, perceptually and behaviorally, with identity-nonverification and negative feelings (Burke 1991). In this way, these theorists have an affinity with McCall and Simmons in terms of how individuals manage negative emotions. However, McCall and Simmons's discussion is far more extensive, giving identity theorists in the perceptual control camp a rich array of further tactics to consider. Also, the defense mechanisms briefly discussed above suggest that identity theorists may need to consider other coping strategies of a psychoanalytic nature that individuals also may use. They may also want to examine the conditions under which these defense mechanisms are used, and whether they facilitate or impede the accomplishment of identity-verification.

The Structural Emphasis

Stryker (2004) maintains that people occupy various roles in a network, and these roles carry meanings in the form of identities. Emotions have an influence on the formation of social networks because people with shared affective meanings will be more likely to enter into and maintain a social relationship. For example, if John and Mary share a love of God, they are more likely to develop a relationship than if they did not share this feeling. They might even join the same religious group. Stryker also maintains that individuals will be more committed to those groups if individuals in the group share the same feelings. Further, he argues that positive affect rather than negative affect is the catalyst for increased commitment to groups. In turn, increased commitment leads to greater positive shared feelings in the group.

While in social networks, individuals behave according to the expectations associated with the roles they are occupying. According to Stryker, when people meet role expectations, they will feel good about themselves and others will feel good about them. Alternatively, if they do not meet role expectations, they will feel bad about themselves and others will feel bad about them. When individuals are highly committed to a role identity, such as the parent identity or friend identity, a greater discrepancy in failing to meet role expectations will result in a greater negative emotional response. At the same time, when others in the situation fail to meet the expectations associated with their own roles, it prevents individuals from meeting their own role expectations, with the result that it will intensify individuals' negative emotional reactions in the situation.

Since salient identities are more likely to be played out across situations and social networks, Stryker argues that affect influences salient identities in the following manner. Salient identities will have more intense affect associated with them. If a person's behavior is consistent with a salient identity, she will feel intense positive emotions. Alternatively, if a person engages in a role performance inconsistent with a salient identity, she will feel intense negative emotions, and she will do something to distance herself from the identity. Intense emotion also is associated with salient identities through commitment. For example, if a person experiences strong negative emotions after enacting an identity, this may decrease his ties to others based on that identity, and the fewer ties will reduce the salience of that identity in one's hierarchy of identities. Alternatively, strong positive emotions increase identity commitment and, in turn, identity salience.

Finally, Stryker discusses the role of intense and uncontrollable emotions for the maintenance of identities, commitment, and identity salience. Intense emotional responses occur when role partners behave in ways that contradict another's identity claims. Intense emotional responses also occur when structural or interactional barriers prevent the enactment of highly positive identities or the denial of highly negative identities. In turn, this decreases commitment to the identity. For example, if one claims the parent identity but spends most of her time in the work setting, she may decrease her ties to others based on the parent identity. Emotional reactions can also be spontaneous and uncontrollable. When spontaneous positive emotions follow from a role performance, commitment and salience to that identity will increase. Correspondingly, when spontaneous negative emotions follow from a role performance, commitment and salience to that identity will decrease.

Stryker acknowledges that the relationships he hypothesizes need to be tested. He also acknowledges that he does not discuss how specific emotions such as love, guilt, embarrassment, anger, and so forth can be incorporated into identity theory. Both theory-testing and the development of specific emotions are needed in identity theory.

Research Using the Interactional and Structural Emphases

There is not much research that examines emotions in either the interactional or the structural version of identity theory. One example is research by Ellestad and Stets (1998). Recall that in chapter 3 we discussed McCall and Simmons's idea that individuals have a hierarchy of *prominent* identities. We compared this with Stryker's notion of individuals having a hierarchy of *salient* identities. Ellestad and Stets examined the relationship between a prominent *and* salient mother identity and jealousy in the family. These identity researchers were the first to examine the simultaneous influence of different kinds of identity hierarchies on a specific emotion: jealousy.

Jealousy is an emotion that is experienced when one perceives or actually experiences a threat or actual loss of a relationship to a third party, often seen as a "rival" or "intruder" (White and Mullen 1989). Applying this idea to the family, Ellestad and Stets suggested that a mother may feel threatened when the father begins to take over caretaker activities typically performed by the mother. Even though a woman may not discourage her spouse from becoming more involved in childrearing, she may be sensitive to how much he becomes involved. The more he gets involved in childrearing, the more she may feel a threat to her primary role as caretaker.

The researchers anticipated that women with a more prominent mother identity, that is, who highly value their identity as caretaker, would feel threatened when their spouse became involved in areas traditionally reserved for her. These areas include activities related to intimate interaction such as nurturance, close attachment, and ongoing attention to a child. Such activities stand in contrast to the more typical father-child interactions revolving around play. Indeed, children often regard fathers as good playmates. Ellestad and Stets anticipated that women with a highly prominent mother identity would feel threatened when they perceive their husbands intruding into their "domain." This threat would reveal itself in the emotion of jealousy.

The researchers also examined the salience of the mother identity. They hypothesized that since identity salience is the likelihood of engaging in *behavior* that is consistent with identity meanings across situations, the more salient the mother identity, the more a woman would try to engage in *coping strategies* designed to reduce the negative effect of jealousy when she feels it. Since coping strategies are designed to manage negative feelings (Lazarus and Folkman 1984), a mother might devise various strategies to reduce her unpleasant feelings, such as spending more time with her child. In doing this, she would be attempting to reassert her role as the principle nurturer, thereby maintaining the mother identity.

Ellestad and Stets used a sample of parents at a number of daycare centers in the Northwest. Mothers and fathers responded to a series of hypothetical situations in which the father intrudes into different mother-child interactions. The parents were to identify how the woman in the story would feel if this occurred and how she would respond given her feelings. The results provided strong support for the fact when the mother identity was more prominent for the woman, she was more likely to report that the woman in the story would experience feelings associated with jealousy. Further, when the mother identity was more salient for the woman, she was more likely to identify coping strategies that the woman in the story might use to reduce the negative feelings associated with the intrusion of the father.

Ellestad and Stets discussed the fact that although a prominent identity is linked to the covert feeling state, identity salience is reflected in individuals' overt coping behavior designed to manage the emotion. Negative emotions indicate a lack of confirmation of a prominent identity. Coping strategies women employ help reassert their identity when it has been challenged. They help foster ways to reduce the negative affect associated with the disconfirmation, with the result that the identity is reaffirmed in the interaction. The thesis that negative emotion stems from a lack of identity-verification is evident in the perceptual control emphasis in identity theory, which we turn to next.

The Perceptual Control Emphasis

The structural and perceptual emphases in identity theory do not differ significantly in how emotions are incorporated into an analysis of identities. The primary difference is in examining emotions by way of the salience hierarchy of identities (in the structural emphasis) or within the control system model (in the perceptual emphasis). In the control model, emotion signals the degree of correspondence between perceptions of the self in the situation and identity-standard meanings (Burke 1991; 1996). Continuous correspondence or identity-verification produces positive emotion, and noncorrespondence or identity-nonverification produces negative emotions. For example, on the one hand, if one sees herself as strong, and she sees that others agree with this view of her in a situation, she will feel good about herself, and she will continue to act in a strong manner. On the other hand, if she sees herself as strong, but she sees that others view her as weak, she will feel bad, and she will increase the "strength" of her performance in order to maintain perceptions of herself as strong.

This idea is similar to the structural version discussed above in which role performances that meet the expectations of others will generate positive affect, while the failure to meet role expectations will generate negative affect. Thus, the idea of a lack of support from others for a role performance is analogous to the idea of nonverification. However, there is one difference. In the perceptual control model, negative emotions emerge even when self-perceptions in the situation go beyond the meanings in the identity standard, as when others see a person as "stronger" than how she sees herself. In the structural version, Stryker does not discuss the valence of the emotions if expectations are exceeded. He simply states the role-performance failure produces negative affect. However, a failure at role performance can involve exceeding one's standard as well as not meeting one's standard, in which case the structural version would be similar to the perceptual version on emotions.

In the perceptual control model, when there is a discrepancy between identity-standard meanings and perceived meanings of the self in a situation, this "error" leads to negative feelings for individuals. In turn, the negative feelings motivate individuals to bring the system under conscious control and remedy the nonverifying state (Burke 1991). Therefore, individuals will engage in various strategies to get out of the negative state and establish a verifying state. They may do something different in the situation that produces new meanings and feedback that verifies their identity. Alternatively, they may disattend to others' feedback or reinterpret others' feedback so they can see themselves as verified in the situation. In later work, these various behavioral and cognitive strategies are labeled *coping responses* (Burke 1996). Again, the goal is to realign perceptions of the meanings of the self in the situation, with the meanings held in the identity standard so that individuals experience positive emotions.

In both the structural and perceptual control emphases, the intensity of emotions is discussed. As mentioned earlier, Stryker maintains that intense emotions result when actors are not able to enact highly positive identities or deny highly negative identities. In turn, this decreases commitment to that identity. Similarly, in the perceptual control emphasis, intense emotions result from the disruption of a more *salient* identity and also a more *committed* identity (Burke 1991). When individuals' salient identities and committed identities are not verified, individuals will experience more intense negative emotions. In addition to salient and committed identities, two other factors influence more intense emotions. These include the *frequency* by which an identity is disrupted and the *significance of the source* of the disruption.

Frequent interruptions in the identity-verification process will produce more intense negative feelings compared to infrequent interruptions (Burke 1991). This happens irrespective of whether the nonverification is in a positive direction (self-perceptions in the situation surpass the identity standard) or a negative direction (self-perceptions in the situation do not meet the standard) (Burke and Harrod 2005). As discussed in chapter 4, the idea that more intense negative feelings are associated with frequent interruption in the identity control system is founded on the interruption theory of stress (Mandler 1982). According to Mandler, we experience distress when our normal activity is disrupted. The distress indicates that something is not right, and a person responds by attempting to adapt so that ongoing activity can resume. The more repeated the interruption, the more the actor is unable to initiate and sustain whatever he or she is doing, and the more distress will be felt.

In the perceptual control emphasis, the frequency of an interruption is the frequency of identity-nonverification. Recall that in chapter 4 we discussed the different types of interruption that can occur in the identity control system that can produce negative emotions. These include one's behavior not having the intended effect of returning the identity to a verifying state, or the inability to maintain multiple identities in a situation, because maintaining one identity simultaneously undermines the maintenance of another identity. An example of the latter would occur when an employer must discipline an employee who is also the employer's friend. The disciplinary action may support the employer identity but undermine the friend identity. Further, there is the interruption that occurs for identities that are played out infrequently. If individuals do not have enough practice in presenting an identity, they may not know how to respond in order to achieve identity-verification when identity-nonverification occurs. In any of the above types of interruptions, the more often they occur, the more intense the negative feelings.

The *source* of a disruption in the identity control system is another important factor. An interruption from a significant other would lead to more intense negative feelings than an interruption from a nonsignificant other (Burke 1991). Significant others would include family, friends, and other close associates. These others are people with whom one has built a set of mutually verified expectations. Past and present interactions result in each actor supporting the other's identity. Further, the meanings that have been built up form a tightly organized system as opposed to a loosely organized system. In addition, more tightly organized identities will lead to greater negative emotions, if interrupted. This is consistent with the assumption in interruption theory that the interruption of a more highly organized process will lead to higher levels of autonomic arousal (Mandler 1982). An example of identity meanings that are more tightly organized might be a parent identity that contains meanings of being dictatorial and controlling compared to a loosely organized parent identity containing meanings of being laissez-faire and relaxed. When the dictatorial parent identity is interrupted, it will be more likely to lead to negative emotions than if the laissez-faire parent identity is interrupted. Again, the identity meanings among significant others are more likely to be tightly organized, thereby producing greater negative feelings.

Research Using the Perceptual Control Emphasis

There has been a significant amount of work within the perceptual control emphasis that has examined emotions. We begin with a discussion of hypotheses on emotions.

In a series of laboratory studies, Stets (2003; 2004; 2005; Stets and Asencio 2008; Stets and Osborn 2008) tested several hypotheses regarding the role of emotions in the identity control system (Burke 1991). The basic design of these laboratory studies was simulating a work situation that invoked the worker identity. Essentially, participants as "workers" carried out three simple tasks, and after each task, they received feedback from a "manager" that either was: (1) expected, given their work (identity-verification), (2) more positive than what was expected (identity-nonverification in a positive direction), or (3) more negative than what was expected (identity-nonverification in a negative direction). Participants always heard from the manager that they accomplished "average" work. Feedback on their work was in the form of points earned for their work. In conditions in which their identity was verified, the manager gave them the expected number of points for average work. For identity-nonverification in a positive direction, the manager gave the workers more points than they expected to get for average work. For identity-nonverification in a negative direction, the workers received fewer points than they expected to get for average work. Workers reported their emotional responses to the different feedback conditions.

The simulations that Stets studied are analogous to many situations in our own lives in which the meanings of feedback we receive from others fall short of the meanings in our identity standard, confirm our identity-standard meanings, or exceed the evaluative meanings in our identity standard. At our job, our employer may give us a pay raise that we expect and we think that we deserve. We are satisfied when we get it. However, sometimes our pay raise may be less than what we expect. Alternatively, it may be more than what we expect. How do we react to this nonverifying situation? How do we feel, and why do we feel this way? In our personal lives, our friends or family members may frequently verify how we see ourselves, but there are times when they may criticize us or shower us with praise and admiration. When we hear this criticism or praise, what are we feeling, and why are we feeling this way? It is difficult for researchers to study these naturally occurring events. They do not have easy access into the lives of individuals in which they could study people's emotional reactions to experiences of identity-nonverification. In Stets's studies, we get a sense as to how individuals are emotionally responding to the verification process (or the lack of it). In turn, the patterns that she found and the ideas she offered for these patterns give us some insight into "what" people are feeling and "why" they are feeling it in the natural setting.

Consistently, Stets has found across her studies that although individuals who received feedback that fell short of their identity standard reported negative emotions, those who received feedback that exceeded their identity standard did not report negative emotions. Instead, they reported positive emotions. This is inconsistent with the identity theory hypothesis (Burke 1991) and stands in stark contrast to other research that used a sample of newly married couples and found that those who experience spousal identity-nonverification reported negative emotions irrespective of whether spousal identity meanings in the situation were overly positive or overly negative (Burke and Harrod 2005).

Stets argued that the theoretical process of enhancement may explain why positive feelings initially emerge for nonverifying feedback in a positive direction. The enhancement process affirms feeling good about oneself and one's world (Sedikides, Gaertner, and Toguchi 2003; Swann 1990). In contrast, the consistency process, from which the identity-verification process derives, affirms a congruent view of oneself and the predictability of one's surroundings. People engage in the enhancement process by simply sorting information into good/positive and bad/negative (Swann 1990). Individuals appear to welcome information that is good (such as a positive feedback) and avoid information that is bad (such as negative feedback). In contrast, the consistency process entails additional mental work. Individuals not only have to categorize the information as good or bad but also must retrieve from memory their identity standard along the dimension of the outcome and then compare that standard with the outcome they receive. This involves additional "steps" (retrieval and comparison) not found in enhancement. In general, the enhancement response is subject to an "automatic process," and the consistency response is subject to a "deliberative process."

The enhancement process may be more likely to occur between uninvolved partners in the laboratory than between married couples. In marriage, the individuals may be motivated to process feedback more thoroughly because the other person and the relationship are important to them compared to the less intimate relationship with a relative stranger in the laboratory. Additionally, in Stets's studies, she might have simulated less committed identities. Participants may not have been highly committed to the worker identity. Consequently, less committed identities initially may be more subject to affective (enhancing) responses of feeling good than to cognitive (consistency) responses of identity-verification. This suggests two situational factors that influence how individuals respond to nonverifying identity feedback: the nature of the actors' relationship in the situation and the degree of commitment they have to the identities in the situation.

Stets's laboratory studies also revealed that as workers repeatedly experienced nonverification, their negative emotions became less intense rather than more intense as predicted by identity theory (Burke 1991). However, Stets found that the dampening of negative emotions only occurred when the meanings in the situation fell short of the meanings in one's identity standard. Stets suggested that individuals may be experiencing some identity change (see next chapter) and are adjusting their identity standards to the feedback they receive. Since a strong emotional reaction would signal a discrepancy between the identity feedback and the identity standard, a weaker emotional reaction over time suggests a closer correspondence between the two. Why would people change their identity standards in the laboratory when feedback falls short of their standard?

It is possible that individuals are not as committed to the identities that are created in a laboratory setting. Greater commitment to an identity leads individuals to work harder in order to maintain a high level of correspondence between self-in-situation meanings and identity-standard meanings by trying to change the responses of others rather than by adjusting the identity standard down (Burke and Reitzes 1981). Alternatively, as we saw in chapter 4, research reveals that if individuals receive feedback that is inconsistent with how they see themselves but are given no opportunity to refute this feedback, they are more likely to align their subsequent view of themselves to the feedback (Swann and Hill 1982). In Stets's laboratory study, participants were not given the opportunity to refute the feedback that they received on their performance. If they had been given the opportunity to interact with the manager and express how they felt about the feedback, they may not have adjusted their standard, and their emotional responses may have been much more intense.

Further, intense emotional arousal to frequent nonverifying feedback may not occur if the feedback is stable and individuals know there is nothing they can do to change the feedback. Indeed, in Stets's study, when participants received persistent, nonverifying feedback, they always received less than what they expected no matter how hard they worked on the task. Thus, workers may have acclimated to the lower amount of points because there was nothing they could do to change their outcomes. This is similar to a state of "learned helplessness" that individuals experience in which they passively resign when they are exposed to stable, uncontrollable events that block their goals (Peterson, Maier, and Seligman 1993). It is common for individuals to experience such situations and resign themselves to it. For example, people often are underpaid, or they are passed over for a promotion. If they do not remove themselves from such situations, over time, they may come to see themselves as less competent and therefore deserving of the feedback.

Studying Moods

Burke (2004b) extended research on emotions in identity theory by studying moods. Moods are different from emotions in that they usually last longer than an emotion, they are lower in intensity, and they are more diffuse and unfocused (Frijda 1993). In terms of being diffused and unfocused, whereas emotions generally are seen to be about something such as being angry at someone or happy about something, moods have no specific target or object. This does not mean that moods do not have a cause; only that the feelings are more imprecise.

Burke examined the two dimensions of mood: unease/distress and activity/arousal. The first reflected the positive-negative or tense-calm dimension of feeling. If an identity is not being verified, one should feel unease/distress. The second reflected the tired-energetic dimension of feeling and is a function more of the natural biological rhythms of the day as well as sugar intake, exercise, and drugs such as caffeine. According to Burke, to the extent that individuals feel unease/distress because of the lack of identity-verification, they subsequently should feel a reduction in the level of their activity/arousal. Indeed, feelings of distress can be taxing and drain individuals, thereby lowering their level of activity.

Using a sample of newly married couples over the first three years of marriage, Burke found that persons who had problems verifying an important identity such as spouse, friend, or worker showed higher levels of unease/distress and lower levels of activity/arousal. The good thing is that the negative mood did not last beyond a day or two. However, if the identity disconfirmation persists, so would the negative mood.

Burke's examination of unease/distress and activity/arousal are analogous to the distinction that Higgins makes in self-discrepancy theory among identity-verification and agitation-related emotions such as anxiety and dejection-related emotions such as depression (Higgins 1987; 1989). Higgins distinguishes between the ought-self (identity expectations held by others about how one ought to be) and the ideal-self (identity expectations held by the self as to how one wishes or hopes to be). He maintained that the lack of verification of the ought-self led to symptoms of distress and anxiety, while the lack of verification of the ideal-self led to depressed symptoms. In a series of studies, Marcussen and Large (Large and Marcussen 2000; Marcussen 2006; Marcussen and Large 2003) have combined Higgins's self-discrepancy theory with Burke's identity control theory to develop identity discrepancy theory (IDT). IDT attempts to predict anxiety from an identity discrepancy in terms of obligations and depression from an identity discrepancy in terms of aspirations. Their results have shown some support for this connection.

Specific Emotions

As indicated earlier, in identity theory, as in most theories that study emotions, the emphasis has been primarily on positive-negative emotions while ignoring the complexity of human emotions that individuals experience (Turner and Stets 2005). Researchers using identity theory have begun to study the various kinds of emotions that individuals may feel in different situations. For example, Stets and Tsushima (2001) investigated whether two different types of identities—the family identity as a social identity and the worker identity as a role identity—are equally likely to result in the negative emotion of *anger* when they are not verified. As discussed in chapter 6, social identities are those identities in which individuals define themselves in terms of their membership in a group. In contrast, role identities are those identities in which individuals define themselves in terms of their role positions in groups and organizations.

Using a national sample, Stets and Tsushima found that the nonverification of group-based identities such as the family identity affected individuals deeply given the strong ties among group members. Consequently, people experienced intense anger when they did not receive support from family members. Alternatively, the nonverification of role-based identities such as the worker identity did not affect a worker as strongly, because the bond among coworkers was not as close. Therefore, individuals experienced less intense anger when they did not receive support from coworkers. The fact that more intense anger emerged in the family identity compared to the worker identity is consistent with the idea that identity disruptions from significant others are more distressful as predicted by identity theory (Burke 1991).

In other work, Stets and Burke (2005b) theorized about how the process of making an internal or external attribution in a situation might influence the different emotional responses individuals have to an identity disruption. When individuals blame themselves (internal attribution) for not being able to verify their identity standards, negative feelings are directed inward. For example, Jane might feel *disappointed* when the meaning of her student identity involves helping a friend pass a course, yet she is unable to provide the help because she is too busy with her own courses. Alternatively, Jane might feel *embarrassed* if her student identity also involved being academically successful, and yet she does poorly on an exam. When actors blame others for an identity disruption in a situation, this is an external attribution because they see another as responsible for the disruption in the verification of their identity. Consequently, they will direct their negative feelings outward onto others. For example, Jane may get *angry* with her friend if the friend does not show up for a meeting in which Jane was going to help the friend with a class. Alternatively, Jane may get *annoyed* if she does poorly on an exam because the instructor wrote a bad exam.

The attribution process might also influence the different emotions individuals experience in a situation when taking into account individuals' positions in the social structure in terms of their status and power relative to the other in the interaction (Stets and Burke 2005b). For example, for two interactants (A and B), A can have higher status compared to B, equal status with B, or lower status than B. If A is responsible for not being able to verify her identity, and if the relative status of B is lower than A in a situation, A might feel slight *uneasiness*. Alternatively, A might feel *shame* if this occurs when interacting with a higher-status B. For example, if Dr. Jackson is lecturing in class and says something in error, he will feel *discomfort* in front of his students. If he is presenting his research to his colleagues at a colloquium series, and he is unable to answer a question about his statistical results, he will feel *embarrassed*. If the audience members are administrators at his institution who have control over his salary increase, he will feel *sadness*.

When others rather than the self are responsible for one's identity discrepancy, the emotions stem from the external attribution process. Here, the emotions are strong when the other in the situation is of lower status or power, and the feelings are mild when the other in the situation is of higher status or power. Indeed, there is more at stake whether the other has more status or power than the self does. Continuing with the example above, if Dr. Jackson is lecturing in class, a student may disrupt his ability to continue by heckling him or interrupting him repeatedly. In that case, Dr. Jackson may feel *hostility*. If his dean does this, Dr. Jackson may feel *fear*.

Another way of studying the specific emotional outcomes that can emerge in a situation is by considering the different types of identities actors take on in interaction (Stets and Burke 2005b). In chapter 6, we discussed how actors have social identities given their membership in different groups, role identities given their participation in various role relationships, and person identities as they define themselves as a unique entity. Recall that when social identities are verified, it leads to feelings of worth, acceptance, and inclusion by others in the group. When role identities are verified, it signifies that one is competent since the individual has met the expectations of self and other while in that role. Finally, when a person identity is confirmed, feelings of authenticity emerge because the individual is meeting his or her own expectations and aspirations.

When a social identity is not verified, there is the threat of rejection from the group. For example, when a young teen skips school, becomes sexually active, and engages in other deviant acts such as underage drinking or drug use, the parents may threaten to disown the teen. If the teen's identity as a member of the "Jones family" is low in salience and prominence, he might feel *embarrassed* when he hears this threat from his parents. In other words, if being a family member is not that salient or important to him, his emotional reaction to not having this identity verified is mild. However, if his identity as a family member of the "Jones'" is salient and prominent, he might feel *shame* in response to his parent's threat. Both embarrassment and shame focus on a negative evaluation of the self for not meeting up to the expectations of others (Tangney and Dearing 2002; Tangney, Miller, Flicker, and Barlow 1996). In turn, the emotions encourage the person to do something about the identity disruption and obtain verification so that one remains a group member.

As mentioned in chapter 6, role identities pertain to one's actions rather than to one's inclusion in a group. Thus, the emotional outcomes related to nonverification of a role identity should focus on having done something that disrupts the identity-verification process. Indeed, guilt and its family of related emotions involve having done a bad thing (Tangney and Dearing 2002). If one's identity is low in salience and prominence, the person may feel *discomfort*; and when the identity is high in salience and prominence, the person may feel *guilt*. In the above example, if the teen's identity as "son" is important to him, and he tries hard in being a "good son," then he may feel *guilt* when he enacts delinquent behaviors because the meanings of these actions do not verify being a "good son." Recognizing one's role in the identity disruption process should motivate the actor to restore identity-verification and prevent future disruptions from arising.

Finally, person identities relate to verifying the "real self." They involve confirming the kind of person one wants to be, whether that is being kind or unkind, responsible or lazy, friendly or unfriendly and so forth. The identity standard can be positive or negative. Indeed, people do take on negative identities, and they seek to have these negative identities verified. Like social and role identities, higher identity salience and prominence to person identities should relate to stronger emotional responses to problems in verification. When the identity is low in salience and prominence, occasional *sadness* should occur for identity-nonverification, while *depression* should emerge when the identity is high in salience, prominence, and commitment. Returning to the above example, if being a "responsible person" is important and salient, the meanings of the delinquent behaviors do not verify this person identity, and he should feel depressed. The inward focus of emotions such as sadness and depression help motivate changes in behaviors so that the meanings will eventually correspond to identity-standard meanings.

Specific emotions can ensue in still another way: through a "mutual verification" context (Stets and Burke 2005b). Mutual verification contexts involve two or more actors who mutually support one another by verifying their own identities and, in doing so, help in the process of verifying the identities of others in the situation. For example, a married couple often develops a mutual verification context in which each partner verifies his or her own spousal identity and in doing so helps maintain the spouse's identity (Burke and Stets 1999). We have found that such mutual verification contexts as marriage result in positive emotions such as love and feelings of trust and commitment (Burke and Stets 1999). However, a disruption can occur in a mutually verifying context. The disruption can be small and minor or large and problematic. When identity discrepancies are small in a mutually verifying context, the individuals within the verifying context should get *annoyed*. If the identity discrepancies are large and persistent, and one person is responsible for the disruption, this person should get *depressed*, and the other(s) in the context should get *angry*.

In the above, the attribution process is again operating. When a person evaluates another as responsible for an identity disruption, the person directs his negative feelings outward toward that other. This is anger. When a person judges himself as responsible for the identity disruption, he directs the negative emotion inward against the self. This is depression. The emotions of anger and depression are strong negative feelings because the mutual verification situation is a well-established identity process that has been interrupted. The interruption of well-established identity processes is more distressful than interruption of less well-established processes (Burke 1991). For example, the large and persistent disruption of a five-year marriage will generate stronger negative emotions than the large and persistent disruption of a three-month dating relationship.

Moral Emotions

Moral emotions are a special case of specific emotions. Stets and her collaborators have examined four major moral emotions: *anger, empathy, shame, and guilt* (Stets, Carter, and Fletcher 2008a; Stets, Carter, Harrod, Cerven, and Abrutyn 2008). Like the research on specific emotions mentioned above, this research on moral emotions moves the role of emotions in identity theory beyond its current boundaries. Emotions are more than just positive or negative feelings. When individuals violate a cultural code or observe another violating a norm, they can experience moral emotions. Moral emotions are actors' response to violations of what is normative, appropriate, or the expected way to behave in a situation.

Stets and her colleagues have examined how moral emotions are related to one's moral identity. The moral identity is a person identity in which the meanings involve sustaining the self as a good/bad entity. Since, according to identity theory, one's identity and behavior are linked through a common system of meaning (Burke 1980; Burke and Reitzes 1981), the moral identity should guide normative behavior compared to counternormative behavior. In other words, if individuals think of themselves in terms of being a good person, this should influence them to do good things rather than bad things. Indeed, research supports the relationship between claiming a moral identity and having a higher propensity to engage in normative rather than counternormative behavior (Stets and Carter 2006; Stets, Carter, and Fletcher 2008a).

Stets and her associates have found, consistent with identity theory, that when individuals with a high moral identity *perceive* that others in the situation do not see them as acting as moral persons, this lack of verification as to who they are brings about feelings of shame and guilt. Stets and her associates also have found that how one *behaves* in a situation influences the verification of their identity. If individuals for some reason act counternormatively while claiming the moral identity, this noncorrespondence between how they have acted and how they should have acted also brings about the moral emotions of guilt or shame. Thus, an identity discrepancy in the situation between input (perceptual) meanings and the identity standard as well as output (behavior) meanings and the identity standard influences moral feelings.

More generally, by studying moral emotions, we get an idea as to what individuals and others value. When one's values are verified, it helps sustain the larger moral order within which the self and her standards are embedded. When one's values are not verified, feelings of shame or guilt help in the development of the self to the extent that individuals learn about themselves, including modifying future actions and moving toward reuniting with the group and sharing the values of the group. In this way, moral emotions monitor one's own behavior when others are not able to monitor it for the person. This makes social order, the moral order, possible.

Conclusion

It wasn't until the 1970s that sociologists began to systematically study emotions (Stets et al. 2008; Turner and Stets 2005), and it took identity theorists another twenty years after that to begin to conceptualize the self and identity in emotional terms rather than strictly cognitive terms. Although identity theorists have been late to recognize the importance of emotions, they have made significant inroads theoretically and empirically in recent years. We now know, for example, that individuals emotionally react negatively when they perceive that they are not being or acting in accord with their identity standard. This negative feeling motivates individuals to do something in the situation to get rid of the negative feeling and to obtain identity-verification. We are less clear as to how a person emotionally reacts when feedback from others in a situation exceeds one's identity standard. Laboratory findings differ from what we find in the natural setting. Future research will have to resolve this inconsistency.

Identity theorists are making efforts to move beyond an analysis of positive-negative emotions to make predictions about specific emotions, including moral emotions. This opens the analysis to a rich array of feelings that individuals experience within and across situations. It facilitates greater precision regarding how individuals are responding to identity-nonverification. Further, it directs identity theorists to additional processes such as internal and external attributions that need to be taken into account when understanding one's emotional experiences. Future research for identity theorists involves systematically examining the contextual factors that interact with the verification process to produce different emotions.

9

Identity Change

Identities are defined by the meanings held in the identity standard. Identity change, therefore, implies that the meanings held in the standard are changing. Identity theory suggests, as we discussed in chapter 7, that the multiple identities people have are arranged in a hierarchical control system. We mentioned at the time that this hierarchical system was central to understanding identity change because the changing output of a higher-level identity control system is the changing standard for a lower-level identity. In this chapter, we elaborate on this and take up two related issues: we examine how identity theory deals with identity change, and we examine how identity theory understands the origins of identity standards and the meanings they contain. In addition, we also look at some research that has explored each of these concerns. We will begin with an exploration of identity change.

Identity Change

Until now, we have primarily talked about the identity-verification process: the process by which people act to change relevant meanings in the situation to bring them into alignment with the meanings held in their identity standard(s). For these discussions, we have implicitly assumed that the identity meanings as held in the standard were constant and unchanging. This assumption, however, was a simplification that made the earlier discussions easier to follow. In fact, identity theory assumes that identity meanings are always changing. However, the rate at which they change is generally assumed to be very slow compared to the action outputs designed to change situational meanings and provide verification. The change in identity meanings is not noticeable except over longer periods ranging from weeks to months or even years. When asked, for example, people will admit they are the same as they were yesterday, but also when asked, they will say they are not the same as they were ten years ago. Nor, for the most part, can they identify when they changed. For most people, the change is gradual and cumulative over some period.

We indicated in chapter 7 that the hierarchical nature of the identity control system was what made change both possible and inevitable. The hierarchical nature of the identity control system in fact accounts for both the stability of our identities over time and the changes that can and do occur. This has always been a puzzle. Many symbolic interactionists have argued that identities are fluid and changing, some even arguing that identities are constructed anew in every situation (Blumer 1969). If that were true, however, we might ask why we don't see many changes in person's identities except over a long span of time. Our argument, as outlined in chapter 4, is that identities, through the verification process, *resist* change. Identities act to change the situation to bring situationally relevant meanings into alignment with the meanings in the identity, thus verifying and supporting the existing self-meanings. Because of this resistance to change, there is stability. However, resisting change is not the same as sustaining no change. The meanings in identity standards do change, but as a general rule, they change very slowly. There are some exceptions to this slowness rule that will be discussed later in the chapter, things such as brainwashing or the changes sometimes sustained by kidnap victims or the changes that might occur when one has an epiphany.

Figure 9.1 reproduces part of the hierarchical structure of identities within a person. The relationship between these two identities is a bit complicated, but it illustrates how the higher-level identity (H) leads to change in the lower-level identity (L). Identity L, the lower identity, is a control system that acts on the meanings in the situation (symbols and resource flows) to bring perceptions of them into alignment with the meanings in its (identity L's) standard. The standard of identity L, which is the set of meanings that defines the identity and serves as a reference for adjusting perceptions, is itself an output of identity H, the higher identity. Identity H is a control system that acts to control its perceptions by altering the standard of identity L in such a way that the behaviors of identity L that act to control its perceptions also alter the meanings that identity H perceives/controls. In this sense, identity L is an agent for identity H. Identity H gets identity L to act (by slowly adjusting its standard) so that the meanings identity H perceives are brought into alignment with identity H's standard. Identity H's perceptions are controlled by identity L, as are identity L's perceptions. Relative to the lower identity (L), the higher identity (H) operates at a much slower pace. This provides stability for the standard of the lower identity because any change in identity L's standard is slow relative to its actions/

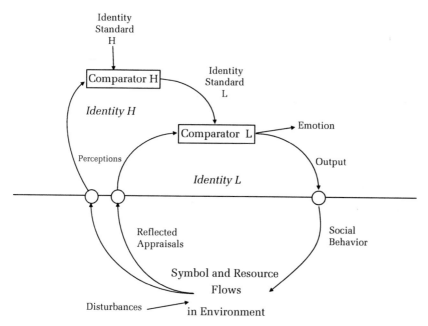

Figure 9.1. Model for Two Hierarchically Arranged Identities within a Person

outputs. Identity change is thus ubiquitous. An identity standard is not fixed and static. It is the (slowly) varying output of an identity at the next level up in the control hierarchy of identities as illustrated in figure 9.1.

For example, Mary has identities as both a wife (spouse identity) and a female (gender identity). One's gender identity is often what is called a master identity; as a high-level identity, it helps set the standard of other lower-level identities. Mary's gender identity is fairly nontraditional, and in order to verify this identity, Mary must make meanings relevant to this identity in the situation consistent with her identity standard.

Mary's spousal identity also needs to be verified when it is activated, so she will act in ways that are consistent with the meanings in the spousal identity standard. Now, if those ways of satisfying her spousal identity standard include gender meanings that do not verify the nontraditional gender meanings held in her gender identity standard, the higher-level perceptions of her gender meanings will not match the gender identity standard. As a result, over time, the output of the gender identity will alter the spousal identity standard so that behaviors that satisfy her spousal identity standard will also satisfy her gender identity standard. The higher-level gender identity has modified the standard of the lower-level spousal identity in order to control the higher-level perceptions.

Although not indicated in the figure, we should point out that identity H, the higher identity, generally controls a number of lower-level identities. Thus, Mary's gender identity may also modify other lower-level identity standards such as mother and teacher, so that the meanings produced in verifying these identities also satisfy the higher-level gender identity. In addition, perceptions controlled by identity H come both directly from the situation and from combinations and patterns of perceptions made by the many lower-level identities. For example, morality in the context of a moral identity is not seen in any particular action but exists in the patterns of actions across a variety of situations. In this way, identity H controls patterns of perceptions across a number of dimensions, with each dimension being controlled by a different lower-level identity.

In addition, each lower identity, L, might have its standard consist of a combination of outputs from a number of higher identities. Burke (1997) explicitly modeled this by showing exactly how a two-level identity system could negotiate in an exchange situation, adjusting its output and the lower identity standard to meet situational exigencies. The model was similar to that in figure 9.1, except that it had three higher-level outputs to the lower-level identity standard. This model is illustrated in figure 9.2.

The lower-level standard controlled the point disparity between its own exchange offer and the exchange offer being made by the other identity. The lower-level identity perceived this point disparity as it unfolded in the immediate exchange situation. The behavior governed by this lower-level identity was the exchange offer being made by the identity. It could be raised or lowered. If this offer were accepted by another identity, an exchange would take place. If it were not accepted, no exchange would take place, and the identities in the model would continue to negotiate over the exchange. The standard for this lower-level identity was the output of the three higher-level control systems and was therefore constantly changing. If the standard changed and became lower (resulting in offering more to reduce the point disparity), an exchange would be more likely to be made. If the standard changed and became higher (increasing the point disparity), an exchange would be less likely to be made.

In this model, there were three identity control systems at the higher level. One of these sought to control the number of exchanges in which the identity would be involved and perceived that quantity in the situation. This standard was usually set at participating in 100 percent of the exchanges. If the perception of participation was not 100 percent, the output from this identity raised the lower standard to make higher offers that would increase the likelihood of being included in an exchange.

Another higher-level identity sought to control the length of time that it took to complete an exchange and perceived that length of time in the situation. The standard for this control system was set at zero, and as perceptions of elapsed time increased from zero, the discrepancy got larger. Because there was a three-minute time limit on each round of negotiation,

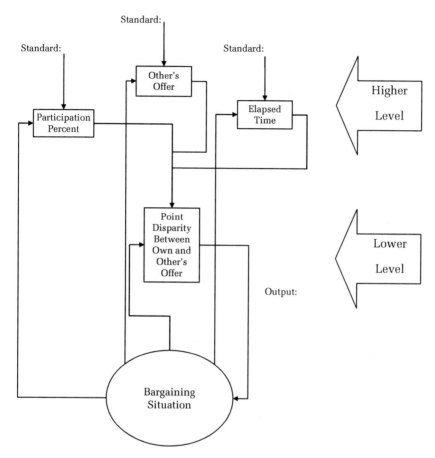

Figure 9.2. Model of Identity for Exchange Bargaining

an exchange that did not take place within the three minutes was lost, which counted against the goal of completing 100 percent of the exchanges. As time increased toward the three-minute mark, that is, as the discrepancy got larger, the error or output from this identity raised the lower-level standard to make higher offers and increase the likelihood of an exchange before time ran out.

A third higher-level identity sought to control the overall exchange price. Over time, as the other higher-level standards were satisfied, the output of this identity sought to raise the lower-level identity standard, lowering the offer price and increasing the profit.

Identity change in this model involved changes in the standard of the lower-level identity. This standard was for point-disparity between the identity's point offer and the exchange partner's identity's offer. If the identity was not involved in 100 percent of the exchange, one of the higher-level identities changed the lower-level standard to raise the offer and make exchanges more likely. If time was running out and an exchange had not been made, another higher-level identity changed the lower-level standard to raise the offer and make exchanges more likely. If the cost of an exchange was too high, the third higher-level identity changed the lower-level identity standard to lower the offer and make a better profit. The lower-level standard was thus constantly changing over time as it interacted with other identities in the exchange situation until all of the identities were verifying each other as much as possible and a stable set of interactions occurred.

Knowing that identity change involves changes in the identity standard and knowing that the identity standard of any identity is the output of a higher-level control system, however, does not tell us the conditions under which identities do change. Burke (2006a) outlines three general conditions under which identities change and illustrates those for the case of the spousal identity. These are: (1) changes in the situation that alter meanings of the self in the situation out of congruence with the identity standard, (2) conflicts between two identities (or more) held by an individual, and (3) conflict between the meanings of an individual's behavior and the meanings in their identity standard. Burke and Cast (1997) present a fourth condition, while Cast, Stets, and Burke (1999) present what could be seen as a special case of this fourth condition. We review these four conditions here. The first three all involve a discrepancy between perceptions and standard of the lower-level identity. This discrepancy leads to change in the output of the higher-level identity in order to control its perceptions and bring them back into alignment with the higher-level standards. The fourth is the result of the identity standard adapting or fitting into the situation—an adaptive response of the identity.

Four Sources of Change

Changes in the Situation

The first source of identity change we consider is the result of changes in a situation that disrupt meanings controlled by an identity in such a way that the changes cannot be countered by actions on the part of the lower identity shown in figure 9.1. Changes in the situational meanings result in a discrepancy between the identity-standard meanings and the self-relevant meanings in the situation. Because of this discrepancy, we know that people will experience some form of distress and uncertainty. Normally, people would attempt to restore the situational meanings to match the identity-standard meanings, but when this is not possible, the only thing that can reduce the discrepancy is for the identity standard to change to match the situational meanings. When that has occurred, there will no longer be a discrepancy, and the distress that was felt will disappear.

Burke and Cast (1997), for example, documented the changes in the meanings of the gender identities of newlywed husbands and wives that occur with the birth of their first child. This birth is an example of a change of identity-relevant meanings in the environment (a disturbance in the model) that persists and is not easily countered. Under these conditions, Burke and Cast found that the gender identity of husbands became somewhat more masculine, while that of wives became somewhat more feminine over the course of the year following the child's birth. The presence of a child changed the meanings in the interactional setting in a way that was not easily changed back or countered, thus leaving a continuing discrepancy between situationally self-relevant meanings and the meanings contained in the identity standards of the couple. This prolonged discrepancy over time allowed the standards of each of the identities to adjust slowly in a direction to match the perceptions of the new self-relevant meanings in the situation, thus slowly reducing the discrepancies over time toward zero. Burke and Cast suggest that this adjustment is probably neither conscious nor planned on the part of the husband and wife; rather, it is an adjustment their identities made without the full awareness of the individuals involved. The experience of the husband and wife is only that over time they become more comfortable with the new situation of the presence of a child in their lives. It is no longer new, strange, or disorienting.

A more dramatic example would be the case of abduction and the adjustments in one's identity that often accompany such a situation. One renowned case was that of Patty Hearst, granddaughter of the legendary newspaper publisher, William Randolph Hearst. She was kidnapped in 1974 by members of a group that called themselves the Symbionese Liberation Army (SLA). According to her own account, Patty was kept blindfolded for two months in a closet at the group's headquarters, unable even to use the bathroom in privacy. In captivity she was isolated and told no one would rescue her. She was physically and sexually abused and told she may die. The SLA members told her how they were oppressed by the establishment. Finally, she was forced to say things against the establishment and the people she loved. In two months, without the ability to verify her old identity, and being forced to act to confirm the new identity her captors gave her, she had a new identity and participated with the SLA in holding up a bank.

These treatments prevented Patty from verifying her former identity. Normal cues as to her identity and proper treatment were removed. All expectations about how she should be treated were violated. No behavior was allowed that served to maintain and verify her former identity. The only identity that she could verify was the one that the SLA provided for her, and so her identity changed.

Other examples of such dramatic changes abound: the American prisoners of war held by the Chinese during the Korean War (Schein 1957; 1958) and the stories of persons "brainwashed" by religious cults. Not all such stories are necessarily true, but enough have been documented to know that it does happen. Identity theory makes the process clear. This change of an identity standard to adjust to a situation over which people have little control is the first way in which identities change. It may be a small change, or it may be a large change, but it happens when perceptions of situational meanings cannot be brought into accord with the meanings in the identity standard.

Other situational changes that have profound effects would be winning the lottery and becoming instantaneously very rich, or conversely, suffering a robbery, a home burning down, living in a city like New Orleans that is devastated by a hurricane, or being removed from the city and not being able to go back. In each of these cases, people's behavior patterns are altered. The decisions they can and must make have important consequences. People may be uprooted from family, friends, and job and lose their normal means of verifying their identities. People become divorced, lose a job, suffer the death of a loved one, survive a terrible traffic accident, or are sent to prison. As a consequence of these types of occurrence, people's identities change, sometimes in unexpected ways. But, again, identity theory makes it clear what is happening in each case. The lack of ability to confirm and verify an identity leads to changes in identity standards, and those new standards are verified.

Less profound, and certainly more common, are the changes that occur because the context in which we play out an identity changes. There may be, for example, a shift in the resources available to a particular role identity. A manager in a growing company that is experiencing increases in its revenues may have more resources to hire more people or divide up the department into two or more functional units. These changes will necessitate changes in the standards for the manager identity. There will be new things to keep track of, new procedures to implement, and new relationships to develop with new employees.

In a similar way, a company that is experiencing losses in revenues may have to consolidate departments or divisions, lay off personnel, and reassign duties. Again, each of these changes means that identities will need to change as new goals, procedures, and standards are implemented. Additionally, promotions, transfers, changes in management, and changes in ownership are common in the workplace, but each will bring about changes in what is expected for a variety of roles and identities and changes in what it means to be the worker that one is.

This kind of exogenous change in situations bringing about changes in identity standards applies not only to role identities as we discussed above but also to social identities, what it means to be a member of a particular category or group. In this case, it is not the role within an organization that changes, but the definition of a group or category within the context of a larger society. In the case of ethnic identities, there are many sociopolitical processes at work. For example, the changes that took place with an influx in the number of Irish immigrating to this country in the early middle nineteenth century. As this group of people tried to fit into the existing society, the meaning of being Irish changed both in the eyes of the non-Irish as well as in the eyes of the Irish. Similar changes occurred for the Polish immigrating into the United States in the early to mid-twentieth century and for every other group that came to the United States willingly or unwillingly: the Koreans in the second half of the twentieth century and the Chinese from the time of the gold rush to the Chinese Exclusion Act in 1882, but then more recently, with the Immigration and Nationality Act of 1965, which brought in a new period in Chinese-American immigration. The changes in what it means to be an Italian-American, a German-American, or a Korean-American shift with the sociopolitical and economic changes that occur in the country. As divisions between groups become larger, meanings of membership in the different groups diverge. All of these are brought about by structural changes in the situations in which our identities are acted on.

Identity Conflicts

A second source leading to identity change exists when people have multiple identities that are related to one another in the sense that the standards of each contain the same dimensions of meaning, but they are set to different (conflicting) levels, and the identities are activated at the same time (Burke 2003; Deaux 1992; 1993; Stets 1995). For example, a man may have a gender identity that defines him as masculine, that is, as rough and tough. He may also have a role identity as a minister that defines him as gentle and caring. Without yet going into how this might come about, it is clear that if he controls perceptions of rough/gentle to match the standard for one identity, these same perceptions are discrepant with the standard for that other identity.

Role conflict and status inconsistency are examples of situations that may be interpreted as identity conflicts. Such conflicts between two identities may come about as a person takes on new role identities. For example, a possible conflict between gender and spousal identities may only come about as the person who had already evolved a comfortable gender identity becomes married and takes on the spousal identity. In a culture that is as diverse as American culture, meanings provided for different identities such as male and spouse may not be fully consistent. The meanings for gender may come from different cultural sources than the meanings for spouse. Mary's gender identity as a woman may suggest that she be strong and independent, but her wife identity may suggest that she let her husband take the lead in family matters. To the extent that these identities are activated at the same time and she cannot act on the basis of one of these identities without creating a discrepancy with respect to the other, then these identities are in conflict. She cannot reduce both discrepancies at the same time.

Continuing this example, as the conflict persists between these two identities of woman and wife, identity theory suggests that Mary will feel some level of distress because of the discrepancies. At the same time, the theory suggests that the identity standards for both her identities will shift slowly toward each other, becoming identical at some "compromise" position so that meaningful behavior can verify both identities at the same time. Mary may become less strong and independent in her gender identity, and she may at the same time become less likely to let her husband always take the lead in family matters. In this case, the meanings in both identity standards have shifted.

Now, one obvious question is, if both identities change, do they change to the same degree? Identity theory suggests that the extent to which each of the identity standards changes depends upon other factors such as the degree of *commitment* to each of the identities (Burke and Reitzes 1991; Burke and Stets 1999; Stryker and Serpe 1982), the degree of *salience* of each of the identities (Callero 1985; Stryker and Serpe 1982; 1994), and the degree to which each identity is tied to other identities in the full set of identities she holds (Burke 2003; Smith-Lovin 2003; Thoits 1986).

Elaborating on this, we suggest that because commitment reflects the number of ties to others because of an identity, stronger commitment means there are ties to more others. With more others expecting to see the meanings of that identity continually portrayed, it would be very costly to change that identity.

Similarly, with one identity being more salient than another, that is, more likely to be activated in a situation, there are many occasions making demands to have particular meanings portrayed. This makes it more difficult to change that identity standard. Finally, if one identity is tied to several others within the hierarchy, it would be less easily changed without disturbing those other identities compared to another identity that is tied to fewer other identities. Alignment among identities that is achieved with fewer adjustments is preferred.

The second source of identity change, then, is the adjustment among the multiple identities that individuals hold (or come to hold) as they take on new identities over time. This adjustment allows the different identities, to the extent that they control the same situational meanings and resources, to work in concert to bring those meanings into common alliance. The change is still governed by higher-level identities as they adjust their outputs to make this possible.

Identity Standard and Behavior Conflicts

The third source of identity change is a conflict between the meanings of one's behavior and the meanings in the identity standard. As we have already discussed, we normally choose behaviors whose meanings are consistent with our identity or whose meanings restore situational meanings to be consistent with our identity. However, as a former mentor and colleague often said, "Life is complex." We cannot always choose the behaviors and meanings we wish. There may be situational reasons for choosing a behavior that is somewhat at odds with our identity. As we have already mentioned, one reason may be that a behavior is at odds with one identity but in accord with another in the case of conflicting identities. However, another reason may be that we don't fully see the consequences of a behavior or a decision.

For example, suppose that Scott is a college basketball player of some repute and skill. He may have a professional contract waiting for him if he has a good season. Bill approaches Scott and makes a proposition. He tells Scott that if Scott will shave a few points off of tomorrow night's game to reduce the expected spread of points between Scott's team and the rivals, Bill will make a certain amount of money and would be willing to share $10 of his winnings with Scott. Of course, Scott would laugh in Bill's face. If Scott is caught, he will lose everything. And he is to do this for $10.

Bill then explains that he was joking. He would be willing to pay Scott $100 for his efforts to shave a few points from the game. Scott pays more attention but still has to refuse. This continues with increased offers and refusals until Bill says he is fronting for his uncle in Las Vegas and that there is a lot of money at stake. He is willing to make a final offer of $100,000. Now Scott is in a quandary. If he turns it down, he loses $100,000. If he takes it (and isn't caught) he loses his self-respect and his feelings that he is an honest person. As a result of this single decision, Scott could be a very changed person. Refusing the money, he may become self-righteous. He may feel he is so good because he refused $100,000 of bad money. Accepting the bribe, he has to justify this. Perhaps he says that is the only rational thing to do; that is how you get ahead; that is how everyone gets ahead; only suckers and losers would turn down the bribe; it is no big deal. Either way, these are big changes for Scott's basketball player identity. And it was nothing he set out to do. The offer was made, and he responded.

This, of course, is a dramatic change. Yet, people make hundreds of decisions everyday: to call in sick in order to do something other than go to work, not to go school on a school day, to fail to tell the cashier about the overpayment in returned change, to let a friend drive home drunk, and to run a red light. These are perhaps small changes, so their effect on one's identity is small. The situational meanings only shift a little. Yet, the higher identity shifts the standard ever so slightly in the direction implied by the chosen behavior, and this makes future behaviors in the same direction more likely and less inconsistent with the changing meanings in the identity standard. These slow, small changes cumulate over time, so that in five years or ten years we can look back and recognize how we have changed.

Negotiation and the Presence of Others

The fourth source in which identities change can be seen as part of an adaptive strategy inherent in identities that helps them establish what we have called mutual verification contexts, that is, situations in which the identities of each participant not only verify themselves but also help verify other participants' identities. As we pointed out in chapter 2, identities are partially formed by the process of taking the role of the other. As will be recalled from that discussion, role-taking is a process identified by Mead (1934), by which persons are able to put themselves into the shoes of another, so to speak, and look at themselves from the other's perspective. In this way persons can see and respond to themselves as a social object much as the other does and in this way see the expectations that the other has of the self. Mead gives the example of the child that cries and then (taking the role of the parent) soothes itself and is thereby soothed. Through this role-taking, the child comes to incorporate expectations of the parent within itself and through this comes to have its identity modified to include these expectations as standards. The child comes to understand how others respond to it and therefore the meanings of its own actions that lead to those responses. In this way the child comes to share the meanings of (responses to) its own actions.

The self can be altered to achieve desired and shared meanings as outcomes. Becoming aware of shared meanings and how to control them brings about greater identity-verification and mutual verification. As pointed out in chapter 2, taking the role of the other is the source of that understanding that becomes incorporated into the identity as a set of standards or guidelines for assessing (perceiving) one's own behavior. Taking the role of the other is thus a mechanism by which identities adapt to the social situation in interacting with others and facilitate the creation of mutual verification contexts in which each identity in verifying itself also verifies the identities of others in the situation.

Summary

We thus have four general sources of systematic identity change in identity theory: *persistent problems with the verification of a particular identity, multiple identities activated together whose verifications require opposing meanings to be manifest in the behavior of the individual, situational exigencies that result in our behavior having different meanings than those embedded in our identity standard*, and *role-taking, which allows us reflexively to change our identity standard to create mutual verification contexts*. The difference between the first two lies in the source of the conflict of meanings. In the first case, it is a disturbance to the meanings in the external situation making them perceived to be discrepant from the meanings of the identity standard. In the second case, it is an internal conflict manifest when two identities become activated at the same time, each controlling the same dimension of meaning but to different levels in their respective standards. This might happen when an identity developed in one context becomes activated in another context, for example, Alice trying to talk on the phone to her boyfriend while her husband is in the same room.

In the third case, the disturbance to situational meanings lies in our own behavior because we don't have full freedom in choosing that behavior; situational exigencies exist that push us in one direction or another. Nevertheless, the result is a discrepancy between the meanings in the situation and the meanings in the identity standard. In the fourth case, it is not necessarily a conflict of meanings, but an adjustment of identity meanings to take into account the identity and perspective of the other. Given each of these conditions, the meanings in the identity standard(s) are likely to change in the service of making identity-verification possible. Under these conditions, what it means to be who we are will change.

To make the first three sources of identity change more concrete, we consider a discrepancy or difference along the dimension of traditional femininity between the meanings in an identity standard and the identity-relevant meanings perceived in a situation. Let us say Mary, in her spouse identity, because of the responses of others to her (reflected appraisals), sees herself in the situation as being more traditionally feminine than she defines herself in her identity standard, that is, she is coming across as too traditionally feminine in her role as wife compared with her spousal identity standard. This discrepancy will have three effects for Mary. First, it will cause some discomfort. Second, it will cause Mary to change her behavior in ways that change the situational meanings (how she is coming across to others) to be less traditionally feminine. Third, at the same time, the discrepancy will slowly result in a change of the meanings held in Mary's identity standard to be more traditionally feminine, moving them closer to a match with the way she is coming across in the situation.

Additionally, other identities that share dimensions of meaning, for example, Mary's gender identity, will, if its standard is set to a different degree of masculinity/femininity, cause a change in the meanings in Mary's spousal identity standard. For example, if Mary sees herself in her gender identity as very feminine, while she sees herself in her spousal identity as only somewhat traditionally feminine, this will influence the degree of femininity of Mary's spousal identity, and the degree of femininity of Mary's spousal identity will influence the degree of femininity of her gender identity. When both identities are activated in the same situation, each will try to control perceived "femininity" meanings in the situation. If these are set at different points in each of the standards, each of the identities will interfere with the other, and neither can be verified until they each change to a level of "femininity" that works for both. One identity standard is telling Mary to be more feminine, while the other identity standard is telling Mary to be less feminine; there needs to be some compromise to allow verification of both identities and reduce the distress associated with not being able to verify either.

Finally, Mary may find that it is convenient for her to take on some of the more traditionally masculine tasks in the household, such as doing some of the household repairs or taking care of the yard. By engaging in these traditionally more masculine tasks, perhaps because her husband is incompetent at them or incapacitated in some way from doing them, Mary is engaging in more masculine behaviors than exist in her spousal identity. Again, there is a discrepancy, and if that discrepancy between situational meanings and identity-standard meanings is not reduced, she will come to see her spousal role identity in more masculine terms.

The mechanisms for these three sources of identity change are really the same: an identity cannot verify itself without in some way changing its standard. It may be that the problem that prevents the verification of an existing identity exists in the environment, such as the way others interpret her behavior; or it may be that the problem is in another identity interfering with the existing identity by trying to control the same meanings to different levels; or it may be that the situation calls for her behavior to convey other meanings, even if only temporarily.

Research on Identity Change

Burke (2006a) used data from newly married couples over the first two years of their marriage to test these ideas. He measured the meanings of each person's gender identity and the meanings of each person's spousal identity, each along a dimension of traditionally masculine to traditionally feminine. Although males and females differed on the average (males being more masculine and females being more feminine), there was variation among males and among females. Some males were more masculine than others; some were more feminine than others. There was similar variation among the females. These measurements were made at three points in time, each separated by a year. In this way, Burke was able to see changes over an extended time. In addition, he was able to measure the extent to which each person engaged in a variety of household activities that also varied along a dimension of traditionally masculine to traditionally feminine. As pointed out in that research, the actual activities were not important, but the meanings underlying them were important. For example, in our culture, working outside around the house on chores is a more masculine kind of activity, while doing the cooking and cleaning is a more feminine activity. The identity meanings (both spouse and gender) and the activity meanings were measured with high reliability.

The research began by looking at the effect of spousal identity meanings on household activity meanings, with the finding that persons with more feminine spousal identities engaged in more feminine household activities. This, of course, is consistent with the basic tenet that people engage in activities that correspond in meaning to the meanings of their identity. However, Burke also found that not everyone engaged in household activities that were totally consistent with their spousal identity meanings. Though generally small, the amount of discrepancy varied across people, so the question was raised as to the consequences of this discrepancy when it occurred.

As we discussed above, when a discrepancy occurs, two things happen. First, the person tries to counteract the disturbance and reduce the discrepancy by engaging in behavior that better reflects the identity meanings. At the same time, the identity meanings slowly change to be more like the perceived situational meanings. Burke (2006a) found both of these consequences. When persons with more feminine spousal identities engaged in more masculine household activities in one year, they reduced the level of masculinity in their household activities in the following year. And when persons with more masculine spousal identities engaged in more feminine household activities in one year, they increased the level of masculinity in their household activities in the following year. At the same time, Burke found that the spousal identities of those persons who were acting too masculine slowly became more masculine while the spousal identities of those who were acting too feminine became more feminine. In both cases, the identity meanings shifted over the year to match the behavior meanings when the two were not fully consistent. Both of these changes, to the situational meanings and to the identity meanings, had the consequence of reducing the discrepancy, as the theory suggests. People tried to move the situational meanings to be closer to the meanings of their identities, but the meanings of their identities became (slowly) closer to the situational meanings.

Because Burke (2006a) measured the meanings of both spousal identities as well as gender identities, he was also able to examine the effect that two identities that share meanings have on each other. As mentioned, both the gender identity and the spousal identity of each person in the study were measured along a dimension of traditionally masculine to traditionally feminine. Identity theory says that when one identity is different than another along the same dimension of meaning, the verification of one interferes with the verification of the other, and over time each will change to be like the other. Such changes will reduce that disparity between these meanings and allow both identities to be verified at the same time. This is, indeed, what Burke found in his study. Persons who had a more feminine gender identity in one year increased the femininity of their spousal identity in the next. Similarly, when the spousal identity of a person was more feminine than their gender identity in one year, the gender identity changed in the following year to be like the spousal identity. Each identity was being modified over time to bring the meanings into alignment.

Burke and Cast (1997) also examined identity change for the gender identities of these newly married couples over the first two years of marriage. Like the Burke study (2006a), they also looked at the consequences of unalterable changes in self-relevant meanings in the situation (in this case, the birth of the first baby). In addition, they looked at the effect of role-taking on the gender identities of the husbands and wives, the third factor that influences identity change discussed above.

Before looking at these sources of change in the respondent's gender identities, however, Burke and Cast simply examined the degree to which gender identities in fact changed over time. Even though the sex of the respondent was, of course, one of the big determinants of gender identity initially, they noted that once the respondent's gender identity had initially been formed, it has a strong persistence, meaning that it did not change substantially over time. They noted that the gender identities of the respondents did change perceptibly from one *year* to the next, but the amount of change over one *month* was hardly enough to be noticeable. They also pointed out that when changes in gender identity do occur, they are kept close to the average of meanings common to their sex. Males overall stay like males, and females stay like females even when changes occur. Thus, they note there is a great deal of stability in one's gender identity. While there is some change over the course of a year; that change is constrained by cultural beliefs to remain consistent with the cultural definitions for the meanings of male and female.

Burke and Cast (1997) next tested the idea that identities change to be more like perceptions of situational self-relevant meanings when those perceptions cannot be controlled through the verification process and made to correspond to the meanings in the identity standard. During the first two years of marriage over which data were collected, several of the couples had children born to them, and this was their first child. Burke and Cast reasoned that such a momentous event would have great meaning for both the husband and the wife. Becoming a mother or father represents a defining event with respect to gender identities (Fein 1976). Adding a baby to the family is a change in the situation that does not go away and cannot be countered. It thus represents an event that alters self-relevant meanings in the situation, for both the husband and wife, to which they must adjust.

And, as indicated earlier in the chapter, this is what Burke and Cast found. The gender identities of men on the average became more masculine after the birth of a child, while those of women became more feminine. Whether the child was born in the first or the second year of marriage, gender identities changed to become more like the new self-relevant meanings in the situation.

Burke and Cast (1997) also examined the third mechanism for identity change: taking the role of the other. As we indicated, this type of identity change comes about because of the adjustment process that identities go through in situations to create mutual verification contexts. Still looking at the gender identities of the newly married husbands and wives, Burke and Cast measured the degree to which each person took the role of their spouse and examined the impact of this on changes in the gender identity of each spouse.

They found that to the extent that both men and women took the role of their spouse, their gender identities became more like the gender identities of their spouse. The gender identities of men became more feminine, to the extent that they took the role of their wife; and the gender identities of women became more masculine, to the extent that they took the role of their husband. In each case, taking the role of the other changed the self, making each person's gender identity more like that of the spouse. This change worked equally for both men and women. Each, by understanding the role of the other in relation to the self, was transformed by that knowledge. These self changes facilitate interaction and verification. Commonalities across identities of masculine and feminine allow a common approach where possible, making mutual verification more likely.

Cast, Stets, and Burke (1999) looked at how the identity of one person can be shaped and changed by others with whom one interacts. They examined the spousal roles of newly married couples. They found that in the negotiation between husbands and wives to develop mutually complementary spousal identities and roles and to prevent the kinds of identity conflicts we spoke of earlier, there is some give and take in defining identity standards for husbands and wives. Cast, Stets, and Burke observed that what it means to be a husband or a wife changes over the first years of marriage. Husbands' views of what a wife should be influence the identities of wives. Also wives' views of what a husband should be influence the identities of husbands. However, they discovered that the influence in each direction was not necessarily equal. They found that whoever had the higher social status in terms of more education and a better job had more influence in defining the identity standard for the spouse. Higher-status wives had more influence on their husbands' identities than the reverse, and higher-status husbands had more influence on their wives' identities than the reverse. Only when the husband and wife had relatively equal status was the mutual influence equal in both directions. People with more power and status have more influence in defining the identities of those around them and are less influenced by those with less power or status.

Asencio and Burke (2008) looked at identity change among 124 incarcerated criminals who were involved in a rehabilitative program for criminals who were also dealing with substance abuse. Because the participants are part of a program, they are housed separately from the rest of the jail population and attend classes and counseling sessions. They also interact with one another more frequently than the offenders who are not in the program. They perform daily chores in cooperation with one another and interact as a group of students might when in the classroom setting. The program encourages them to provide moral and emotional support for one another in the quest to overcome drugs and come "clean." Because of this, these particular inmates tend to have a greater camaraderie among them than inmates in the general jail population have.

Three different identities were examined, with measures being taken at the beginning, after eight weeks, and again after another eight weeks. The three identities were a criminal identity, a drug-user identity, and a worker identity, and each respondent rated himself or herself on scales that reflected the degree to which they saw themselves as a criminal (versus law abiding), a drug user (versus not a drug user), and a worker (versus a nonworker). These self-appraisals indicate the identity standard for each of the three identities in question. Each of the respondents was also asked how others, including significant others (spouse and important family members) and peers (others in the same rehabilitative program), saw them in terms of each of these identities. These are the reflected appraisals.

With these data, Asencio and Burke examined three things. First, they looked at the change in each of the identities over time. Second, they looked at the influence of reflected appraisals on identities (does how you think others see you influence how you see yourself?) and the effect of changes in the reflected appraisals on the self-views over time. Finally, they looked at how self-appraisals influence reflected appraisals (as would be expected if people try to get others to see them the way they see themselves, thus allowing verification of the self-views).

Without going into all of the details of the study, these researchers found a different pattern for each of the identities. They found that the criminal identity maintained some stability over time, which would be expected if it was internalized and maintained through some verification. At the same time, however, the criminal identity was strongly influenced by the reflected appraisals. How these respondents saw themselves in terms of their criminal identity was a function of how they saw themselves defined by their significant others and peers. Because the reflected appraisals decreased over time with respect to the degree to which the respondents were seen as criminals, the respondents decreased the degree to which they saw themselves as criminals. However, the reflected appraisals were not influenced by the way the respondents saw themselves. The respondents' self-views did not influence the way they thought others saw them. Thus, for this identity, verification is obtained not so much by changing meanings in the social environment to be consistent with the self-definitions, but by changing the self-definitions to match the way others view the self. This is an instance, therefore, of an identity being defined by others but taken on and internalized within the individual and maintained over time.

Asencio and Burke found a different pattern with respect to the drug-user identity. Again, as for the criminal identity, the drug-user identity was strongly influenced by the reflected appraisals, and the self-view did not influence the reflected appraisals. Unlike the criminal identity, however, the drug-user identity showed no evidence of internalization and continuity. It was as if the drug-user identity was freshly defined from day to day by the way the respondent felt others viewed him or her. Incidentally, the self-view did change over the period of observation as the result of the changing reflected appraisals, which shifted in the direction of seeing the respondent less and less as a drug user.

Still a third pattern was found with respect to the third identity that was studied, the worker identity. Like the criminal identity, the worker identity displayed continuity over time, suggesting that it, too, had been internalized and was maintained through the verification process. However, unlike the criminal identity, the worker identity was not influenced by the reflected appraisals. How each person saw himself or herself as a worker was not a function of how each thought others saw him or her. Rather, how they thought others saw them was a function of their own self-definitions. This suggests that the worker identity not only was internalized but also was verified and maintained in spite of other's views. Other's views came, over time, to reflect how each respondent saw himself or herself.

The Sources of Identity

We have been considering changes to existing identities. Another type of identity change is the creation of an identity. This is perhaps the first kind of identity change we experience—the development of an identity standard where there was none. Where do the meanings that define an identity come from? How do they get to be part of the identity standard? We suggest three mechanisms are involved: social learning, direct socialization, and reflected appraisals. In this section we turn to examine these mechanisms.

Social Learning

The first source of identity standards is the general culture in which we grow up. As mentioned before, it is here that we come to learn the categories and meanings that define the positions and expectations we will take on. Children learn from their parents, books, television, and movies about the different roles that exist in the culture. They often play at these roles, such as doctor, nurse, police officer, and firefighter. In playing at these roles, they experience vicariously what it might be like to be a doctor or nurse, to have that identity. They begin to play at controlling the actual and potential resources through sign and symbolic meanings (though often in make-believe) that would be controlled by a person with the identity. This is *anticipatory socialization,* and it includes all of the practice and rehearsing we do before we take on a new role and identity.

As children grow, they become more aware of the different positions in society and learn what it means to be in one of those positions and how to fulfill the expectations associated with the position. It is here that the concept of taking the role of the other as discussed in chapters 1 and 2 becomes important. And, importantly, they learn how the different positions relate to, and the extent that they relate to, one another. Children learn what parents do by observing their parents. When children go to school, they learn about teachers and what teachers do. They learn about how teachers relate to one another and how teachers relate to students. They learn about the principal and the school nurse. They learn about guidance counselors and teachers' aides.

In addition, people observe others in similar positions or in complementary positions. They see and learn from these observations about what to do, what not to do, what constitutes best practices, as well as how to do things that must be done. This is *modeling* and constitutes an important part of the social learning that takes place as people take on the identity associated with the new position.

In addition, as people try out aspects of the role or position, their own experience of reward and punishment guides the learning. Some things work, and others don't. People approve of some behaviors and disapprove of other behaviors. All of these create understandings of what we have called "the way things are supposed to be" that are used in the creation of identity standards. People also see the successes and failures of others whom they observe in the situation. For example, when we see someone reprimanded by the boss for failing to do something, we make a vow to ourselves not to make the same mistake. In this way we alter the identity standard for the worker identity we have.

Direct Socialization

In addition to observation and social learning from models or from rein-forcements and punishments for one's own behaviors, there is both formal and informal instruction about what is expected for fulfilling a new posi-tion one has taken on. There may be job training for a new job, orientation meetings for new college students, or premarital counseling for taking on the spousal role and identity. In larger, more complex societies, there seems to be more reliance on education and direct socialization than on the more informal social learning that takes place. This is true partly because of the complexity of the learning that must take place, but also because of the inter-connectivity of positions, groups, and organizations and the number of oth-ers that depend upon the correct performance. There is no time for trial and error; we must be up and running from the beginning. Direct socialization will assure that as people move into new positions and take on new identi-ties, they have the correct identity standards from the beginning. They will act correctly to control the signs and symbols representing the actual and potential resources that must be controlled by the position.

Reflected Appraisals

The last mechanism for the sources of an identity lies in the reflected appraisals held by a person, that is, how that person thinks others define him or her, as we discussed in chapter 2. We have discussed the effect of reflected appraisals on the spousal identity and on the identities of crimi-nal, drug user, and worker held by incarcerated individuals earlier in the chapter. These effects were assumed to be on existing role identities and were assumed to change those existing identities over time. However, if those reflected appraisals exist from the time when a person first comes into the position for which an identity might exist, for example, when a person first gets married and takes on the spousal identity or when a person first becomes a criminal and takes on the criminal identity, then the reflected appraisals play an important part in shaping and defining that identity. This would especially be true for children in the development of person identities, identities that define them as persons, as they are just beginning to develop senses of themselves.

We saw for the spousal identity that persons who had lower status than their partner had their identity shaped in part by their partner's view of them. They came to take on the spousal identity that their partner wanted them to have. We also saw the changes in the criminal and drug-user identity for the incarcerated persons who had no power or control over these identities in the jail context. Young children in the family context are even less powerful with respect to their parents than either the spouses or the felons. Children come to define themselves in terms of how they think their parents see them. If their parents see them as worthless or incompetent, they will come to define themselves as worthless or incompetent. If their parents define them as valued and capable, then they will come to define themselves as valued and capable.

In part these effects are strong because there is no prior identity that the children act to maintain and verify by resisting alternative definitions. But we also know that even if there are some prior self-definitions that are different than the way the parents treat them, with no power to counteract this "disturbance," their identities will change to ultimately conform to the set of meanings being portrayed by the parents.

Summary

In this chapter we examined how identities come to be formed and, once formed, how they change. By identity change, we mean that the identity standard, which contains the identity meanings and expectations, is transformed. For this to happen, the levels or degrees along some dimension of meaning are changed, either increased or decreased from their prior position. For example, Mary may decrease the degree of assertiveness in her gender identity, or Hector may increase the degree to which he maintains an "on time" schedule for his gasoline deliveries.

Because an identity standard is the output from a higher-level identity, it is change in the output of that higher-level identity as it tries to control its perceptions (inputs) to achieve verification that brings about change in the standard of the lower-level identity. We discussed four sources for this type of change in identities. The first was changes in the meanings in the situation that cannot be counteracted by the lower-level identity. The second was identity conflict that exists when two identities are each trying to control the same dimensions of meaning to different levels. The third occurs when a person for one reason or another acts in ways that are at odds with his or her identity. Behavioral decisions may be forced on a person, or their behavior may have the consequence of unanticipated changes in self-relevant meanings in the situation. Finally, we discussed a fourth source that was the adaptive changes that occur to an identity in the presence of others when establishing mutual verification contexts in which each person adapts so that in verifying one's own identity, he or she also helps verify the identities of those others.

Each of these four sources of identity change is something that occurs to some extent in most situations with the consequence that the meanings held in identity standards are always in a state of flux but generally in small amounts and generally very slowly. Mostly, people act to maintain their identities and resist the forces that might cause their identities to change. Each of these processes has been the subject of research, though, as we pointed out, much more is needed.

10

Future Research

A number of areas serve as fertile ground for the future development of identity theory. Although some research already is underway in these areas, which we will mention, there is still much work to be done in advancing identity theory. Working within these areas will help extend the theory beyond its current boundaries as well as identify the scope conditions of the theory. Broadly defined, these areas include: (1) theory development, (2) methodological innovations, and (3) substantive advances.

Theoretical Development

Integrating the Structural and Perceptual Control Emphases

There are several ways theoretical development is needed. The first involves an integration of the social structural emphasis in identity theory with the perceptual emphasis (Stryker and Burke 2000). To briefly review, Stryker's work emphasizes how social structure is made up of interconnecting positions and roles and how these interconnections increase the salience and commitment of certain identities (over others) in interaction. Because identity meanings of salient and committed identities become relevant in multiple situations as persons define more situations they enter as an opportunity to play out these identities, we begin to see the trans-situational aspect of the self. Further, when salient and committed identities regularly are invoked across situations, we see that they not only serve to guide the self in specific situations but also help maintain the very network of others to which the self is tied in the social structure. Thus, the society-self relationship is mutually reinforcing.

The perceptual control emphasis we highlight in this book starts from the internalized identity standards within the self, rather than from the social structure, and examines how individuals perceptually control the meanings of who they are in situations to match their identity-standard meanings. Within this perspective, we examine how the self takes on roles, how action and interaction are embedded in and affected by social structural contexts (although we need to examine contexts in more detail as we discuss below), and how the perceptual control process maintains simultaneously the self and the social structure. We do not disregard the social structure any more than Stryker ignores the internal mechanism of the identity process. What distinguishes the two approaches is simply what is emphasized. Nevertheless, there is no reason to continue to see the theory in these two different ways. They can be integrated.

To illustrate this integration, let us take the idea of committed and salient identities from social structural identity theory and incorporate it into the perceptual control process of the identity model. The identity standard in the identity control process reflects the meanings of a particular identity. Let us think of the student identity. The more strongly one is committed to this identity, the greater should be the salience of the identity. If the identity is salient, the more likely it is that the identity meanings of being a student will be perceived as relevant in situations, and the greater the motivational force to respond to the nonverification of student identity meanings when they arise. One should work hard to move the self from a nonverifying state to a verifying state. When one persistently cannot align the meanings of the self in the situation with the student identity-standard meanings, the student identity should reduce in salience and result in decreased commitment to the relationships on which the identity is premised. In general, integrating theoretical elements from each version of identity theory, such as the above, can move us toward a more general theory of identity processes.

Types of Discrepancies

Recall that in the perceptual control model of the identity process, identity-verification (or the lack thereof) occurs when the meanings individuals attribute to themselves in a situation based on (a) the reflected appraisal process (how persons *think* that others see them in the situation) and (b) the self-appraisal process (how persons actually see themselves in the situation) correspond (or fail to correspond) with the meanings in their identity standard. Correspondence in meanings produces positive emotions, and noncorrespondence in meanings produces negative emotions. In general, identity-verification or nonverification reveals itself on the input (perceptual) side of the identity model. Meanings regarding how one is perceived in a situation in terms of a particular identity are compared to the meanings in one's identity standard. These self-in-situation meanings may be based on, among other things, (1) how the person is behaving in the situation, (2) the actual meaning of the situation that suggests invoking a particular identity (for example, if a person attends a religious service, we may assume the person is claiming a religious identity; if the person is at work, we assume the work identity is activated, and so forth), (3) the meanings implied by how others in the situation treat the person (for example, if others defer to the person, they may see the person as claiming a dominant identity or masculine identity), and (4) the display of identity cues by the person such as how the individual is dressed or the particular style of speech that is used. All of these elements contribute to perceptions of the self in the situation.

Identity-verification also can occur on the output (behavioral) side of the identity model. According to identity theory, the meanings in one's identity standard guide the meanings of one's behavior (Burke and Reitzes 1981). There should be a correspondence in meanings between how individuals see themselves and what they do. Following from this, we suggest that a special class of perceptions has to do with reflecting on one's own behavior. At issue is how much the meanings that follow from one's behavior corresponds to the meanings in his or her identity standard or to some other identity standard. For example, if one has the identity standard of being ethical, then the person should behave normatively rather than counternormatively in situations. Individuals may experience negative emotions if they perceive that what they are doing in a situation does not correspond with what they should do given the meanings in their identity standard. They evaluate that the meanings their behavior gives off are incongruent with their identity-standard meanings. Thus, the behavioral discrepancy would be high.

This evaluation can occur independently of the feedback that people obtain from others in the situation. For example, even if others provide feedback that how a person is presenting herself in a situation is consistent with the individual's identity claims, the individual may still judge her behavior meanings as incongruent with the identity standard. In this way, a person may ignore the feedback of others in the situation and be more attentive to her own self-appraisals. Thus, when identity-nonverification occurs, individuals may experience negative emotions through different pathways in the identity model.

We make one further point about behavior in identity theory. Researchers have developed and tested identity theory based on the meanings related to the *presence* of particular acts or the *commission* of certain behaviors. Thus, the identity process has been developed and extended by examining what people *do* in situations. What have not been examined are meanings as they relate to the *absence* of particular acts or the *omission* of behavior. For example, in examining the moral identity, it is important not only to examine people committing bad acts, but also to examine people failing to commit good acts. Both types of behavior fail to meet the expectations in the identity standard, and both kinds of acts challenge the moral order. At issue is whether the identity process operates differently when the meaning of the behavior (commission or omission) is different from the meaning held in the identity standard. If the identity process is general, then that process should influence both the omission of meaningful behavior as well as the commission of such behavior.

Testing Key Processes from Other Theories

Another way to develop identity theory is to incorporate key processes into the theory that are the hallmark of alternative social psychological theories. In doing this, the predictive power of identity theory is put to the test, and ideas are examined across theoretical programs. For example, a key process in expectation states theory and status characteristics theory is the status process. This process is reflected in the idea that when individuals enter interaction, they develop corresponding evaluations and expectations of one another by locating one another's status relative to themselves. Those who are evaluated as having higher status (given the ordering of status value and influence in the social structure) will be evaluated as more competent, be expected to contribute more to the interaction, receive more deference from others, and be held in high esteem.

Recently, identity theorists have examined the role accorded to status in the identity-verification process and have found that the greater the influence and esteem of higher-status actors, the greater the likelihood that they will have their identities verified (Burke 2008; Cast, Stets, and Burke 1999; Stets and Harrod 2004). These findings reveal that status influences not only task-oriented judgments in interaction, as expectation status and status characteristics theorists have found, but also judgments related to perceptions of individuals. Thus, the effects of status occur not simply for external (task) assessments in which the reference is outside the self but also for internal (self) assessments. Further, if higher-status individuals are more likely than lower-status individuals to experience identity-verification, this means that they enjoy the positive benefits of identity-verification such as greater esteem and efficacy more than lower-status individuals (Stets and Harrod 2004). In turn, this greater enjoyment verifies and helps sustain their higher status in the social structure. Indeed, higher-status actors should be better off not only materially but also psychologically. In general, with more research that applies identity theory to social psychological processes emphasized in other theories, we can determine the limits and possibilities of identity theory as a general theory of social behavior.

Showing Commonalities across Theories

Still another way of theoretically developing identity theory is to identify the key processes it shares with other theories in order to find common ground and overlapping ideas. In identifying these similarities, we may be able to apply identity theory to previously unexplored areas that ordinarily have been the domain for testing other theories. For example, the identity process operates in a manner similar to the justice process in distributive justice theory (Stets 2003; 2005). In both identity theory and distributive justice theory, there is the idea that in situations, (1) people have a *standard* that guides self-perceptions and behavior, (2) they engage in a *comparison process* to assess whether actual outcomes match their expected outcomes, and (3) they feel particular *emotions* following the comparison between their actual and expected outcomes (Burke 1991; Hegtvedt and Markovsky 1995; Markovsky 1985). In identity theory, the standard is the self-meanings of identities that guide behavior in situations. In distributive justice theory, the standard is perceptions of justice that guide the evaluation as to whether outcomes are allocated in a fair manner. In both theories, individuals compare their feedback or outcomes in the situation with what they expect to receive given their standard. If a discrepancy emerges between the two, people feel negative emotions. If there is no discrepancy between expected outcomes and actual outcomes, people feel positive emotions. Finally, there is *behavior* that exists to either maintain congruence between expected and actual outcomes or change the incongruence to congruence.

In distributive justice theory, researchers study the processes associated with individuals receiving an over-reward, just reward, or an under-reward. This reward structure is analogous, in identity theory, to individuals being nonverified in a positive direction (that is, the meaning of the feedback they receive in a situation exceeds their identity-standard meanings), verified (the meaning of the feedback is consistent with their identity-standard meanings) or nonverified in a negative direction (the feedback falls short of their identity standard) (Stets 2003; 2005). For example, a boss may tell a worker that his job performance is very outstanding, and thus he will receive a large salary increase. Alternatively, the boss may tell him that his job performance is abysmal, and he will not receive any salary increase. Either feedback disconfirms the worker's identity of being an average worker. In the above ways, we have applied identity dynamics to dynamics typically conceived in terms of justice.

Furthermore, when we apply the identity process to justice situations, the findings may not only develop identity theory but also extend distributive justice theory. For example, when considering the worker identity, we found that when individuals receive nonverifying feedback that exceeds their identity standard (that is, they receive more than what they expect for average job performance), they initially react by feeling good about getting more (Stets 2005). This finding was unexpected given the predictions of identity theory. Nonverifying feedback that exceeds one's identity standard should produce negative emotions rather than positive emotions. Stets argued, as we discussed earlier, that if individuals had more time to process the nonverifying feedback they were given in the study, they might have reacted more negatively. Time gives one the opportunity to compare actual and expected outcomes. Without available time, individuals simply provided an automatic reaction to getting more than what they expected—it makes them feel good. In a related way, distributive justice theorists have argued that more of an over-reward is needed to generate a negative state of a magnitude equal to that of an under-reward and that emotional responses to an over-reward are positive unless the departure from the standard is large (Hegtvedt 1990; Jasso 1980). The positive emotions resulting from an over-reward initially may ensue because actors are guided by the motive to feel good. Only when the over-reward significantly exceeds the expected standard do individuals begin to see the difference between actual and expected outcomes and, in turn, feel negative emotions.

Let us turn to another theory and show its affinity to identity theory: exchange theory. Theorists in both the exchange and identity tradition are interested in the nature of commitment. In exchange theory, commitment is influenced by repeated exchange agreements between people (Lawler and Yoon 1996). For instance, A and B may enter repeated exchanges in which A gives B money and B provides A some service. Over time, the repeated exchanges between A and B build commitment. In identity theory, repeated exchange agreements are analogous to a person's identity repeatedly verified in interaction (Burke and Stets 1999). To the extent that one gives the other money in exchange for a service, each person is confirming the view of the other in the encounter. A treats B as having competency to provide a particular service, and B treats A as having the resources to compensate B for his service.

What's more, we find that repeatedly verifying one another in an interaction leads to important emotional outcomes for the individual and for the relationship. Repeated identity-verification generates positive feelings for an individual and, in turn, trust in the other. Enhanced trust and positive self-feelings give rise to a positive emotional attachment to the relationship and commitment to one's partner. The positive emotional attachment to the relationship fosters the creation of a collective orientation and view of the actors in the context of a unit—a "we." In this way, we see how identity theory offers a rich avenue in understanding the development of a relationship between individuals who have a history of interaction with each other. Indeed, most of our daily interactions involve familiar or intimate others compared with interactions among strangers that exchange theorists typically focus on.

Exchange theory and identity theory do differ, and the differences highlight the strength of identity theory as a general theory. In exchange theory, value preferences guide exchanges in that one seeks to obtain from the other what he values. In identity theory, the meanings in one's identity standard set the value in the encounter and guide one's behavior. In exchange theory, resources are one's value preferences, whether they are commodities or possessions such as money or power. In identity theory, as discussed in chapter 5, the resources involved in an encounter are typically broader than those resources understood in the usual exchange model, such as value preferences. Resources include all the signs and symbols, for example, dress, talk, and demeanor, as well as information, support, tasks, food, air, love, and so forth that refer to the meanings in the identity standard and that function to verify the self and sustain interaction (Freese and Burke 1994). For this reason, by using identity theory rather than exchange theory to understand commitment, we begin to extend our analysis of commitment to a wider range of situations and relationships than those characterized by exchange theory. We go beyond exchange agreements based on what each values in the encounter. We also avoid the problem of value because the identity standard defines the relevant meanings that individuals seek in the situation whether they are scarce, negotiable, or even tangible. Essentially, the strength in identity theory is that it offers a theoretical avenue by which we can broaden the conditions to which the process of commitment in exchange applies.

Given the above, we see how identity theory becomes a theory that can be applied to a wide range of interactions such as justice situations and exchange situations. The more we can apply identity theory to situations that are test sites for other theories, the more we have identified identity theory as a general theory of human behavior. For example, identity theory has been applied to network exchange theory to understand the processes involved in the emergence of power in exchange networks (Burke 1997). Current network exchange theory, using a rational choice model, suggests that power emerges in exchange networks due to the advantage that some network positions have over others because of the number of alternatives for exchange they have. Positions with few or no alternatives are at a bargaining disadvantage relative to positions with many alternative sources of exchange.

Burke (1997) argued that in place of a rational choice model, one can substitute an identity model in which people are not seeking to maximize their payoff but are seeking simply to exchange as many times as they can (their identity standard is set such that they seek to participate in one hundred percent of the available exchanges). Burke showed that using this alternative identity model, one can predict the distribution of power differentials better than most existing exchange theories. Further, Burke showed that if one changes the identity standard, many different power distributions can emerge. He argued that the assumption that people want to participate in every exchange possible is not realistic, because people in fact have many different obligations and competing goals to which they must attend. By using identity theory in this context opens up these possibilities.

Methodological Innovations

Survey versus Experimental Method

In identity theory, most researchers have examined the identity process using the survey approach. A good example is an analysis of identity processes based on surveying individuals during the first three years of their marriage (Burke and Cast 1997; Burke and Stets 1999; Cast 2003; 2004; Cast, Stets, and Burke 1999; Stets 1997; Stets and Burke 1996). This particular line of research addressed identities in natural groups (marriage), in which individuals are typically committed to the identities they claim (for example, spouse, parent, worker), the situation is somewhat predictable (interactions are within the routine environment of home living), and individuals are familiar with the others (their spouses) in the setting. As we will see below, the experimental setting can be very different in terms of why the individuals have come together, the degree of commitment to their identities, the novelty of the situation, and how much they know each other in the situation.

When the survey approach is used to investigate the identity process, we obtain information on individuals' identity meanings, their behavior, and their feelings. Individuals' self-reports largely result from a deliberative and cognitive activity in which they attempt to accurately represent themselves to a researcher. Often, researchers do not capture the context within which the identity emerged, because that would require detailed information from respondents, which becomes time consuming. Therefore, we typically learn about identities in isolation from their surroundings.

Experimental research enables researchers to study the identity process within a specific context created in the laboratory. The context can be unique or novel and one that individuals may not experience in a natural setting. To the degree that it approximates settings in the natural environment, we can capture individuals' immediate thoughts, actions, and emotions. As we mentioned in chapter 9, we have begun to examine identity processes in the laboratory (Stets 2003; 2004; 2005; Stets and Asencio 2008; Stets, Carter, and Fletcher 2008b; Stets and Osborn 2008). In these studies, individuals may not be as committed to the identity they are invoking in the situation, the situation is novel, and they are generally interacting with others whom they have never met before. As we discussed in chapter 9, when we compare the identity process using different methodologies, we get slightly different results. For example, we have found that people feel good when their outcomes exceed their identity standard in the laboratory (they are overevaluated), but they feel bad when their outcomes exceed their identity standard using a survey in marriage (Burke and Harrod 2005; Cast and Cantwell 2007; Stets 2005; Stets and Asencio 2008). We have suggested that individuals may be guided by the enhancement principle in the laboratory, while people in a marriage relationship may be guided by the verification principle. This raises the issue of whether theorizing the identity process is contingent upon the methodology used or if there are different underlying conditions that need to be taken into direct account.

On the one hand, recent evidence examining the moral identity from a self-administered survey *and* a laboratory study revealed that the identity process operates in the same manner when explaining individuals' self-reports on their surveys as well as their behavior and feelings in the laboratory (Stets,

Carter, and Fletcher 2008b). For example, if people experience an identity discrepancy with their moral identity (that is, how they think others see them in the situation is inconsistent with the meanings in their identity standard), they report experiencing negative emotions. Irrespective of whether the inconsistency is reported in the survey or in the laboratory, individuals still indicate experiencing negative emotions. This suggests that identity theory is a general theory that can be tested across different methodologies.

On the other hand, since identity processes emerge in weak as well as strong relationships, short-term as well as long-term interactions, novel as well as routine settings, it is possible that some identity predictions are contingent on certain conditions being met. For example, perhaps the same identity needs to be examined across methodologies as was done with studying the moral identity in order to test the impact of these conditions. When one begins to compare different identities across different methodologies and conditions, there may be a great deal of variability both in terms of the identities and in terms of the methods that it may be difficult to identify what is producing the different effects. Still, identifying the significant dimensions along which identities may vary may help.

For instance, as we mentioned in chapter 9, it is possible that in an intimate relationship such as a marriage, spouses are motivated to process nonverifying feedback in a deliberate manner by thinking more deeply about it because the relationship is important to them and they are committed to the identity of a spouse. In processing this feedback, they will recognize the incongruence between how they see themselves and how others see them, and they will feel bad. In contrast, in interactions between strangers in the laboratory in which the worker identity is made salient, individuals may be less motivated to process nonverifying feedback in a deliberate, thoughtful way. This may be because the interaction is not important to them, and they are not committed to the worker identity they are asked to take on in the laboratory. Consequently, when they receive nonverifying feedback that is more positive than what they expect, they may be more likely to feel good.

The above suggests two contextual factors that may make the negative response to nonverifying identity feedback conditional: the nature of the relationship and the degree of commitment to the identity enacted. A negative reaction to nonverifying identity feedback may be more likely between intimates than between strangers and also more likely when one is committed to the identity than when one is not committed to the identity. Thus, we may need to specify the conditions under which our predictions hold. When they do not hold, we need to identify the mechanisms or processes that are intruding into the theoretical relationships.

The Role of Context

We are seeing that we need to take the context or features of the situation into account in the development of identity theory. There are two ways in which the situation or context can be examined. First, a researcher can bring contextual factors into the laboratory such as obtaining individuals of different ages, ethnic groups, or social classes. This may give us ideas as to how identity processes interact with status processes. Since most daily interactions involve familiar others compared to unfamiliar others, it might be more fruitful to bring friends or spouses into the laboratory to study identity processes as they interact with status processes. A second approach is for researchers to study the identity process in their natural environment. The problem with this approach is the researcher may not be able to isolate the many factors in the environment that may make the identity processes conditional.

Another way of examining contextual factors is to use the experiential sampling method (ESM). Early on, identity researchers used experience sampling, but it did not become widely adopted (Burke and Franzoi 1988). Recently, we have encouraged others to revisit this method as a way of capturing social psychological processes including identity processes in natural settings (Osborn and Stets 2007). ESM is a procedure that collects data on the *context* and *content* of people's everyday experiences. As individuals go about their daily lives, they identify their current situations (context), and they record their thoughts, feelings, and behaviors (content) very soon after they occur either through a computerized method such as a personal digital assistant (PDA) or by a pencil and paper method (Hektner, Schmidt, and Csikszentmihalyi 2007).

In our recent pretest of ESM, we were interested in how people with different identities, especially the moral identity, responded in situations in which they had a choice between doing what they believe to be the right thing and doing what they believe to be the wrong thing (Osborn and Stets 2007). Given these situations, we asked individuals about their physical and social location, how they responded in the situation, and how they felt. Participants carried around a PDA over a ten-hour day. During every ninety-minute interval, the alarm on the PDA would randomly go off, signaling that the respondent was to answer a brief survey on the context and content of what they recently experienced.

In general, the identity-verification process has not been tested in one's natural environment, and this served as the opportunity to test it. Whether contextual factors may make the identity-verification process operative, conditional, or nonexistent in one's natural environment will help us determine the robustness of the identity process.

Measuring Concepts

We need improved measures of our concepts. For example, identity salience is typically measured using individuals' self-reports. Additional measurement strategies could be invoked. For instance, the likelihood of a person enacting an identity in a situation alternatively might be measured by people's response latency, that is, how long it takes people to respond to questions or cues about particular identities. Identity cues might be pictures or symbols that individuals can identify with regarding an identity such as a cross symbolizing a religious identity. The quicker the response to the cue or question, the more likely it is that the identity is accessible in memory, higher in their identity salience hierarchy, and thus more likely to be activated in a given situation.

The implicit association test (IAT) is another technique available to measure identity salience (Nosek, Greenwald, and Banaji 2007). IAT is designed to measure aspects of thinking and feeling that may not be easily accessed or available in consciousness. It is possible that if we were interested in the salience of a particular identity for an individual, we could operationalize that identity in the IAT and then track individuals' latency responses when presented with the identity stimulus. For example, we might test the salience of the moral identity in the following manner. IAT involves the use of *four categories*, for example, "self" and "other" and "moral" and "immoral," and *stimulus items* that serve as exemplars of those categories such as self and other faces and characteristics that describe a moral person (e.g., honest, caring, fair, and principled) and an immoral person (e.g., unkind, not compassionate, unjust, and selfish). The IAT effect is a comparison of the combined association strengths of two associative pairs such as "self" with the "moral" items and "other" with the "immoral" items contrasted with the strength of the other two associative pairs, that is, "self" with the "immoral" items and "other" with "moral" items. This comparison might capture the salience of one's moral identity. For example, if a person responded more quickly to associative pairs such as "self" and "moral" compared to "other" and "moral," then this would suggest the greater salience of the moral identity for the individual.

Essentially, it may be fruitful to move to the use of multiple indicators of identity constructs in order to capture the different dimensions of those constructs. In the example above, while one's self-reports of the salience of identities may get at the conscious aspects of identity salience, the IAT may get at the unconscious aspect of identity salience. Both may influence behavior.

To the above, we add the idea that identity theorists need to begin to measure other concepts that may be important for the theory. For example, what is termed a salient identity in social identity theory is an identity that is *activated* in a situation (Oakes 1987; Stets and Burke 2000). A particular identity becomes activated or salient as a function of the interaction between the characteristics of the perceiver (accessibility) and the situation (fit). As indicated earlier in chapter 6, accessibility is the readiness of a given category to be called up into awareness, and fit is the congruence between characteristics of an identity and stimuli that are present in the situation.

While identity theory focuses on the link between persons that a salient identity promotes (by way of commitment), social identity theory focuses on characteristics of the situation in which an identity may be activated. Rather than merging the concepts of identity activation and identity salience as do social identity theorists or focusing only on salience to the neglect of activation as is true of identity theorists, we can examine both identity salience and identity activation as distinct processes that occur in a situation. For instance, in a study of the moral identity in which this identity is examined using both the survey and experimental method, the salience of the moral identity is measured in the survey, and then two weeks later, these individuals participate in a laboratory experiment in which they are given the opportunity to engage in a good, normative behavior such as not cheating on an exam or bad, counternormative behavior such as cheating on an exam (Stets, Carter, and Fletcher 2008b). For half of these individuals, the moral identity is activated prior to them engaging in their behavior of choice. Following procedures used by others (Aquino, Reed, Thau, and Freeman 2006), identity activation occurs in the following way.

Individuals engage in a handwriting task in which nine traits that comprise the moral identity appear down a column on a page. They are asked to write down (in their own handwriting) these nine traits across the remaining four columns on the page, thereby writing down each trait four times. Then, on the following page, they are to use each of the nine traits at least once and write a brief story about themselves in one or two paragraphs. For those exposed to the nonidentity activation condition, they are exposed to traits that do not contain moral identity characteristics but are positively valenced. The expectation is that compared to nonactivation of the moral identity in the situation, activation of the moral identity should produce a stronger positive relationship between the meanings of persons' behavior and the moral identity-standard meanings.

Still another concept from social identity theory that should be important in identity theory is the idea of group membership, that is, individuals claiming a social identity. At issue is how role, social, and person identities operate within a situation. Again, in the study discussed above on the moral identity, what is also studied is whether individuals will be more likely to engage in normative or counternormative behavior alone or as a member of a group. While in one condition, individuals have the opportunity to act normatively or counternormatively (not cheat or cheat) on their own, in another condition, individuals are placed in a group with two other members (the in-group) and compete with another group (the out-group) to obtain a higher score on a test. The prediction is that when alone, individuals will behave normatively or counternormatively based on whether the meanings held in the moral identity standard are high or low. However, when they become a member of an in-group, they will be more inclined to behave counternormatively (for example, cheat) if the counternormative act gives their own group an advantage over the out-group. In this way, the meanings associated with the social identity may exert an important influence on behavior; and depending upon the meanings in one's moral identity, they may support or conflict with the moral person identity.

Substantive Advances

Substantively, there are many rich and unexplored issues in identity theory, which leads us to the future of identity theory. We divide these issues into five main areas in the order in which we discussed them in this book. These include the areas of resources, the multiple bases of identities (role, group, and person), multiple identities, emotions, and identity change. As we discuss these areas below, we offer a series of hypotheses that help direct avenues for future research. In testing these hypotheses, we have the potential to extend identity theory beyond its current boundaries. The hypotheses throughout are not exhaustive. Rather, they serve as a guide for future directions. We place our hypotheses in a series of tables at the end of the chapter as a way of summarizing our predictions. In general, the reader should leave this chapter with the conclusion that this book is not the last word on identity theory. There is still much that needs to be done.

Resources

In chapter 5, we discussed the role of resources in identity theory. Research that has tested the role of resources in the identity-verification process has focused on status (Burke 2008; Stets and Harrod 2004). For example, the higher people's status in terms of education, occupation, and income, the more resources they have at their disposal to use to achieve their goals. Since one goal is identity-verification, high-status individuals will use their resources to obtain identity feedback in a situation that is consistent with their own identity views. In this way, they are better equipped at verifying their identity within and across situations than low-status persons.

We have been expanding the study of resources as they influence the identity-verification process by investigating the role of personal resources (such as self-worth and self-efficacy), interpersonal resources (such as taking the role of the other, being trusted and liked), and structural resources (such as status) (Stets and Cast 2007). We have found that access to more resources of these different kinds leads to greater identity-verification. Further, we have found that the verification of people's identities places them in an advantageous position from which they can access additional resources for potential use to maintain identity-verification in the future and sustain the self during those times when verification might not be possible.

Most recently, we have begun to investigate emotions as a resource for individuals (Stets and Osborn 2008). We find this line of research important in expanding our understanding of how resources, in general, and emotions, more specifically, operate in situations. In particular, we argue that *positive emotions* serve as a personal resource. When individuals feel good, it enhances their ability to withstand problematic situations such as identity-nonverification. Negative emotions act in the opposite way, draining individuals and leaving them vulnerable to stressors. This conceptualization of positive emotions as a resource is similar to the idea that high self-esteem is a resource for persons, operating as a buffer during stressful times (Cast and Burke 2002).

Just as self-esteem can be "built up" through verification and depleted through lack of verification, the same can occur for emotions. In this way, resources not only help in the verification process as discussed above but also serve as a "protective shield," preventing strong negative emotional reactions when identity-verification is not forthcoming. Recently, we have labeled the "dual purpose" that resources serve, that is, as *facilitating* identity-verification and *buffering* the self when problems in identity-verification emerge as resolving "first-and second-order" problem issues (Burke 2008). On the one hand, resources can be used to verify who one is. On the other hand, if identity-verification is not imminent, the same or additional resources can be called upon to temper the negative experiences felt when identity-nonverification occurs, allowing a person to continue seeking alternative means for verification.

The above returns us to an important idea about resources that we discussed in chapter 5. Resources are those processes that sustain persons and interaction. Sustaining the self involves both verifying the self and building up the self so that it can withstand nonverifying situations when they come along. Resources service the self in both ways. Sustaining interaction involves making sure that interaction can proceed. This means that there is space for the interaction; that the necessary tools, furniture, lighting, and setting are available and appropriate; that the participants have been notified and are present at the appropriate time; and so on.

Most work in the past has examined the failure of verification in terms of identity-relevant symbolic meanings in the situation not being in accord with one's identity standard. But we can hypothesize the same is true with respect to the manipulation of sign meanings and bringing actual resources to the level specified in the identity standard. Thus we hypothesize that:

> H1: *The failure to bring identity-relevant actual resources to the level specified in an identity standard will result in the feeling of distress.*

Multiple Bases of Identity

As we discussed in chapter 6, future research needs to carefully examine the different bases of identities, that is, role, group, and person identities, and how they are interrelated in a situation. This would lead to a more integrated and stronger theory of identity. Identity theorists have been preoccupied with role identities to the neglect of group and person identities. Role identities are beneficial to the self, but so too are group and person identities. As we mentioned in chapter 6 and as shown in table 10.1, because the verification of role, group, and person identities may have distinct consequences for individuals such as generating feelings of competency, belongingness, and authenticity, we hypothesize that:

Table 10.1. Role, Social, and Person Identities (Hypotheses 2–6; 27–29)

Dimension	Bases of Identities		
	Role	Social	Person
Verification	Competence	Self-Worth	Authenticity
Nonverification	Discomfort-Guilt	Embarrassment-Shame	Sadness-Depression
Choice	Person influences Role	Person influences Social	
No Choice	Role influences Person	Social influences Person	

H2: *Verification of role identities will lead to increased feelings of competence and effectiveness.*

H3: *Verification of group identities will lead to increased feelings of self-worth and acceptance.*

H4: *Verification of person identities will lead to increased feelings of authenticity.*

Although individuals' claim role, group, or person identities, often these identities emerge simultaneously in a situation. Within *groups*, there are *roles*, and *persons* play out these roles. Thus, we need to examine how these identity meanings interrelate in situations. Since, as we discussed earlier, person identities are more likely to be "master identities" operating across situations, groups, and roles, it is expected that person identities will influence the selection of role and social identities; one will select role and social identities that are consistent with the meanings in one's person identities (Burke 2004a). However, this assumes that individuals can choose the roles and groups that they enter into. Sometimes, choice is not possible as when one must obtain an education or is drafted into the military. Here, individuals will find themselves in situations in which they must adjust to the demands of the situations, and this adjustment may extend to modifying person identity meanings so that they are more consistent with role or social identity meanings. Therefore, also as shown in table 10.1, we predict that:

H5: *The meaning of person identities will influence the meanings of role and group identities when persons have a choice in the roles and groups they adopt.*

H6: *The meanings of role and group identities will influence the meaning of person identities when persons have no choice in the roles and groups they adopt.*

Multiple Identities

As we discussed in detail in chapter 7, social actors hold multiple positions in the social structure, and correspondingly, have multiple identities. Early work examined how multiple identities relate to psychological well-being (Thoits 1983; 1986; 2003). Recently, we have begun to see how multiple identities may be activated in a group as when one takes on both the task leadership identity and socioemotional leadership identity (Burke 2003). Alternatively, we have seen how within a single situation each person has an identity, and as they interact, each tries to verify his or her identity as when each person in a marriage is trying to verify his or her spousal identity (Burke and Stets 1999). However, we have not gone far enough in studying the "'multiple identities' conception of the self" (Stryker and Burke 2000, p. 291).

Some have examined the person as a container of multiple identities as when one takes on the identity of worker, friend, and student and seeks verification of these identities in nonoverlapping groups (Stets and Harrod 2004). However, this does not capture how these identities may simultaneously emerge in one situation. For example, one may regularly interact with a friend who is also a fellow student at school and coworker at one's place of work. At issue would be how the meanings of these multiple identities are managed when they begin to conflict. What happens when the person finds out that his friend has cheated on an exam, has stolen some money from the register at work, or has been saying unkind words about the person to other friends? When multiple identities emerge in the same situation, as when spouses seek to verify not only their spouse identity in a marriage but also their person identity as sociable (Stets and Cast 2007), we need to better understand how these identities are related to each other either in a complementary or contradictory manner. For instance, a husband may desire his wife's sociable identity to be passive, quiet, and docile. What happens when the wife seeks to maintain meanings in her sociable identity of being active, loud, and unruly?

It therefore makes sense to move away from the procedure of examining one identity at a time. This views the self in narrow terms. The self is much more complex given the many roles, groups, and characteristics that it can claim. Identity researchers need to examine this complexity. Derived from our discussion of multiple identities in chapter 7, the following hypotheses can be tested as presented in table 10.2:

> *H7: Identities with common meanings will tend to be activated together.*

> *H8: Identities that often are activated together will develop similar levels of prominence.*

> *H9: Identities that often are activated together will develop similar levels of salience and commitment.*

Table 10.2.   The Nature of Identities (Hypotheses 7–18; 33–34)

Identities that are activated together:
- will have common meanings
- will develop similar levels of prominence
- will develop similar levels of salience and commitment

Identities more likely to be verified will be:
- more prominent
- more salient and more committed

Accumulating identities that are:
- multiple will make people feel good if they are all verified
- obligatory will make people feel good if they are all verified

Nonverified identities will produce more negative emotions:
- in more intimate relationships
- in more invested identities
- in more committed identities
- in more salient identities
- when the source of identity discrepancy is higher in the social structure
- if a person enters the situation in a negative affective state

Identity change will be more likely to occur:
- for lower status persons
- in organizations or groups which experience changes in resource levels

H10: Identities higher in prominence will guide behavior and take preference in the verification process compared to identities lower in prominence.

H11: Identities higher in salience or commitment will guide behavior and take preference in the verification process compared to identities lower in salience or commitment.

H12: Accumulating multiple identities will make people feel good if the identities are all verified.

H13: Accumulating obligatory identities compared to accumulating voluntary identities will make people feel better if they are all verified.

Emotions

In chapter 8, we reviewed the empirical tests to date on the relationship between identity-verification and emotions. Our review revealed that the role of emotion in identity theory needs further investigation because it is likely to be far more complex and contextual than originally thought. For example, we indicated that whether nonverification leads to negative emotions may depend upon the nature of the relationship as well as the degree of commitment one has in an identity and the salience of the identity. Therefore, continuing with the hypotheses in table 10.2, we predict that:

H14: *Nonverified identities will be more likely to produce negative emotions in more intimate relationships compared to less intimate relationships.*

H15: *Nonverified identities will be more likely to produce negative emotions in more committed identities compared to less committed identities.*

H16: *Nonverified identities will be more likely to produce negative emotions when the identity is salient compared to when it is not salient.*

Emotions emerge from the identity-verification process, but their nature may depend on the *source* of the identity feedback and the degree to which this person has power and status in the interaction (Stets and Burke 2005b). While power is the ability to control resources, status reflects the respect and esteem one obtains from others. For example, if the boss remarks that a worker is not performing at the expected level, the worker will feel worse than if the remark came from a fellow coworker. In this way, power and status carry additional meanings in a situation beyond the identity feedback that can influence one's feelings in a situation.

Recent research reveals that individuals react more negatively to those who have high power and status and who do not verify one's identity than those who have low power and status and who do not verify one's identity (Stets and Asencio 2008). When high-status others act in an unfair manner by not verifying one's identity, they appear to be perceived as behaving incompetently and inappropriately. It is perceived as illegitimate because they are expected to know better, that is, to provide others the feedback they deserve. Therefore, emotions have multiple sources in a situation, and these need to be taken into account. Thus, as shown in table 10.2, we predict that:

H17: *Nonverified identities will be more likely to produce negative emotions when the source of the identity discrepancy is a person higher in power or status than lower in power or status.*

In a related manner, we need to consider the emotions that individuals bring into a situation (Stets and Osborn 2008). Individuals' emotions are not always created anew in each situation. There is often a "carry-over" effect from previous situations and encounters. Part of one's current set of feelings is the result of previous experiences as well as feelings from yesterday, last week, or even months ago. Thus, if one enters a situation feeling good but then experiences identity-nonverification, the earlier positive feelings help temper the negative feelings that emerge as a result of identity-nonverification. Further, the experiences in one's current situation that generate particular feelings will be carried into future interactions, thereby influencing later emotional reactions. In this way, emotions are not simply a consequence of the identity-verification process, but they may also be an antecedent to the verification process as individuals move from one situation to the next, carrying with them feelings from the past.

We take one example to show how emotions are antecedent to the verification process. There is evidence that when people are in a particular affective state (either positive or negative), they are more likely to attend to details of an outcome that are congruent with their affective state than incongruent with their affective state (Forgas 1995). Thus, if one enters a situation in a positive affective state and then does not obtain identity-verification, the person may not attend to the nonverifying information to the degree that they would attend to it if they were in a negative affective state. By tempering the nonverifying information either by temporarily distracting oneself, deprecating the source of the feedback, or attending to some but not all of the nonverifying feedback, a person is able to maintain positive feelings in the situation. In turn, this facilitates withstanding the nonverifying feedback and continuing to navigate oneself through the situation. Given the above, we hypothesize, as summarized in table 10.2, that:

> H18: *Nonverified identities will be more likely to produce negative emotions if the person enters the situation in a negative affective state compared to a positive affective state.*

Finally, as we mentioned in chapter 8, to further advance the study of emotions in identity theory, we need to test a series of predictions that we recently offered to researchers (see Stets and Burke 2005b for further details). First, we need to move beyond studying the general affective states of negative and positive feelings and begin to make predictions about specific emotions. In making predictions about particular emotions, we sharpen the outcome associated with identity-verification and identity-nonverification. Second, we need to consider the role of attributions in influencing feeling states. The attribution process can emerge at two different points in the identity model. First, attributions may emerge on the input side of the identity model. Here, persons evaluate whether the source of their identity-verification or identity-nonverification is themselves or others in the situation. When individuals attribute responsibility for identity-verification or the lack thereof to themselves, they are making an internal attribution. When they find another responsible for identity-verification or nonverification, they are making an external attribution. Second, attributions may also emerge with respect to the identity standard. Here, individuals may build up a set of expectations that they hold for themselves in a particular identity as a kind of ideal; others may not share these expectations. This is an internal attribution to their identity meanings. Alternatively, they may build up a set of expectations that others have of them in the identity. This is an external attribution to their identity meanings. Combining the attribution processes mentioned above with specific emotions, we derive the following hypotheses that are outlined in table 10.3:

> H19: *When the source of meanings in the identity standard is the self and the source of the discrepancy is the self, the self will experience emotions ranging from disappointment to sadness.*

Table 10.3.   Emotions (Hypotheses 19–26)

Source of Meaning	Source of Discrepancy	
	Self	Other
Self	Disappointment-Sadness	Anger-Rage
Other	Embarrassment-Shame	Annoyance-Hostility
	Relative Status of Other	
Higher	Shame	Anxiety
Equal	Embarrassment	Annoyance
Lower	Discomfort	Hostility
	Relative Power of Other	
Higher	Sadness	Fear
Equal	Disappointment	Anger
Other	Displeasure	Rage

H20: When the source of meanings in the identity standard is the other and the source of the discrepancy is the self, the self will experience emotions ranging from embarrassment to shame.

H21: When the source of meanings in the identity standard is the self and the source of the discrepancy is the other, the self will experience emotions ranging from anger to rage.

H22: When the source of meanings in the identity standard is the other and the source of the discrepancy is the other, the self will experience emotions ranging from annoyance to hostility.

Notice that the above emotions range from the mild to the severe. As we discussed more fully in our earlier work, we anticipate that more prominent and salient identities that are not verified will produce more severe emotional reactions than less prominent and salient identities.

Another dimension to our hypotheses involves the relative power and status of actors in the situation that may produce different emotions. When considering individuals' status vis-à-vis others in the situation, and whether the source of an identity discrepancy rests with the self or the other in the situation, we predict (as shown in table 10.3) that:

H23: When the source of the discrepancy is the self, the self will experience

    a. shame when the relative status of the other in the situation is higher than the self,

    b. embarrassment when the relative status of the other is equal to the self, and

   c. *discomfort when the relative status of the other is lower than the self.*

H24: *When the source of the discrepancy is the other, the self will experience*

   a. *anxiety when the relative status of the other in the situation is higher than the self,*

   b. *annoyance when the relative status of the other is equal to the self, and*

   c. *hostility when the relative status of the other is lower than the self.*

When taking into account persons' relative power in the situation, and whether the source of an identity discrepancy is the self or the other in the situation, we expect (as summarized in table 10.3) that:

H25: *When the source of the discrepancy is the self, the self will experience*

   a. *sadness when the relative power of the other in the situation is higher than the self,*

   b. *disappointment when the relative power of the other is equal to the self, and*

   c. *displeasure when the relative status of the other is lower than the self.*

H26: *When the source of the discrepancy is the other, the self will experience*

   a. *fear when the relative power of the other in the situation is higher than the self,*

   b. *anger when the relative power of the other is equal to the self, and*

   c. *rage when the relative status of the other is lower than the self.*

We point out that when you compare the emotions in column 1 of table 10.3 with the emotions in column 2 of table 10.3, the emotions are positioned where they are to reflect the idea that some feelings are directed inward against the self, while other emotions are directed outward toward others. Indeed, when the self is perceived as responsible for an identity discrepancy, negative affect such as shame is directed inward. Alternatively, when another is viewed as responsible for an identity discrepancy, negative affect such as anger is directed outward.

Still another dimension to our hypotheses pertains to the different emotional outcomes given the nonverification of different identities: role, social, and person. Returning to the top of table 10.1, we anticipate that:

H27: Nonverification of a role-based identity will lead to feelings ranging from discomfort to guilt.

H28: Nonverification of a group-based identity will lead to feelings ranging from embarrassment to shame.

H29: Nonverification of a person-based identity will lead to feelings ranging from occasional sadness to depression.

Finally, we need to study how emotions emerge in mutual verification contexts. Recall that mutual verification contexts are situations in which two or more individuals mutually support each other by verifying their own identities and in so doing help in the process of verifying the identities of others in the situation. For example, a married couple often develops a mutual verification context in which each partner verifies his or her own spousal identity and in so doing helps maintain the spouse's identity (Burke and Stets 1999). As summarized in table 10.4, we hypothesize that:

H30: If the discrepancy is not large or not persistent in a mutual verification context, the feeling of annoyance will emerge.

H31: A discrepancy in a mutual verification context that is large or persistent and caused by another will result in feelings of anger.

H32: A discrepancy in a mutual verification context that is large or persistent when caused by the self will result in feelings of depression.

Identity Change

Although some identity theorists have examined identity change (Asencio and Burke 2008; Burke 2006a; Burke and Cast 1997; Cast and Cantwell 2007; Kiecolt 1994; 2000; Serpe 1987), more generally, this has been a neglected area of research. We have been making important advances in theoretically understanding the roots of identity change as discussed in chapter 9, but there is a dearth of empirical work. Part of the difficulty lies in obtaining longitudinal data that captures identity changes taking place, particularly when the change may occur very slowly. We can only encourage more research. In so doing, we offer some hypotheses for future research.

Table 10.4.   Mutual Verification (Hypotheses 30–32)

	Source of Discrepancy	
Degree of Discrepancy	Self	Other
Not large or not persistent	Annoyance	Annoyance
Large or persistent	Depression	Anger

In chapter 9, we discussed identity change in which the source of the change was endogenous, that is, the change stemmed from a lack of identity-verification in the perceptual control model. Here, the source of the identity change is internal or rooted in processes occurring within the self. For example, if perceptions as to who one is in a situation cannot be controlled to match the meanings in the identity standard, the identity-standard meanings will slowly change to match the situational self-perceptions. This is accomplished through higher-level identities changing their outputs. These outputs are the identity standards for lower-level identities.

However, the source of identity change may also be exogenous or external to the perceptual control system. Here, the placement of identities in the larger social structure, the corresponding resource levels of the actors, and the changes in the flow of resources within the social structure can influence identity change. For instance, people's identity meanings may change in a situation when someone with more resources in the situation defines or redefines the meanings and expectations associated with a particular role or group membership. For example, a "resource rich" manager may redefine the expectations associated with a particular work role, and a "resource poor" worker may have to adjust. A worker can challenge the redefined roles, and if the worker persists in the resistance, the worker either may quit or be fired. However, the individual will be replaced with another who will take on the newly defined role identity. "Resource rich" individuals can even have influence over identity meanings in intimate relationships such as marriage. We saw (for example, in research that studied the meanings individuals take on as "spouse" in a marriage) lower-status spouses, that is, persons who had a lower education and occupational status compared to their partner, were more likely to take on the meanings of spouse as it was defined by their higher-status spouses than vice versa (Cast, Stets, and Burke 1999). Consequently, as outlined in the bottom of table 10.2, we expect that:

H33: Identity change will be more likely to occur for persons with lower status or power compared to persons with higher status or power.

Another exogenous source of identity change occurs when there is a change in resource levels in the social structure as when organizations or groups expand or contract. When organizations or groups grow or shrink, there will likely be changes in the expectations associated with the many roles within the organization. For example, in times of growth, expectations may be added to specific roles within an organization, thereby encouraging the adoption of new role identity meanings. Alternatively, as an organization shrinks, expectations may be reduced, once again influencing the content of the role identity meanings. For example, if a grocery store is downsizing, it may begin by letting its newest workers go. In turn, the store manager may require the expectations associated with the newest workers (such as "grocery baggers") to be fulfilled by the workers at the register in addition to their duties of tallying the costs of groceries and keeping the register balanced such as cleaning the track belt, calling for price checks, and so forth. Given this and again on the bottom of table 10.2, we expect that:

> *H34:   In organizations or groups in which there are significant changes in resource levels, a role identity is more likely to change than in organizations that have relatively constant resource levels.*

The above implies that changing resource levels in organizations and groups influence not only changes in expectations associated with the many roles within an organization but also the many counterroles to which these roles interrelate. In this way, changing expectations spread from roles to counterroles and change the meanings of identities and counteridentities. In the above example, while the cashier now has additional expectations to fulfill, the role identity of customer also has changed. No longer can the customer expect "quick" service in the grocery line. Instead, the customer is expected to be patient as the cashier fulfills more duties. Further, we might begin to see the customer taking on additional expectations to help the cashier such as working harder to find products that may be shelved in odd places rather than having the cashier or bagger find it, bagging one's own groceries, and so on.

In organizations in which there are significant changes in resource levels, changing expectations in role and counterrole identities may come not only from the "top down" but also from the "bottom up" as when individuals innovate. For example, workers may find new and resourceful ways in which to accomplish an important part of a role, thereby changing the expectations and meanings associated with a role identity. If this innovation also helps verify a counterrole in the situation, then the role partner may endorse the changes in the role expectations. For example, the cashier who now has to take on additional duties may suggest to the manager to have certain registers in which customers bag their own groceries in exchange for the customer moving through the grocery line quicker. If the cashier was appointed to such a register, they would be shifting the expectation associated with their role onto the person in the counterrole who may freely accept it because of the incentive to get out of the store faster. Innovation from the "bottom up" is more likely to occur in organizations in which resource levels are changing. Therefore, we anticipate that:

> *H35:   Role identity change due to individual innovation is more likely to occur in organizations that have significant changes in resource levels compared to organizations that have relatively constant resource levels.*

Conclusion

This is an exciting time in the development of identity theory. By integrating the different emphases in identity theory (the structural and the perceptual), we are poised to bridge the gap between the individual and society. We can address issues of a more macro concern, such as the origins of the patterns of activity that constitute social structure, as well as issues of a more micro concern, such as the various meanings of the self in a role, as a group member, and as a person. In advancing identity theory beyond its current boundaries, identity theorists must remain open to new ways of thinking about and testing identity processes. Different methodologies can be employed, and the theory is wide open for substantive advances. Over the past thirty years, identity theory has been formulating a coherent and cumulative theory of social behavior. The next thirty years of theory-building can only sharpen and deepen our understanding of self, identity, meaning, behavior, and emotion, all of which constitute the very foundation of society.

Appendix

Identity Measures

Identity Prominence—How Important an Identity Is to the Self

1. Prominence relative to other identities: A paired comparison procedure of five identities (academic, athletic, extracurricular, friend, dater). Respondents compare each identity with the four other identities in terms of which is more important to the way they think about themselves. They assign a 1 to the more important identity and a 0 to the other. There are a total of 10 comparisons, with each activity/role/identity appearing four times in the comparisons. The scores are added, and a constant (1) is added so that scores range from 1–5 rather than 0–4. Source: (Stryker and Serpe 1994).

2. Prominence of an identity: A one-item question that asks individuals how important the identity is to them. Response categories include "Not at all important," "Somewhat important," "Important," and "Very important" (coded 1–4). Source: (Stets and Biga 2003).

3. Indirect measure of prominence relative to other identities: Compares the emotional responses associated with being "Good" or "Bad" in one identity compared to other identities. For example, with respect to the mother identity, two sets of items are presented: one is positively worded, and one is negatively worded. In the positive set, women are asked how they would respond if complimented for being "Pretty," "Intelligent," "A good friend," "A good mother," and "Physically fit." Response categories are "Feel ok" to "Feel fantastic" (coded 1–4). For the negative set, they are asked how they would respond if told they "Looked old," "Were a poor

student," "Poor mother," "Stubborn," and "Overweight." Responses are "Down a few minutes" to "Terribly upset" (coded 1–4). The responses of each positive and negative identity items (for example, being a "Good mother" and being a "Poor mother") are averaged and compared to the other eight items. An ordinal ranking is established of the mothering identity relative to the other items. A score of 8 is a mother identity that is highest in prominence hierarchy. Source: (Nuttbrock and Freudiger 1991).

4. Indirect measure of prominence: Compares the emotional responses associated with being "Good" or "Bad" in an identity. Again, with respect to the mother identity, women are asked to rate how they would feel if a friend commented that they were a "Good" mother. Response categories included feeling "Ok," "Nice," "Very good," and "Terrific" (coded 1–4). Then they are asked how they would feel if a friend told them that they were a "Poor" mother. Response categories include "Feeling slightly upset," "Moderately upset," "Very upset," or "Extremely upset" (coded 1–4). The two items are averaged, and a high score reflects a very prominent mother identity. Source: (Ellestad and Stets 1998).

5. Prominence of an identity and an indirect measure of prominence: A two-item scale. Examining the student identity, individuals are asked to rate the importance of the student role. Responses include "Not very important," "Somewhat important," "Important," "Very important" (coded 1–4). Then individuals are asked to respond to how they would feel if someone said they had no right to call themselves real students. Responses categories include "Not very upset," "Only somewhat upset," "Moderately upset," "Upset," or "Very upset" (coded 1–5). The two items are averaged, and a high score reflects a very prominent student identity. Source: (Burke and Reitzes 1991).

Identity Salience—The Likelihood of An Identity Being Invoked across Situations

1. Salience of one identity relative to other identities: Subjects are asked to report what they would tell another in meeting the person for the first time in various situations. Situations may include "Meeting a roommate for the first time," "Meeting someone at a party," "Meeting a friend of a close friend," and "Telling a speech about oneself." Among a list of descriptors are various identities that persons may claim such as "Academic," "Athletic," "Friend," "Dater," and "Worker." Subjects report which role identity they would tell another first, which they would tell another second, and so on in each of the situations. Responses range from "Least likely to tell" to "Most likely to tell" (coded 1–5). The responses for each identity are summed across the situations, with a high score representing a more salient identity. Source: (Nuttbrock and Freudiger 1991; Stets and

Biga 2003; Stets, Carter, Harrod, Cerven, and Abruytn 2008; Stryker and Serpe 1994).

2. A two-item measure examining salience of the religious identity: Respondents are to rank the religion role relative to other roles (that is, parent, spouse, and worker). The first item asked them to think about meeting people the first time. They are then asked which of the following they would tell others about first: doing the work they do, being a husband or wife, being a parent, doing the religious activities they do, or something else? Which would they tell them next? They continue until all activities are ranked. The second item asks individuals to think about a weekend in which they had a choice to do something. They are then asked which of the following they would choose to do first: go to a religious service or activity, go on an outing with/visit their children, catch up on work, spend time with their husband or wife, or none of these? Which would they do next? They continue until all activities are ranked. Source: (Stryker and Serpe 1982).

Identity Commitment—The Costs Associated with Not Playing Out An Identity

Costs are examined along two dimensions: the number of ties (quantitative— the more ties, the greater the cost of giving up the identity) and the strength of the ties to others in one's social networks based on an identity (qualitative—the stronger the ties, the greater the cost of giving up the identity).

1. Quantitative Commitment: A two-item scale. Respondents are asked whether they joined any organizations related to an identity, and whether they had made any friends through activities related to the identity. Responses are "No" or "Yes" (coded 0–1). Source: (Stets and Biga 2003; Stryker and Serpe 1994).

2. Qualitative Commitment: A four-item scale. For the first two items, individuals are asked how important it is to them that their parents (and best friend) view them as being involved in activities related to a role identity. Responses include "Not at all important" to "Very important" (coded 1–4). For the last two items, they are asked how good their parents (and best friend) think they are at activities related to a role identity. Responses include "Below average" to "Excellent" (scored 1–4). Source: (Stets and Biga 2003; Stryker and Serpe 1994).

3. Cognitive Bases (Positive and Negative) and Socioemotional Bases (Extensive and Intensive) of Commitment: Four factors comprise identity commitment. The focus is on the student identity. The first two factors are the cognitive bases that involve the rewards (positive) and costs (negative) that result from interacting with others as a student. There are five positive/reward items that include the degree to which: (1) individuals get satisfaction or fulfillment from being a student; (2) they feel being a student is beneficial or rewarding in terms of the future; (3) people say they are right in placing

importance on being a student; (4) they obtain strong praise as a student; and (5) they perceive disappointment by others in their failure as a student. There are three negative/cost items and they include: (1) the frequency of mild criticism as a student, (2) the frequency of strong criticism as a student, and (3) the balance of criticism and praise as a student. There are three items that make up extensive commitment including identifying the number of: (1) people individuals would miss if they were not longer a student, (2) friends made in college, and (3) people they would no longer see if they were no longer a student. Finally, five items make up intensive commitment including how important it is to individuals that the following people see them as a student: brother/sister, high school friends, intimate met in high school, parents, and an intimate (lover, fiancée, or spouse). Source: (Burke and Reitzes 1991).

4. For slight variations on the above, Burke and Reitzes measure, see Serpe (1987) and Stryker and Serpe (1982).

Role Identity Standard—The Meanings Associated with Holding Particular Roles in the Social Structure

A semantic differential format is used in which respondents are to choose between two opposite characteristics/meanings of the identity.

1. Gender Identity: Male and female items are drawn from the M (Masculinity), F (Femininity), and MF scales of the Personal Attributes Questionnaire (PAQ) (Spence and Helmreich 1978). There are 24 bipolar items. These include: (1) not at all aggressive/very aggressive, (2) not at all independent/very independent, (3) not at all emotional/very emotional, (4) very submissive/very dominant, (5) not at all excitable in a major crisis/very excitable in a major crisis, (6) very passive/very active, (7) not at all able to devote self completely to others/able to devote self completely to others, (8) very rough/very gentle, (9) not at all helpful to others/very helpful to others, (10) not at all competitive/very competitive, (11) very home oriented/very worldly, (12) not at all kind/very kind, (13) indifferent to others' approval/highly needful of others' approval, (14) feelings not easily hurt/feelings easily hurt, (15) not at all aware of feelings of others/very aware of feelings of others, (16) can make decisions easily/has difficulty making decisions, (17) gives up very easily/never gives up easily, (18) never cries/cries very easily, (19) not at all self-confident/very self-confident, (20) feels very inferior/feels very superior, (21) not at all understand of others/very understanding of others, (22) very cold in relations with others/very warm in relations with others, (23) very little need for security/very strong need for security, and (24) goes to pieces under pressure/stands up well under pressure. Source: (Burke and Cast 1997; Burke, Stets, and Pirog-Good 1988; Burke and Tully 1977; Stets 1995; 1997; Stets and Biga 2003; Stets and Burke 1996).

2. Student Identity: A 24-item bipolar scale. Individuals are asked to think of themselves as a college student. They are to identify where they would place themselves between each bipolar statement including: (1) pressured/not pressured, (2) competitive/noncompetitive, (3) studious/nonstudious, (4) ambitious/not ambitious, (5) motivated/not-motivated, (6) dedicated/undedicated, (7) hardworking/lazy, (8) responsible/irresponsible, (9) critical/accepting, (10) social/antisocial, (11) apathetic/interested, (12) involved/uninvolved, (13) friendly/unfriendly, (14) concerned/unconcerned, (15) aggressive/nonaggressive, (16) sensitive/insensitive, (17) dependent/independent, (18) open-minded/closed-minded, (19) mature/immature, (20) realistic/idealistic, (21) individualistic/group-oriented, (22) inquisitive/bored, (23) optimistic/pessimistic, and (24) creative/dull. Responses range from 1–5, in which 1 reflects agreement with one bipolar statement, 5 reflects agreement with the other bipolar statement, and 3 places the respondent in between the two statements. Source: (Reitzes and Burke 1980).

3. Spouse Identity: Individuals rate 11 spousal role activities by how much they feel that they should engage in the role activity. Role activities include: (1) cleaning the house, (2) preparing and serving the meals, (3) washing, ironing, and mending the clothes, (4) home repair, (5) yard work, (6) taking care of bills and accounts, (7) shopping for groceries, (8) maintaining contact with parents and in-laws or other members of the family, (9) initiating sexual activity, (10) providing income for the family before children are born, and (11) providing income for the family after children are born. Responses range from "Not doing that activity in the household" to "Doing all of that activity in the household" (coded 0–4). Source: (Burke and Stets 1999; Cast and Burke 2002; Stets and Burke 2005a).

4. Parent Identity: Individuals rate 6 parenting role activities by how much they are expected to be responsible for the activity. Activities include teaching the child: (1) to get along, (2) right from wrong, (3) to dress himself/herself properly, (4) to take responsibility, (5) to do one's schoolwork, and (6) discipline. Response range from "Entirely spouse" to "Entirely self" (coded 0–4). Source: (Cast 2004).

5. Task Leader Identity: A 5-item Likert scale. Individuals are asked to rate themselves on items that indicate the degree to which they tend to act as leaders. The items include "I try to maintain my own opinions even though other people may have a different point of view," "When I work on committees, I like to take charge of things," "I try to influence strongly other people's actions," "When I work with a group of people I like to have things done my way," and "I try to be the dominant person when I am with other people." Responses range from 1–5 reflecting the answer categories of "Often," "Sometimes," "Occasionally," "Rarely," and "Never." Source: (Riley and Burke 1995).

Person Identity Standard—The Meanings Associated with Being a Particular Kind of Person

A semantic differential format is used in which respondents are to choose between two opposite characteristics/meanings.

1. Environment Identity: An 11-item bipolar scale. Respondents are asked to think of how they view themselves in relationship to the environment. They are to identify where they would place themselves between each statement including: (1) in competition with the natural environment/in cooperation with the natural environment, (2) detached from the natural environment/connected to the natural environment, (3) very concerned about the natural environment/indifferent about the natural environment, (4) very protective of the natural environment/not at all protective of the natural environment, (5) superior to the natural environment/inferior to the natural environment, (6) very passionate toward the natural environment/not at all passionate toward the natural environment, (7) not respectful of the natural environment/very respectful of the natural environment, (8) independent from the natural environment/dependent on the natural environment, (9) an advocate of the natural environment/disinterested in the natural environment, (10) wanting to preserve the natural environment/wanting to utilize the natural environment, and (11) nostalgic thinking about the natural environment/emotionless thinking about the natural environment. Responses range from 1–5, in which 1 reflects agreement with one statement, 5 reflects agreement with the opposite statement, and 3 is half way between the two statements. Source: (Stets and Biga 2003).

2. Moral Identity: A semantic differential is used. Respondents are given a list of 12 bipolar characteristics. They are to identify where they would place themselves between each bipolar statement including: (1) honest/dishonest, (2) caring/uncaring, (3) unkind/kind, (4) unfair/fair, (5) helpful/not helpful, (6) stingy/generous, (7) compassionate/hard-hearted, (8) untruthful/truthful, (9) not hardworking/hardworking, (10) friendly/unfriendly, (11) selfish/selfless, and (12) principled/unprincipled. Responses ranged from 1 to 5, in which 1 reflects agreement with one bipolar characteristic, 5 reflects agreement with the other bipolar characteristic, and 3 places the respondent in between the two bipolar characteristics. Source: (Stets et al. 2008).

3. Control Identity: Respondents are asked how often in the past year they had engaged in 10 acts with their spouse. These include: (1) I make my spouse do what I want, (2) I keep my spouse in line, (3) I impose my will onto my spouse, (4) I keep tabs on my spouse, (5) I regulate who my spouse sees, (6) I supervise my spouse, (7) I keep my spouse from doing things I do not approve of, (8) I let my spouse do what she or he wants, (9) If I don't like what my spouse is

doing, I make him/her stop, and (10) I set the rules in my relationship with my spouse. Response categories include "Never," "Seldom," "Sometimes," "Fairly often," or "Very often" (coded 1–5). Source: (Stets and Burke 1994, 1996).

4. Sociable Identity: This represents the degree to which individuals see themselves as possessing the attributes and skills important to smooth and supportive interactions. There are three dimensions: friendly, understanding, and likeable. Responses are on a scale from 0 to 100 that reflects how much individuals see themselves along each dimension. Source: (Stets and Cast 2007).

Identity-Verification—Individuals' Identity-Standard Meanings Match the Meanings Others' Attribute to Them

1. Individuals' identity-standard meanings minus the *perceptions* of others' identity meanings of themselves: the worker, academic, and friend identities are examined. Respondents first report their evaluation of themselves. For the worker identity, they rate how good they are at their job from "Not at all good" to "Very good." For the academic identity, they indicate how satisfied they are with the level of education they have attained from "Not at all satisfied" to "Very satisfied." For the friend identity, they identify how good they see themselves as a friend from "Not at all good" to "Very good." All three ratings are coded 0–10. Then, respondents report how they *think* others see them in each identity. For the worker identity, respondents identify how they think: (1) family members, (2) coworkers, (3) friends, and (4) their partners (if applicable) rate them in the worker identity. Responses are on a scale from "Not at all good" to "Very good" at one's job. For the academic identity, respondents indicate how satisfied they think: (1) family members, (2) friends, and (3) their partners (if applicable) are with the level of education they have attained. Responses are on a scale from "Not at all satisfied" to "Very satisfied. For the friend identity, they rate how they think friends and close friends see them as a friend. Responses are on a scale from "Not at all good" to "Very good." All three ratings are coded 0–10. Identity-verification scores are then calculated by taking the absolute difference between a significant other's rating of oneself on a particular identity and the respondent's rating on that identity, averaging the absolute differences across significant others, and finally subtracting them from 10 within each identity to form a scale of identity-verification for each identity. Source: (Stets and Harrod 2004).

2. Individuals' identity-standard meanings minus others' *actual* identity meanings: Actual meanings serve as a proxy of perceived meanings. The degree of verification is determined by calculating the average absolute difference between one's own meanings and the meanings held by another about the self. For example, verification of the spousal identity involves one's rating of oneself on the 11

spousal activities mentioned above on the spouse identity minus the spouse's rating of the individual on the 11 spousal activities. A score of 0 indicates perfect agreement or verification of the spousal identity; a score of 4 indicates maximum disagreement or discrepancy. Source: (Burke and Stets 1999; Cast and Burke 2002; Stets and Burke 2005a). This procedure also has been used for verification of the parent identity. Source: (Cast 2004).

3. Perceptual discrepancy measure: The above verification measure by Stets and Harrod (2004) in later work is labeled a perceptual discrepancy to represent a discrepancy in the input side of the identity model. Applying this measure to the moral identity, for example, a perceptual discrepancy is a difference in the ratings of individuals across the 12 bipolar moral identity items above minus how individuals perceive that others see them as moral persons. The difference between these two values is then squared so that a departure from 0 in either a negative or positive direction means an increased discrepancy between the person's moral identity standard and perceptions of how he or she thinks others see them. Source: (Stets, Carter, and Fletcher 2008b).

4. Behavioral discrepancy measure: A discrepancy in the output side of the identity model: This occurs when the meanings that are given off by one's behavior in a situation are inconsistent with the meanings held in one's identity standard. This is applied to an analysis of the moral identity. The ratings by individuals across the 12 bipolar moral identity items above are multiplied by 0 if they behaved morally in the situation and by 1 if they did not. Source: (Stets and Carter 2006; Stets, Carter, and Fletcher 2008b).

Resources—Anything that Sustains or Enhances An Interaction and the People Connected to It

1. Personal Resources: Two proposed resources are feeling good and feeling effective in one's environment. Feeling good is measured from seven items that operationalize self-worth in the Rosenberg (1979) self-esteem scale including: (1) I feel I am a person of worth, at least on an equal basis with others; (2) I feel that I have a number of good qualities; (3) I feel I do not have much to be proud of; (4) I take a positive attitude toward myself; (5) On the whole, I am satisfied with myself; (6) I wish I could have more respect for myself; and (7) At times, I think I am no good at all. Response categories include "Strongly disagree," "Disagree," "Agree," and "Strongly Agree" (coded 0–4). Feeling effective is measured from five items from a mastery scale (Pearlin, Lieberman, Menaghan, and Mullan 1981), two items from the Rosenberg self-esteem scale, and one item from an efficacy-based self-esteem scale (Gecas 2000). The final scale includes the following items: (1) There is really no way I can solve some of the problems I have; (2) Sometimes I feel that I'm being pushed around in life; (3) I have little control over the things that

happen to me; (4) I often feel helpless in dealing with the problems of life; (5) There is little I can do to change many of the important things in my life; (6) All in all, I am inclined to feel that I am a failure; (7) I am able to do things as well as most other people; (8) I certainly feel useless at times; (and 9) confident versus lack confidence. Responses include "Strongly disagree," "Disagree," "Agree," and "Strongly Agree" (coded 0–4). Source (Stets and Cast 2007).

2. Interpersonal Resources: Three interpersonal resources include taking the role of the other, being trusted, and being liked. Role-taking is measured through a 5-item scale (Stets 1993): (1) I have difficulty seeing my spouse's viewpoint in an argument; (2) When something affects my spouse, I am understanding; (3) I see myself in the same way that my spouse sees me; (4) I understand my spouse's feelings quite well; and (5) My spouse does things I do not understand. Responses range from "Never" to "Very often" (coded 1–5). Trust is measured from an 8-item trust scale (Larzelere and Huston 1980): (1) My partner is primarily interested in his/her own welfare; (2) There are times when my partner cannot be trusted; (3) My partner is perfectly honest and truthful with me; (4) I feel that I can trust my partner completely; (5) My partner is truly sincere in his/her promises; (6) I feel that my partner does not show me enough consideration; (7) My partner treats me fairly and justly; and (8) I feel that my partner can be counted on to help me. Responses are from "Strongly agree" to "Strongly disagree" (coded 1–7). Liking is measured using Rubin's (1973) 13-item scale. Items include: (1) When I am with (spouse), we almost always are in the same mood; (2) I think that (partner) is unusually well adjusted; (3) I would highly recommend (partner) for a responsible job; (4) In my opinion, (partner) is an exceptionally mature person; (5) I have great confidence in (partner's) good judgment; (6) Most people would react favorably to (partner) after a brief acquaintance; (7) I think that (partner) and I are quite similar to each other; (8) I would vote for (partner) in a class or group election; (9) I think that (partner) is one of those people who quickly wins respect; (10) I think that (partner) is an extremely intelligent person; (11) (Partner) is one of the most likeable people I know; (12) (Partner) is the sort of person whom I myself would like to be; and (13) It seems to me that it is very easy for (partner) to gain admiration. Respondents indicate the degree of truth of a statement from "Not at all true" to "Definitely true" (coded 0–8). Source: (Stets and Cast 2007).

3. Structural Resources: These are an individual's education, income, occupational status, and race. Source: (Burke 2008; Stets and Cast 2007; Stets and Harrod 2004).

Notes

Chapter 1

1. In chapter 5, we will introduce another view of social structure that focuses not on the patterns of individual behavior but on the flow of resources that is initiated and maintained by that behavior.

2. Even so-called simple societies have fairly complex differentiation among clans, families, lineages, occupational specializations, and so on.

3. It is not likely that the responses in different individuals are exactly identical. Rather, the symbol representation process in one individual functions in the same way as the symbol representation process in another individual. The functional equivalence of meanings gives symbols their shared quality.

4. It is important to realize that naming is itself a social process. What names are to be used may be negotiated and may change over time. However, for interaction to proceed, there must be some consensus on the names and meaning, even though that may change over time.

5. Identities are the internal processes (agents) that give rise to the external behaviors (actions), the patterns of which constitute roles. The correspondence between roles and identities has often given rise to the term "role identity" to signify the close relationship between the two concepts.

6. Some identities are obviously more inclusive than other identities in the sense that meanings from one identity spill over into another identity. For example, husbands and wives may talk about things that are relevant to their work identities, to identities tied to friends, and so on. In each of these cases, however, the identity is likely to be talked about and concerns expressed. The identity is not likely to be enacted.

7. It should be understood that some social structures are more open to different potential responses than are others (Serpe 1987; Stryker 1980 [2002]). For example, some schools require the students to follow a dress code or even to wear uniforms, while other schools allow more freedom of expression in clothing.

8. As we will see in chapter 5, the resources that sustain identities and interactions are not necessarily physical things. Information, love, and support also can be resources, as well as things that are even more abstract such as ordering and sequencing.

Chapter 2

1. Of course, the complete act is needed to accomplish the goals that are indicated in the gesture. Behavior is not just goal oriented but also goal attaining. Thus, although the use of gestures and communication may modify the process of attaining goals, and even the goals that are obtained, the ultimate survival of the organism, the interaction, groups, and societies ultimately depends upon the attainment of goals; at some point we have to stop talking and act.

2. The degree of correction of the input is important. Too much and the system becomes unstable. Too little and the system is not controlled.

Chapter 4

1. These are the dimensions of meaning that Reitzes and Burke (1981; 1980) found relevant to distinguishing the college student identity from other relevant identities including graduate student identity, high school student identity, college graduate identity, and noncollege peer identity.

2. For the mathematically inclined, the set of meanings may be represented as a vector. If there are four dimensions of meaning that are relevant, then a four-dimensional vector may represent them, with vector lengths a function of the location of the person on each of the dimensions.

3. In chapter 5, we will see that meanings are responses.

4. It is an open question as to how such information is conveyed in the situation. How do we know that the meanings pertain to us? Research is needed to address this issue.

5. Identity theory, like symbolic interaction generally, distinguishes perceptions that arise from three distinct processes related to role performance within groups: reflected appraisals (how we think others see us), social comparisons (how we see ourselves in comparison to others), and self-attributions (how we see ourselves [Rosenberg 1990]).

6. The notion of unit here is arbitrary. It is assumed that meanings can be measured as quantities along various dimensions. Although those dimensions might be the "universal" dimensions of evaluation, potency,

and activity suggested by Osgood and his associates (1975), they may also be other situationally relevant dimensions such as masculinity/femininity for gender identities (Burke and Tully 1977), "intellectualism" for college student identities (Reitzes and Burke 1980), or "feeling useless" for old-age identities (Mutran and Burke 1979a).

7. Strictly speaking, the meanings do not occur in the environment. Rather, the stimuli that come from the environment are transformed into meanings once perceived by persons.

8. These interruptions may occur within a role, for example, when an ER physician moves from patient to patient before being able to treat any one of them fully in accord with the standards held in their identity, or they may occur between roles, for example, when a volunteer firefighter must drop everything to respond to an alarm.

Chapter 5

1. This procedure bases the differences between boys and girls on stereotypic perceptions of the two categories. That is, the ratings were based on the children's views of what it means in general to be a boy or a girl. An alternative procedure is to base the differentiating dimensions on the differences in the way boys see themselves and the way girls see themselves. This would allow us to distinguish not between ratings of how people see girls and how people see boys but between self-ratings of boys and self-ratings of girls. If the former are stereotypical differences, the latter are typical or average differences.

2. As introduced in chapters 1 and 2, the term "sign" is a generic label that includes both natural signs and conventional signs. Conventional signs are referred to as symbols. In the present context, we are using the term "sign" to refer to *natural signs*. Thus, we will speak of signs and symbols rather than of natural and conventional signs.

3. We are reminded of the finding by Benjamin Whorf (1956), a prominent linguist in the first half of the last century who also worked as a fire investigator for an insurance firm. One of the fires he investigated was started by an explosion set off by a worker throwing a cigarette butt into an "empty" gasoline drum, not realizing that there continued to be gasoline vapors in the supposedly "empty" drum. Here, the gasoline vapors served more as a disturbance to the resources supporting the workers at this plant.

Chapter 6

1. For Rosenberg (1979), a personal identity is classifying a person into a category with one case. The individual is assigned a unique label, usually a name.

Chapter 7

1. It is, of course, possible that an identity will be dropped and the individual will no longer consider himself or herself to have that identity. For example, Cast and Burke (2002) show that spouses who have trouble verifying their spousal identity are more likely to become divorced.

2. Stryker and Statham (1985) and Stryker and Macke (1978) have nicely summarized much of this work.

3. Levels of commitment to each identity, as well as situational demands, would influence which identity is dominant in the situation even though both are activated.

4. Additionally, identities that one does not want known may also become known.

Chapter 8

1. These strategies are analogous to Burke's (1991) coping responses in his perceptual control theory.

References

Abrams, Dominic, and Michael A. Hogg. 1990. *Social identity theory: Constructive and critical advances.* London: Harvester-Wheatsheaf.

Aquino, Karl, Americus II Reed, Stefan Thau, and Dan Freeman. 2006. "A grotesque and dark beauty: How moral identity and mechanisms of moral disengagement influence cognitive and emotional reactions to war." *Journal of Experimental Social Psychology* 43:385–92.

Asencio, Emily K., and Peter J. Burke. 2008. "Identity change among incarcerated criminal offenders." Social Psychology Seminar, Riverside, CA.

Baddeley, A. D. 1972. "Selective attention and performance in dangerous environments." *British Journal of Psychology* 63:537–46.

Bailey, James R., and John H. Yost. 2000. "Role theory: foundations, extensions, and applications." Pp. 2420–25 in *Encyclopedia of sociology*, vol. 4, edited by E. F. Borgatta and R. J. V. Montgomery. New York: Macmillan.

Baldwin, James Mark. 1906. *Mental development in the child and the race.* New York: Macmillan.

Baumeister, Roy F. 1998. "The self." Pp. 680–740 in *The handbook of social psychology*, vol. 2 (4th ed.), edited by D. T. Gilbert and S. T. Fiske. Boston: McGraw-Hill.

Baumgardner, Ann H., Cynthia M. Kaufman, and Paul E. Levy. 1989. "Regulating affect interpersonally: When low esteem leads to greater enhancement." *Journal of Personality and Social Psychology* 56:907–21.

Blaine, Bruce, and Jennifer Crocker. 1993. "Self-esteem and self-serving biases in reactions to positive and negative events: An integrative view." Pp. 55–85 in *Self-esteem: The puzzle of low self-regard*, edited by R. F. Baumeister. New York: Plenum Press.

Blumer, Herbert. 1962. "Society as symbolic interaction." Pp. 179–92 in *Human behavior and social processes*, edited by A. M. Rose. Boston: Houghton Mifflin.

——. 1969. *Symbolic interactionism.* Englewood Cliffs, NJ: Prentice-Hall.

Bryant, Fred B., and Paul R. Yarnold. 1990. "The impact of type A behavior on subjective life quality." *Journal of Social Behavior and Personality* 5:369–404.

Burke, Peter J. 1980. "The self: Measurement implications from a symbolic interactionist perspective." *Social Psychology Quarterly* 43:18–29.

——. 1991. "Identity processes and social stress." *American Sociological Review* 56:836–49.

——. 1996. "Social identities and psychosocial stress." Pp. 141–74 in *Psychosocial stress: Perspectives on structure, theory, life-course, and methods,* edited by H. B. Kaplan. San Diego: Academic Press.

——. 1997. "An identity model for network exchange." *American Sociological Review* 62:134–50.

——. 2001. "Multiple identities and network exchange." Paper presented at the conference on Theory and Research on Group Processes.

——. 2003. "Relationships among multiple identities." Pp. 195–214 in *Advances in identity theory and research,* edited by P. J. Burke, T. J. Owens, R. T. Serpe, and P. A. Thoits. New York: Kluwer Academic/Plenum.

——. 2004a. "Identities and social structure: The 2003 Cooley-Mead award address." *Social Psychology Quarterly* 67:5–15.

——. 2004b. "Identities, events, and moods." *Advances in Group Processes* 21:25–49.

——. 2006a. "Identity change." *Social Psychology Quarterly* 69:81–96.

——. 2006b. "Perceptions of leadership in groups: An empirical test of identity control theory." Pp. 267–91 in *Purpose, meaning, and action: Control systems theories in sociology,* edited by. K. McClelland and T. J. Fararo. New York: Palgrave Macmillan.

——. 2006c. "Preface" Pp. xi–xiv in *Contemporary social psychological theories,* edited by P. J. Burke. Stanford: Stanford University Press.

——. 2008. "Identity, social status, and emotion." Pp. 75–93 in *Social structure and emotion,* edited by J. Clay-Warner and D. T. Robinson. San Diego: Elsevier.

Burke, Peter J., and Alicia D. Cast. 1997. "Stability and change in the gender identities of newly married couples." *Social Psychology Quarterly* 60:277–90.

Burke, Peter J., and Stephen L. Franzoi. 1988. "Studying situations and identities using experiential sampling methodology." *American Sociological Review* 53:559–68.

Burke, Peter J., and Michael M. Harrod. 2005. "Too much of a good thing?" *Social Psychology Quarterly* 68:359–74.

Burke, Peter J., and Donald C. Reitzes. 1980. "College student identity: Measurement and implications." *Pacific Sociological Review* 23:46–66.

——. 1981. "The link between identity and role performance." *Social Psychology Quarterly* 44:83–92.

——. 1991. "An identity theory approach to commitment." *Social Psychology Quarterly* 54:239–51.

Burke, Peter J., and Jan E. Stets. 1999. "Trust and commitment through self-verification." *Social Psychology Quarterly* 62:347–66.

Burke, Peter J., Jan E. Stets, and Maureen A. Pirog-Good. 1988. "Gender identity, self-esteem, and physical and sexual abuse in dating relationships." *Social Psychology Quarterly* 51:272–85.

Burke, Peter J., and Judy C. Tully. 1977. "The measurement of role identity." *Social Forces* 55:881–97.

Callero, Peter L. 1985. "Role-identity salience." *Social Psychology Quarterly* 48:203–14.

Campbell, Jennifer D. 1990. "Self-esteem and clarity of the self-concept." *Journal of Personality and Social Psychology* 59:538–49.

Campbell, Jennifer D., Barry Chew, and Linda S. Scratchley. 1991. "Cognitive and emotional reactions to daily events: The effects of self-esteem and self-complexity." *Journal of Personality* 59:473–505.

Carver, Charles S., and Michael F. Scheier. 1988. "A control-process perspective on anxiety." *Anxiety Research* 1:17–22.

Cast, Alicia D. 2003. "Power and the ability to control the definition of the situation." *Social Psychology Quarterly* 66:185–201.

———. 2004. "Identity verification and the well-being of parents." *Sociological Perspectives* 47:55–78.

Cast, Alicia D., and Peter J. Burke. 2002. "A theory of self-esteem." *Social Forces* 80:1041–68.

Cast, Alicia D. and Allison M. Cantwell. 2007. "Identity change in newly married couples: Effects of positive and negative feedback." *Social Psychology Quarterly* 70:172–85.

Cast, Alicia D., Jan E. Stets, and Peter J. Burke. 1999. "Does the self conform to the views of others?" *Social Psychology Quarterly* 62:68–82.

Charng, Hong-wen, Jane A. Piliavin, and Peter L. Callero. 1988. "Role identity and reasoned action in the prediction of repeated behavior." *Social Psychology Quarterly* 51:303–17.

Cohen, Albert. 1959. "Some implications of self-esteem for social influence." Pp. 102–20 in *Personality and persuasibility*, edited by C. I. Hovland and I. L. Janis. New Haven: Yale University Press.

Coleman, James S. 1990. *Foundations of social theory*. Cambridge, MA: Belknap Press of Harvard University Press.

Conway, J. 1978. *Men in mid-life crisis*. Elgin, IL: Cook.

Cook, Karen S. and Eric Rice. 2003. "Social exchange theory." Pp. 53–76 in *Handbook of social psychology*, edited by J. DeLamater. New York: Kluwer Academic.

Cooley, Charles H. 1902. *Human nature and social order*. New York: Scribner.

———. 1909. *Social organization*. New York: Scribner.

Coopersmith, Stanley. 1967. *The antecedents of self-esteem*. San Francisco: W.H. Freeman.

Couch, Carl J., Stan L. Saxton, and Michael A. Katovich. 1986. *Studies in symbolic interaction: The Iowa School*. Greenwich, CT: JAI Press.

Damasio, Antonio R. 1994. *Descartes' error: Emotion, reason, and the human brain*. New York: Putnam.

Deaux, Kay. 1992. "Personalizing identity and socializing self." Pp. 9–33 in *Social psychology of identity and the self-concept*, edited by G. M. Blackwell. London: Surry University Press.

——. 1993. "Reconstructing social identity." *Personality and Social Psychology Bulletin* 19:4–12.

Derogatis, Leonard R. 1977. *SCL-90: Administration, scoring and procedures manual for the R version and other instruments of the psychopathology rating scale series.*

Durkheim, Emile. 1893 [1984]. *The division of labor.* Trans. G. Simpson. New York: Free Press.

Ekman, Paul. 1992. "An argument for basic emotions." *Cognition and Emotion* 6:169–200.

Ellestad, June, and Jan E. Stets. 1998. "Jealousy and parenting: Predicting emotions from identity theory." *Sociological Perspectives* 41:639–68.

Elliott, Gregory C. 1982. "Self-esteem and self-presentation among the young as a function of age and gender." *Journal of Youth and Adolescence* 11:135–53.

Emerson, Richard M. 1962. "Power-dependence relations." *American Sociological Review* 27:31–40.

Erikson, Erik H. 1950. *Childhood and society.* New York: Norton.

Fazio, Russell H., David M. Sanbonmatsu, Martha C. Powell, and Frank R. Kardes. 1986. "On the automatic activation of attitudes." *Journal of Personality and Social Psychology* 50:229–38.

Fein, Robert A. 1976. "Men's entrance to parenthood." *The Family Coordinator* 25:341–48.

Ferguson, Adam. 1792. *Principles of moral and political science: Being chiefly a retrospect of lectures delivered in the College of Edinburgh,* vol. 1. Edinburgh; Printed for A. Strahan and T. Cadell, London and W. Creech, Edinburgh.

Foote, Nelson N. 1951. "Identification as the basis for a theory of motivation." *American Sociological Review* 26:14–21.

Forgas, Joseph P. 1995. "Mood and judgment: The affect infusion model (AIM)." *Psychological Bulletin* 117:39–66.

Freese, Lee. 1988. "The very thought of resources." Paper presented at the annual meetings of the American Sociological Association.

Freese, Lee, and Peter J. Burke. 1994. "Persons, identities, and social interaction." *Advances in Group Processes* 11:1–24.

Frijda, Nico H. 1993. "Moods, emotion episodes, and emotions." Pp. 381–403 in *Handbook of emotions,* edited by L. Michael and J. M. Haviland. New York: Guilford Press.

Gecas, Viktor. 1982. "The self-concept." *Annual Review of Sociology* 8:1–33.

——. 1989. "The social psychology of self-efficacy." *Annual Review of Sociology* 15:291–316.

——. 2000. "Value identities, self-motives, and social movements." Pp. 93–109 in *Self, identity, and social movements,* edited by S. Stryker, T. J. Owens, and R. W. White. Minneapolis: University of Minnesota Press.

Goode, William J. 1960. "A theory of role strain." *American Sociological Review* 25:483–96.

Gross, Neal, S. Mason Ward, and Alexander W. McEachern. 1958. *Explorations in role analysis.* New York: John Wiley and Sons.

Hegtvedt, Karen A. 1990. "The effects of relationship structure on emotional responses to inequity." *Social Psychology Quarterly* 53:214–28.

Hegtvedt, Karen A., and Barry Markovsky. 1995. "Justice and injustice." Pp. 257–80 in *Sociological perspectives on social psychology*, edited by K. S. Cook, G. A. Fine, and J. S. House. Boston: Allyn and Bacon.

Heise, David R. 1979. *Understanding events: Affect and the construction of social action*. Cambridge: Cambridge University Press.

Hektner, Joel M., Jennifer A. Schmidt, and Mihaly Csikszentmihalyi. 2007. *Experience sampling method: Measuring the quality of everyday life*. Thousand Oaks: Sage.

Higgins, E. Tory. 1987. "Self-discrepancy: A theory relating self and affect." *Psychological Review* 94:319–40.

———. 1989. "Self-discrepancy theory: What patterns of self-beliefs cause people to suffer?" Pp. 93–136 in *Advances in experimental social psychology*, vol. 22, edited by L. Berkowitz. New York: Academic Press.

Hitlin, Steven. 2003. "Values as the core of personal identity: Drawing links between two theories of self." *Social Psychology Quarterly* 66:118–37.

Hochschild, Arlie Russell. 1983. *The managed heart: Commercialization of human feeling*. Berkeley: University of California Press.

Hogg, Michael A. 2006. "Social identity theory." Pp. 111–36 in *Contemporary social psychological theories*, edited by P. J. Burke. Stanford: Stanford University Press.

Hogg, Michael A., and Dominic Abrams. 1988. *Social identifications: A social psychology of intergroup relations and group processes*. London: Routledge.

Hogg, Michael A., and Barbara A. Mullin. 1999. "Joining groups to reduce uncertainty: Subjective uncertainty reduction and group identification." Pp. 249–79 in *Social identity and social cognition.*, edited by D. Abrams and M. A. Hogg.Malden, MA: Blackwell.

Hogg, Michael A., Deborah J. Terry, and Katherine M. White. 1995. "A tale of two theories: A critical comparison of identity theory with social identity theory." *Social Psychology Quarterly* 58:255–69.

Homans, George C. 1950. *The human group*. New York: Harpers.

———. 1974. *Social behavior: Its elementary forms* (2nd ed.). New York: Harcourt Brace and World.

Jackson, Elton. 1962. "Status consistency and symptoms of stress." *American Sociological Review* 27:469–80.

Jackson, Elton F., and Peter J. Burke. 1965. "Status and symptoms of stress: Additive and interaction effects." *American Sociological Review* 30:556–64.

James, William. 1890. *Principles of psychology*. New York: Holt Rinehart and Winston.

Jasso, Guillermina. 1980. "A new theory of distributive justice." *American Sociological Review* 45:3–32.

Kemper, Theodore D. 1987. "How many emotions are there? Wedding the social and autonomic components." *American Journal of Sociology* 93:263–89.

Kiecolt, K. Jill. 1994. "Stress and the decision to change oneself: A theoretical model." *Social Psychology Quarterly* 57:49–63.

———. 2000. "Self change in social movements." Pp. 110–31 in *Identity, self, and social movements*, edited by S. Stryker, T. Owens, and R. White. Minneapolis: University of Minnesota Press.

Kirmeyer, Sandra L. 1988. "Coping with competing demands: Interruption and type A pattern." *Journal of Applied Psychology* 73:621–29.

Koestler, Arthur. 1969. "Beyond atomism and holism—The concept of the holon." Pp. 192–216 in *Beyond reductionism*, edited by A. Koestler and J. R. Smythies. Boston: Beacon Press.

Kuhn, Manford H. 1964. "Major trends in symbolic interaction theory in the past twenty-five years." *The Sociological Quarterly* 5:61–84.

Kuhn, Manford H., and Thomas S. McPartland. 1954. "An empirical investigation of self-attitudes." *American Sociological Review* 19:68–76.

Large, Michael D., and Kristen Marcussen. 2000. "Extending identity theory to predict differential forms and degrees of psychological distress." *Social Psychology Quarterly* 63:49–59.

Larzelere, R. E., and T. L. Huston. 1980. "The dyadic trust scale." *Journal of Marriage and the Family* 42:595–604.

Lawler, Edward J., and Jeongkoo Yoon. 1996. "Commitment in exchange relations: Test of a theory of relational cohesion." *American Sociological Review* 61:89–108.

Lazarus, Richard S., and Susan Folkman. 1984. *Stress, appraisal, and coping.* New York: Springer.

Lenski, Gerhard E. 1954. "Status crystallization: A non-vertical dimension of social status." *American Sociological Review* 19:405–13.

Linton, Ralph. 1936. *The study of man.* New York: Appleton-Century-Crofts.

Linville, Patricia. 1985. "Self-Complexity and affective extremity: Don't put all of your eggs in one cognitive basket." *Social Cognition* 3: 94–120.

———. 1987. Self-complexity as a cognitive buffer against stress-related illness and depression. *Journal of Personality and Social Psychology* 52: 663–76.

Longmore, Monica A., and Alfred DeMaris. 1997. "Perceived inequity and depression in intimate relationships: The moderating effect of self-esteem." *Social Psychology Quarterly* 60:172–84.

MacKinnon, Neil J. 1994. *Symbolic interaction as affect control.* Albany: State University of New York Press.

Mandler, George. 1982. "Stress and thought processes." Pp. 88–104 in *Handbook of stress: Theoretical and clinical aspects*, edited by L. Goldberger and S. Breznitz. New York: Free Press.

Marcussen, Kristen. 2006. "Identities, self-esteem, and psychological distress: An application of identity-discrepancy theory." *Sociological Perspectives* 49:1–24.

Marcussen, Kristen, and Michael D. Large. 2003. "Using identity discrepancy theory to predict psychological distress." Pp. 151–66 in *Advances in identity theory and research*, edited by P. J. Burke, T. J. Owens, R. T. Serpe, and P. A. Thoits. New York: Kluwer Academic/Plenum.

Markovsky, Barry. 1985. "Toward a multilevel distributive justice theory." *American Sociological Review* 50:822–39.

McCall, George. 2003. "The me and the not-me: Positive and negative poles of identity." Pp. 11–26 in *Advances in identity theory and research*, edited by P. J. Burke, T. J. Owens, R. T. Serpe, and P. A. Thoits. New York: Kluwer Academic/Plenum.

McCall, George J., and J. L. Simmons. 1978. *Identities and interactions.* New York: Free Press.

Mead, George H. 1934. *Mind, self, and society.* Chicago: University of Chicago Press.

———. 1938. *The philosophy of the act.* Chicago: University of Chicago Press.

Meltzer, Bernard N. 1972. "Mead's social psychology." Pp. 4–22 in *Symbolic interaction: A reader in social psychology,* edited by J. G. Manis and B. N. Meltzer. Boston: Allyn and Bacon.

Meltzer, Bernard N., John W. Petras, and Larry T. Reynolds. 1977. *Symbolic interactionism: Genesis, varieties and criticism.* Boston: Routledge and Kegan Paul.

Merton, Robert K. 1957. *Social theory and social structure.* Glencoe, IL: Free Press.

Mirowsky, John, and Catherine E. Ross. 1989. *Social causes of psychological distress.* New York: Aldine de Gruyter.

Mutran, Elizabeth, and Peter J. Burke. 1979a. "Feeling 'useless': A common component of young and old adult identities." *Research on Aging* 1:188–212.

———. 1979b. "Personalism as a component of old age identity." *Research on Aging* 1:37–64.

Nadel, S. F. 1957. *The theory of social structure.* Glencoe, IL: Free Press.

Nosek, Brian, Anthony G. Greenwald, and Mahzarin R. Banaji. 2007. "The implicit association test at age 7: A methodological and conceptual review." Pp. 265–92 in *Automatic processes in social thinking and behavior,* edited by J. A. Bargh. New York: Psychology Press.

Nuttbrock, Larry, and Patricia Freudiger. 1991. "Identity salience and motherhood: A test of Stryker's theory." *Social Psychology Quarterly* 54: 146–57.

Oakes, Penelope. 1987. "The salience of social categories." Pp. 117–41 in *Rediscovering the social group,* edited by J. C. Turner, M. A. Hogg, P. J. Oakes, S. D. Reicher, and M. S. Wetherell. New York: Basil Blackwell.

Oakes, Penelope J., S. Alexander Haslam, and John C. Turner. 1994. *Stereotyping and social reality.* New York: Basil Blackwell.

Osborn, Shelley N., and Jan E. Stets. 2007. "The experience sampling method and social psychological research." Paper presented at the annual meetings of the American Sociological Association.

Osgood, Charles E., William H. May, and Murray S. Miron. 1975. *Crosscultural universals of affective meaning.* Urbana: University of Illinois Press.

Osgood, Charles E., George J. Suci, and Percy H. Tannenbaum. 1957. *The measurement of meaning.* Urbana: University of Illinois Press.

Parsons, Talcott. 1949. *The structure of social action.* Glencoe, IL: Free Press.

Pearlin, Leonard I., and Morton A. Lieberman. 1979. "Social sources of emotional distress." Pp. 217–48 in *Research in community mental health,* edited by R. Simmons. Greenwich, CT: JAI Press.

Pearlin, Leonard I., Morton A. Lieberman, Elizabeth G. Menaghan, and Joseph T. Mullan. 1981. "The stress process." *Journal of Health and Social Behavior* 22:337–56.

Pescosolido, Bernice A., and Beth A. Rubin. 2000. "The web of group affiliations revisited: Social life, postmodernism, and sociology." *American
Sociological Review* 65:52–76.

Peterson, Christopher, Steven F. Maier, and Martin E. P. Seligman. 1993.
Learned helplessness: A theory for the age of personal control. New
York: Oxford University Press.

Piliavin, Jane Allyn. 1991. "Is the road to helping paved with good intentions? Or inertia?" Pp. 259–79 in *The self-society dynamic: Cognition,
emotion, and action,* edited by J. A. Howard and P. L. Callero. New York:
Cambridge University Press.

Pinel, Elizabeth C., and William B. Swann, Jr. 2000. "Finding the self through
others: Self-verification and social movement participation." Pp. 132–52
in *Self, identity, and social movements,* edited by S. Stryker, T. J. Owens,
and R. W. White. Minneapolis: University of Minnesota Press.

Plutchik, Robert. 1980. *Emotion: A psychoevolutionary synthesis.* New York:
Harper and Row.

Powers, William T. 1973. *Behavior: The control of perception.* Chicago:
Aldine.

Reitzes, Donald C., and Peter J. Burke. 1980. "College student identity measurement and implications." *Pacific Sociological Review* 23:46–66.

Riley, Anna, and Peter J. Burke. 1995. "Identities and self-verification in the
small group." *Social Psychology Quarterly* 58:61–73.

Rosenberg, Morris. 1979. *Conceiving the self.* New York: Basic Books.

———. 1990. "The self-concept: Social product and social force." Pp. 593–624
in *Social psychology: Sociological perspectives,* edited by M. Rosenberg
and R. H. Turner. New Brunswick, NJ: Transaction Publishers.

Rubin, Zick. 1973. *Liking and loving: An invitation to social psychology.*
New York: Holt Rinehart and Winston.

Scheff, Thomas J. 1988. "Shame and conformity: The deference-emotion
system." *American Sociological Review* 53:395–406.

———. 1990. "Socialization of emotion: Pride and shame as causal agents."
Pp. 281–304 in *Research agendas in the sociology of emotions,* edited
by T. D. Kemper. Albany: State University of New York.

———. 2000. "Shame and the social bond: A sociological theory." *Sociological
Theory* 18:84–99.

Schein, Edgar H. 1957. "Reaction patterns to severe, chronic stress in American army prisoners of war." *Journal of Social Issues* 13:21–30.

———. 1958. "The Chinese indoctrination program for prisoners of war:
A study of attempted 'brainwashing.'" Pp. 311–34 in *Readings in social
psychology,* edited by E. E. Maccoby, T. M. Newcomb, and E. L. Hartley.
New York: Henry Holt and Company.

Secord, Paul F., and Carl W. Backman. 1974. *Social psychology.* New York:
McGraw-Hill.

Sedikides, Constantine, Lowell Gaertner, and Yoshiyasu Toguchi. 2003.
"Pancultural self-Enhancement." *Journal of Personality and Social Psychology* 84:60–79.

Serpe, Richard T. 1987. "Stability and change in self: A structural symbolic
interactionist explanation." *Social Psychology Quarterly* 50:44–55.

Serpe, Richard T., and Sheldon Stryker. 1987. "The construction of self and reconstruction of social relationships." *Advances in Group Processes* 4: 41–66.

Sewell, William H. 1992. "A theory of structure: Duality, agency, and transformation." *American Journal of Sociology* 98:1–29.

Smith, Adam. 1966 [1759]. *The theory of moral sentiments.* New York: Kelley.

Smith-Lovin, Lynn. 2003. "Self, identity, and interaction in an ecology of identities." Pp. 167–78 in *Advances in identity theory and research,* edited by P. J. Burke, T. J. Owens, R. T. Serpe, and P. A. Thoits. New York: Kluwer/Plenum.

Smith-Lovin, Lynn, and David R. Heise. 1988. *Analyzing social interaction: Advances in affect control theory.* New York: Gordon and Breach Science Publishers.

Smith-Lovin, Lynn, and Dawn T. Robinson. 2006. "Control theories of identity, action, and emotion: In search of testable differences between affect control theory and identity control theory." Pp. 163–88 in *Purpose, meaning, and action: Control systems theories in sociology,* edited by K. McClelland and T. J. Fararo. New York: Palgrave Macmillan.

Spence, Janet T., and Robert L. Helmreich. 1978. *Masculinity and femininity: Their psychological dimensions, correlates and antecedents.* Austin: University of Texas Press.

Spencer, Steven J., Robert A. Josephs, and Claude M. Steele. 1993. "Low self-esteem: The uphill struggle for self-integrity." Pp. 21–36 in *Self-esteem: The puzzle of low self-regard,* edited by R. F. Baumeister. New York: Plenum Press.

Stager, Susan F., and Peter J. Burke. 1982. "A reexamination of body build stereotypes." *Journal of Research in Personality* 16:435–46.

Steele, Claude M. 1988. "The psychology of self-affirmation: Sustaining the integrity of the self." Pp. 261–302 in *Advances in experimental social psychology,* vol. 21, edited by L. Berkowitz. New York: Academic Press.

Stets, Jan E. 1993. "Control in dating relationships." *Journal of Marriage and the Family* 55:673–85.

——. 1995. "Role identities and person identities: Gender identity, mastery identity, and controlling one's partner." *Sociological Perspectives* 38:129–50.

——. 1997. "Status and identity in marital interaction." *Social Psychology Quarterly* 60:185–217.

——. 2003. "Justice, emotion, and identity theory." Pp. 105–22 in *Advances in identity theory and research,* edited by P. J. Burke, T. J. Owens, R. T. Serpe, and P. A. Thoits. New York: Kluwer Academic/Plenum.

——. 2004. "Emotions in identity theory: The effects of status." *Advances in Group Processes* 21:51–76.

——. 2005. "Examining emotions in identity theory." *Social Psychology Quarterly* 68:39–56.

Stets, Jan E., and Emily K. Asencio. 2008. "Consistency and enhancement processes in understanding emotions." *Social Forces* 86: 1055–78.

Stets, Jan E., and Chris F. Biga. 2003. "Bringing identity theory into environmental sociology." *Sociological Theory* 21:398–423.

Stets, Jan E., and Peter J. Burke. 1994. "Inconsistent self-views in the control identity model." *Social Science Research* 23:236–62.

———. 1996. "Gender, control, and interaction." *Social Psychology Quarterly* 59:193–220.

———. 2000. "Identity theory and social identity theory." *Social Psychology Quarterly* 63:224–37.

———. 2005a. "Identity-verification, control, and aggression in marriage." *Social Psychology Quarterly* 68:160–78.

———. 2005b. "New directions in identity control theory." *Advances in Group Processes* 22:43–64.

Stets, Jan E., and Michael J. Carter. 2006. "The moral identity: A principle level identity." Pp. 293–316 in *Purpose, meaning, and action: Control systems theories in sociology*, edited by K. McClelland and T. J. Fararo. New York: Palgrave MacMillan.

Stets, Jan E., Michael J. Carter, and Jesse Fletcher. 2008a. "Examining the moral identity across different methodologies." Social Psychology Seminar, Riverside, CA.

———. 2008b. "Testing identity Theory: identity discrepancies, behaviors, and emotions." Paper presented at the annual meetings of the American Sociological Association.

Stets, Jan E., Michael J. Carter, Michael M. Harrod, Christine Cerven, and Seth Abrutyn. 2008. "The moral identity, status, moral emotions, and the normative order." Pp. 227–51 in *Social structure and emotion*, edited by J. Clay-Warner and J. T. Robinson. San Diego: Elsevier.

Stets, Jan E., and Alicia D. Cast. 2007. "Resources and identity verification from an identity theory perspective." *Sociological Perspectives* 50:517–43.

Stets, Jan E., and Michael M. Harrod. 2004. "Verification across multiple identities: The role of status." *Social Psychology Quarterly* 67:155–71.

Stets, Jan E., and Shelley N. Osborn. 2008. "Injustice and emotions using identity theory." *Advances in Group Processes* 25: 151–79.

Stets, Jan E., and Teresa Tsushima. 2001. "Negative emotion and coping responses within identity control theory." *Social Psychology Quarterly* 64:283–95.

Stone, Gregory P. 1962. "Appearance and the aelf." Pp. 86–118 in *Human behavior and social processes*, edited by A. Rose. Boston: Houghton Mifflin.

Stotland, Ezra, and Michael Pendleton. 1989. "Workload, stress, and strain among police officers." *Behavioral Medicine* 15:5–17.

Stryker, Sheldon. 1968. "Identity salience and role performance." *Journal of Marriage and the Family* 4:558–64.

———. 1980 [2002]. *Symbolic interactionism: A social structural version.* Caldwell, NJ: Blackburn Press.

———. 1987. "Identity theory: Developments and Extensions." Pp. 89–104 in *Self and identity: Psychological perspectives*, edited by K. Yardley and T. Honess. Chichester, UK: Wiley.

———. 1997. "'In the beginning there is society': Lessons from a sociological social psychology." Pp. 315–27 in *The message of social psychology: Perspectives on mind in society*, edited by C. McGarty and S. A. Haslam. Malden, MA: Blackwell.

———. 2000. "Identity competition: Key to differential social movement participation?" Pp. 21–40 in *Self, identity, and social movements*, edited by S. Stryker, T. Owens, and R. White. Minneapolis: University of Minnesota Press.

———. 2004. "Integrating emotion into identity theory." *Advances in Group Processes* 21:1–23.

Stryker, Sheldon, and Peter J. Burke. 2000. "The Past, present, and future of an identity theory." *Social Psychology Quarterly* 63:284–97.

Stryker, Sheldon, and Anne S. Macke. 1978. "Status inconsistency and role conflict." *Annual Review of Sociology* 4:57–90.

Stryker, Sheldon, and Richard T. Serpe. 1982. "Commitment, identity salience, and role behavior: A theory and research example." Pp. 199–218 in *Personality, roles, and social behavior*, edited by W. Ickes and E. S. Knowles. New York: Springer-Verlag.

———. 1994. "Identity salience and psychological centrality: Equivalent, overlapping, or complementary concepts?" *Social Psychology Quarterly* 57:16–35.

Stryker, Sheldon, and Anne Statham. 1985. "Symbolic interaction and role theory." Pp. 311–78 in *Handbook of social psychology*, edited by G. Lindzey and E. Aronson. New York: Random House.

Stryker, Sheldon, and Kevin D. Vryan. 2003. "The symbolic interactionist frame." Pp. 3–28 in *Handbook of social psychology*, edited by J. DeLamater. New York: Kluwer Academic/Plenum.

Swann, William B., Jr. 1983. "Self-verification: Bringing social reality into harmony with the self." Pp. 33–66 in *Psychological perspectives on the self*, edited by J. Suls and A. Greenwald. Hillsdale, NJ: Erlbaum.

———. 1987. "Identity negotiation: Where two roads meet." *Journal of Personality and Social Psychology* 53:1038–51.

———. 1990. "To be adored or to be known?: The interplay of self-enhancement and self-verification." Pp. 408–50 in *Handbook of motivation and cognition*, edited by E. T. Higgins and R. M. Sorrentino. New York: Guilford Press.

———. 2005. "The self and identity negotiation." *Interaction Studies* 6:69–83.

Swann, William B., Jr., John J. Griffin, Steven C. Predmore, and Bebe Gaines. 1987. "The cognitive-affective crossfire: When self-consistency confronts self-enhancement." *Journal of Personality and Social Psychology* 52:881–89.

Swann, William B., Jr., and Craig A. Hill. 1982. "When our identities are mistaken: Reaffirming self-conceptions through social interaction." *Journal of Personality and Social Psychology* 43:59–66.

Swann, William B., Jr., Brett W. Pelham, and Douglas S. Krull. 1989. "Agreeable fancy or disagreeable truth? Reconciling self enhancement and self-verification." *Journal of Personality and Social Psychology* 57:782–91.

Swann, William B., Jr., and Stephen J. Read. 1981. "Self-verification processes: How we sustain our self conceptions." *Journal of Experimental Social Psychology* 17:351–72.

Swann, William B., Jr., Peter J. Rentfrow, and Jennifer S. Guinn. 2003. "Self-verification: The search for coherence." Pp. 367–83 in *Handbook of self and identity*, edited by M. R. Leary and J. P. Tangney. New York: Guilford Press.

Tajfel, Henri, and John C. Turner. 1979. "An integrative theory of intergroup conflict." Pp. 33–47 in *The social psychology of intergroup relations*, edited by W. G. Austin and S. Worchel. Pacific Grove, CA: Brooks/Cole.

Tallman, Irving, Peter J. Burke, and Viktor Gecas. 1998. "Socialization into marital roles: Testing a contextual, developmental model of marital functioning." Pp. 312–42 in *The developmental course of marital dysfunction*, edited by T. N. Bradbury. New York : Cambridge University Press.

Tangney, June Price, and Rhonda L. Dearing. 2002. *Shame and guilt.* New York: Guilford Press.

Tangney, June Price, Rowland S. Miller, Laura Flicker, and Deborah Hill Barlow. 1996. "Are shame, guilt, and embarrassment distinct emotions?" *Journal of Personality and Social Psychology* 70:1256–69.

Thoits, Peggy A. 1983. "Multiple identities and psychological well-being: A reformulation and test of the social isolation hypothesis." *American Sociological Review* 49:174–87.

——. 1986. "Multiple identities: Examining gender and marital status differences in distress." *American Sociological Review* 51:259–72.

——. 1991. "On merging identity theory and stress research." *Social Psychology Quarterly* 54:101–12.

——. 1995. "Identity-relevant events and psychological symptoms: A cautionary tale." *Journal of Health and Social Behavior* 36:72–82.

——. 2003. "Personal agency in the accumulation of role-identities." Pp. 179–94 in *Advances in identity theory and research*, edited by P. J. Burke, T. J. Owens, P. A. Thoits, and R. T. Serpe. New York: Kluwer Academic/Plenum.

Thoits, Peggy A., and Lauren K. Virshup. 1997. "Me's and we's: Forms and functions of social identities." Pp. 106–33 in *Self and identity: Fundamental issues*, edited by R. D. Ashmore and L. J. Jussim. New York: Oxford University Press.

Thomas, William Isaac, and Dorothy Swain Thomas. 1928. *The child in America.* New York: Knopf.

Tsushima, Teresa, and Peter J. Burke. 1999. "Levels, agency, and control in the parent identity." *Social Psychology Quarterly* 62:173–89.

Turner, John C., Michael A. Hogg, Penelope J. Oakes, Stephen D. Reicher, and Margaret S. Wetherell. 1987. "Rediscovering the social group: A self-categorization theory." New York: Basil Blackwell.

Turner, Jonathan H. 2000. *On the origins of human emotions: A sociological inquiry into the evolution of human affect.* Stanford: Stanford University Press.

———. 2002. *Face-to-face: Towards a sociological theory of interpersonal behavior*. Stanford: Stanford University Press.

———. 2006. "Psychoanalytic sociological theories and emotion." Pp. 276–94 in *Handbook of the sociology of emotions*, edited by J. E. Stets and J. H. Turner. New York: Springer.

Turner, Jonathan H., and Jan E. Stets. 2005. *The sociology of emotions*. New York: Cambridge University Press.

Turner, Ralph H. 1962. "Role-taking: Process versus conformity." Pp. 20–40 in *Human behavior and social processes*, edited by A. M. Rose. Boston: Houghton Mifflin.

———. 1978. "The role and the person." *American Journal of Sociology* 84:1–23.

Ward, Lloyd G., and Robert Throop. 1992. "Emotional experience in Dewey and Mead: Notes for the social Ppychology of emotion." Pp. 61–94 in *Social perspectives on emotion*, edited by D. D. Franks and V. Gecas. Greenwich: JAI Press.

Weiner, Norbert. 1948. *Cybernetics: Or the control and communication in the animal and the machine*. Cambridge: MIT Press.

Weinstein, Eugene A., and Paul Deutschberger. 1963. "Some dimensions of altercasting." *Sociometry* 26:454–66.

White, Gregory L., and Paul E. Mullen. 1989. *Jealousy: Theory, research, and clinical strategies*. New York: Guilford Press.

Whorf, Benjamin Lee. 1956. *Language, thought, and reality; Selected writings*. Cambridge: MIT Press.

Wolff, Kurt H. 1950. *The sociology of Georg Simmel*. Glencoe, IL: Free Press.

Zanna, Mark and Joel Cooper. 1976. "Dissonance and the attribution process." Pp. 199–217 in *New directions in attribution research*, edited by J. H. Harvey, W. J. Ickes, and R. F. Kidd. Hillsdale, NJ: Erlbaum.

Index

CPSIA information can be obtained at www.ICGtesting.com
Printed in the USA
BVOW030358190213

313622BV00001B/4/P